Who Is to Blame for Judges 19?

Contrapuntal Readings of the Bible in World Christianity

Series Editors: K. K. Yeo, Melanie Baffes

Just as God knows no boundaries and incarnation happens in shared space, truth does not respect borders and its expression in various contexts is kaleidoscopic. As God's church is birthed forth from local cultures, it is called into a catholic community—namely world Christianity. This series values the twofold identity of biblical interpretations that seek to engage in contextual theology and, at the same time, become part of a global and "many-voiced" conversation for the sake of mutual understanding. By promoting contrapuntal readings that hold contextual and global biblical hermeneutics in tension, this series celebrates interpretations in three movements: (1) those based on the biblical text that honor multiple and interacting worldviews (reading the world biblically/theologically); (2) those that work at the translatability of the biblical text to uphold various dynamic vernaculars and faithful hermeneutics for the world (reading the Bible/theology contextually); and (3) those that respect the cross-cultural and shifting contexts in which faithful communities are embedded, and embody, real-life issues.

International Advisory Board

Walter Brueggemann, William Marcellus McPheeters Professor Emeritus of Old Testament, Columbia Theological Seminary (USA)

Adela Yarbro Collins, Buckingham Professor of New Testament Criticism and Interpretation, Yale Divinity School (USA)

Kathy Ehrensperger, Research Professor of New Testament in Jewish Perspective, University of Potsdam (Germany)

Justo L. González, Emeritus Professor of Historical Theology, Candler School of Theology, Emory University (USA)

Richard A. Horsley, Distinguished Professor of Liberal Arts and the Study of Religion Emeritus, University of Massachusetts—Boston (USA)

Robert Jewett (1933–2020), Emeritus Professor of New Testament, Heidelberg University (Germany)

Brigitte Kahl, Professor of New Testament, Union Theological Seminary (USA)

Peter Lampe, Professor of New Testament Theology, Heidelberg University (Germany)

Tremper Longman III, Robert H. Gundry Professor Emeritus of Biblical Studies, Westmont College (USA)

Daniel Patte, Professor Emeritus of Religious Studies, New Testament, and Christianity, Vanderbilt University (USA)

Volumes in the Series (2018–2022)

Volume 1: *Text and Context: Vernacular Approaches to the Bible in Global Christianity*, edited by Melanie Baffes

Volume 2: *What Has Jerusalem to Do with Beijing? Biblical Interpretation from a Chinese Perspective* (Twentieth Anniversary Edition), K. K. Yeo

Volume 3: *Chinese Biblical Anthropology: Persons and Ideas in the Old Testament and in Modern Chinese Literature*, Cao Jian

Volume 4: *Cross-textual Reading of Ecclesiastes with Analects: In Search of Political Wisdom in a Disordered World*, Elaine Wei-Fun Goh

Volume 5: *The Cambridge Dictionary of Christianity*, 2 vols., edited by Daniel Patte

Volume 6: *An Ethic of Hospitality: The Pilgrim Motif in Hebrews and the Refugee Problem in Kenya*, Emily Jeptepkeny Choge

Volume 7: *The Diffused Story of the Footwashing in John 13: A Textual Study of Bible Reception in Late Imperial China*, Yanrong Chen

Volume 8: *Who Is to Blame for Judges 19? Interplay Between the Text and a Chinese Context*, Grace Kwan Sik Tsoi

Volume 9: *Scripture, Cultures, and Criticism: Interpretive Steps and Critical Issues Raised by Robert Jewett*, edited by K. K. Yeo

Who Is to Blame for Judges 19?

Interplay between the Text and a Chinese Context

Grace Kwan Sik Tsoi

FOREWORD BY
Mark G. Brett

☙PICKWICK *Publications* • Eugene, Oregon

WHO IS TO BLAME FOR JUDGES 19?
Interplay between the Text and a Chinese Context

Contrapuntal Readings of the Bible in World Christianity 8

Copyright © 2022 Grace Kwan Sik Tsoi. All rights reserved. Except for brief quotations in critical publications or reviews, no part of this book may be reproduced in any manner without prior written permission from the publisher. Write: Permissions, Wipf and Stock Publishers, 199 W. 8th Ave., Suite 3, Eugene, OR 97401.

Pickwick Publications
An Imprint of Wipf and Stock Publishers
199 W. 8th Ave., Suite 3
Eugene, OR 97401

www.wipfandstock.com

PAPERBACK ISBN: 978-1-6667-3063-0
HARDCOVER ISBN: 978-1-6667-2238-3
EBOOK ISBN: 978-1-6667-2239-0

Cataloguing-in-Publication data:

Names: Tsoi, Grace Kwan Sik, author. | Brett, Mark G., foreword.

Title: Who is to blame for Judges 19? : interplay between the text and a Chinese context / Grace Kwan Sik Tsoi ; foreword by Mark G. Brett.

Description: Eugene, OR: Pickwick Publications, 2022. | Contrapuntal Readings of the Bible in World Christianity 8. | Includes bibliographical references and index.

Identifiers: ISBN 978-1-6667-3063-0 (paperback). | ISBN 978-1-6667-2238-3 (hardcover). | ISBN 978-1-6667-2239-0 (ebook).

Subjects: LCSH: Bible.—Judges XIX—Criticism, interpretation, etc. | Concubinage. | Concubinage—China—History. | Bible—Ideological criticism. | Bible—Literary criticism. | Bible—Translations—Chinese.

Classification: BS1305.6 T76 2022 (print). | BS1305.6 (ebook).

06/17/22

Scripture quotations marked (ERV) are taken from the Holy Bible, English Revised Version, which is in the public domain.

Scripture quotations marked (NKJV) are taken from the New King James Version®. Copyright © 1982 by Thomas Nelson. Used by permission. All rights reserved.

Scripture quotations marked (NRSV) are taken from New Revised Standard Version Bible, copyright © 1989 National Council of the Churches of Christ in the United States of America. Used by permission. All rights reserved worldwide.

Scripture quotations marked (CNV) are from Chinese New Version, copyright © 1976, 1992, 1999, 2001, 2005 by Worldwide Bible Society.

Scripture quotations marked (CUV) are from the Chinese Union Version, which is in the public domain.

Scripture quotations marked (RCUV) are from the Revised Chinese Union Version © 2006, 2010, 2017 Hong Kong Bible Society. Used by permission.

Scripture quotations marked (DV) are from the Delegates' Version, which is in the public domain.

Contents

Foreword by Mark G. Brett | ix
Acknowledgments | xi
Introduction | xiii
Abbreviations | xx

1. Reading Judges 19 in a World with Concubines:
   A Chinese Contextual Perspective | 1

2. Reading the *Pîlegeš* (Concubine) in Judges 19
   in the Historical Context | 28

3. Reading Judges 19 as a Narrative:
   Gaps, Ambiguities, and Point-of-View | 52

4. Reading Judges 19 Intertextually:
   Motifs of Hospitality, Rape, and Sacrifice | 86

5. Reading Judges 19 with Ideological Lenses:
   Gender and Politics | 129

6. Chinese Christian Reading of Judges 19:
   Reflections on Translation and Implications | 159

7. Concluding Reflections | 186

Bibliography | 189
Author Index | 201
Subject Index | 205
Scripture Index | 209

Foreword

GRACE TSOI ADDRESSES A number of key questions related to biblical studies in Asia, and she opens up the field in important ways. Some of the questions at issue in this book will be familiar to international biblical scholars if formulated in a very general way: for example, how are we to understand the biblical texts of terror in the book of Judges? How are we to understand the ancient meanings of violence against women? But there is a problem hiding in the pronoun "we" in such general questions. Who exactly is the reading audience? What if the "we" are, more specifically, modern readers whose first language is Chinese? What difference does this make?

An older set of scholarly assumptions might presume that such a specific contextual question does not really belong to biblical studies properly conceived. One could simply recognize where the historic resources for biblical study are housed, identify the prestigious institutions where doctoral studies can be undertaken, and move to Europe or the US. One should certainly recognize the research languages that are required: Hebrew, Greek, English, German; and French. Perhaps after completing a doctorate, one might write an article on how modern Chinese readers can understand the violence in Judges 19. The fact that concubinage existed in China up until 1950, when it was prohibited by the Peoples Republic of China, could go in a footnote.

Thankfully, Grace Tsoi did not take this route. Instead, she plunged straight into the problem of what might count as "contextual" biblical interpretation, accepting neither the imperialist assumptions of Western biblical scholarship nor the nationalist countermovement that would neglect Euro-American scholars as a matter of poetic justice. Responding to her location as a diaspora Chinese reader in Australia, she contributes to the project of Australasian contextual biblical studies and confronts all the complexities of cultural hybridity and intersectional identity. She does not imagine that all Chinese readers will be interested in the Bible in the same way. The diversity is self-evident. But through a wide-ranging international scholarly dialogue, she arrives at extraordinary insights into a very specific history of reception. It is a pleasure to see the fruit of Grace Tsoi's research now accessible to a wide audience, and in particular, to younger readers who are seeking to open up the space of Asian biblical scholarship by remaining precisely in their own context.

Mark G. Brett

Acknowledgments

I would like to thank the editors of the series, Dr. K. K. Yeo and Dr. Melanie Baffes, for accepting my manuscript and for their patience in guiding me through my first publication. I would like to express my sincere gratitude to the principal supervisor of my thesis, Professor Mark Brett. It was his critical mind and breadth of knowledge that shaped my thinking, and his timely encouragements kept me from despair. I would also like to thank my second supervisor, Dr. Philip Chia, whose advice on Chinese biblical scholarship was invaluable. A special thanks to Rev. Ming Leung, who introduced me to the world of biblical studies and inspired my passion.

To Gary, my husband, who has tirelessly supported me in every way throughout my ministry, I thank the Lord every day for you. To my dear friends, who had more confidence in me than I had in myself, you kept me sane amidst head-spinning readings. And to Pang Lai-Chun, my Ah-yee, who loved me unconditionally since birth and brought me to Jesus, I dedicate this work to you. I so wish that you had lived to see its completion.

Introduction

JUDGES 19 IS PROBABLY the most horrific narrative in the Hebrew Bible. A Levite thrusts his concubine into a situation of gang rape, murder, and dismemberment. There is no explicit comment in the narrative about his brutality, let alone any condemnation. This passage has attracted much attention from biblical scholars; many have wrestled with the agenda of the narrator in this gruesome scene. To Western scholarship, it is almost taken for granted that the concubine is the victim in the narrative, and feminist commentators in recent years have proposed various interpretations that resist such marginalization of women.

This, however, might not necessarily be the case in the reading context of a Chinese Christian. Embedded in a cultural heritage of concubinage, where concubines are stigmatized as promiscuous women who bring destruction to families, a Chinese reader of Judges 19 could be heavily weighted with value judgment against this character. As the issue of concubinage has been a major concern since Western missionaries entered China, and the practice is strongly condemned as an adulterous relationship defying Christian standards of monogamy, it is unlikely for interpretations that sympathize with the concubine to flourish in this context. Instead, the Chinese translation of the passage in the CUV—which glosses over the brutal actions of the Levite—might even be understood as ascribing culpability to the concubine. In a way, the text could be used as a warning to women and a way to justify submission to the patriarchal system.

The question then becomes: who indeed is the victim in the narrative? Is the text for or against the marginalization of women? Is this evaluation arbitrary, depending on the context of the readers, or are there clues from literary features of the narrative that can shed light on the rhetorical purpose of the narrator? To put it simply, on whom is the narrator intending to place blame in the discourse?

All these questions demand further investigation of the text and the contexts. The difference in interpretations between Chinese and Western readers highlights the important contribution of context to the reading of a text, which echoes the development of contextual hermeneutics in biblical scholarship in the past two decades. The basic emphasis in this recent discussion is the recognition of context in any interpretation, which has always been present in some respects.[1] What is new is its recognition and highlighting by those performing the reading, particularly scholars who come from outside the old European centers of scholarship.[2] As fruitful as the outcomes have been thus far, the practice of the methodology is not without its challenges.

In the opening session of the 2016 Society of Biblical Literature International Meeting held in Seoul, Athalya Brenner-Idan criticized the current practice of contextual interpretation. She urged contextual biblical studies to go beyond descriptions of how a community reads a text in a certain context. Instead, we need to ask "in what way reading the Bible in the light of your present life, and vice versa, illuminates both back and forth, and the reading should follow the tools of the trade. Then it will be helpful and has value way beyond your own context."[3] Indeed the task of biblical scholars does not stop at locating a reading potential of a certain context. Rather, with the tools of biblical criticisms, one should encourage a dialogue between the text and the reader's context, and thus contribute toward an understanding of the text that is not limited by a context, whether past or present. In other words, one is not only concerned about what might the text mean to me, but also what might the text mean to others, including, possibly, the first audiences.[4]

When one examines Chinese contextual biblical studies in light of Brenner-Idan's insights, it is obvious that we are still looking for an approach that lives up to the expectations. Pioneered by Archie Lee, Chinese contextual hermeneutics has so far been focused on cross-textual studies, which read the Bible in the light of Chinese classics.[5] Although interesting parallels or contrasts have been observed, the value of this exercise is in fact rather limited. Seldom does the approach involve in-depth examination of

---

1. As John Riches convincingly demonstrates, the influence of context has always been present though it may not always be acknowledged; "Cultural Bias," 431–48.

2. For example, Punt, "Dealing (with) the Past," 29–45; and Chia, "Biblical Studies in a Rising Asia," 81–95.

3. Brenner-Idan, "So Where Are We?," 3.

4. By first audiences, I refer to the original intended readership of the biblical texts.

5. The effort of Archie Lee in this area can be seen in the selection of his articles from 1991–2008 in Lee, *Kua wenben yuedu*. Examples of scholars who follow in his footsteps include Meng, "Remembering Ancestors," 257–68; Tian, "Confucian Catholics' Appropriation of the Decalogue," 163–80; Yan, "'Who Is More to You than Seven Sons,'" 47–55.

the Hebrew text using tools of biblical criticism such as historical or literary methodologies, which, as Brenner-Idan implies, may be influenced in some way by the Chinese context of reading. The product of the Chinese cross-textual readings are often only meaningful to the Chinese audience, and they do not yield any significance for other contemporary cultures, let alone to the ancient Hebrew context.

Moreover, understanding the Chinese context constructed merely from classical Chinese texts in itself is highly questionable. At the time when these ancient texts were popular and well received among Chinese literati, that is, before the end of the Imperial era, Christianity had hardly exerted any influence in China. And by the time the Bible reached more people in China with the expansion of Christian churches in the past century, these classical texts are no longer a major part of the educational system. Certainly, they are not entirely forgotten, and we may still find the roots of some phrases or traditional values in them, but apart from that, the influences they have for the Chinese context today is doubtful.

Furthermore, the apparent authority and status the cross-textual approach grants to the Chinese classics in relation to the Bible can hardly find resonance in the community that actually reads the Bible—the Chinese Christian churches.[6] Unlike in Western civilizations, Christianity remains foreign to the Chinese culture until today, and it is well recognized among Chinese Christians that the values and elements from their own culture are often found to be in tension with the teachings from the Bible.[7] To Chinese Christians, especially Protestants, the Bible is their Holy Scripture that has unsurpassable authority over their ways of thinking and living, and anything from the Chinese culture should be subjected to its authority. It would be unimaginable for the Chinese classics to be read with any comparable status as the Bible. A contextual Chinese reading of the Bible that has relevance to the community of faith would instead uphold the authority of the

---

6. For example, in Archie Lee's cross-textual reading between the Chinese creation myths and Genesis, he considers the concept of apotheosis from these myths a challenge to monotheism in Christianity that cannot be dismissed; Lee, *Kua wenben yuedu*, 23. This seems to take the Chinese myths to a status comparable to the Bible and does not acknowledge the authority of Scripture in the Chinese communities of faith. I will confine my discussion of Chinese Christian churches to the scope of Protestant Christian churches from the Republican China to recent years in this study (as the focus of my consideration is the Chinese Union Version), while acknowledging that there are other religious affiliations that may fit under this umbrella.

7. For an analysis of the clash between Christianity and the Chinese culture from both ideological and historical perspectives, see Zhuo, *Jidujiao yu zhongguo wenhua chujing*, 39–109.

Bible above any elements in their culture, including classical texts, and seek to read the biblical text within this perceived authority.[8]

Besides, the cross-textual approach that focuses on Chinese classics neglects the role of Western cultures in Chinese biblical interpretation. As Chloë Starr points out, "If two cultural matrices are always involved in interpreting biblical texts in the West, for the Chinese this was [sic] three."[9] The Chinese context of biblical reading involves more than an interaction between their own culture and the ancient biblical culture; it also involves the Western culture that belonged to the missionaries who converted them and translated their Bible. For late nineteenth- and early twentieth-century Chinese readers of the Bible:

> [T]he matrix from which the text emerged was overlaid with a deep layer of nineteenth-century Western interpretation. The mission context, and the particular concerns and interests of the sending churches, pressed between Chinese readers and their interpretations. This was in part a matter of what was translated, and of what secondary and explanatory texts were printed for the Chinese market.[10]

To Chinese readers, a contextual reading of the Bible is inseparable from this Western influence that shaped the very foundation of their faith.

The influence of Western missionaries did not cease with their departure from China in the middle of the twentieth century. It has continued, in the form of the CUV, for almost a century, until the present day. Since its publication in 1919, this version translated by Western missionaries has dominated Chinese churches and governed the interpretations of generations of Chinese Christians. Since translation is not a value-neutral exercise, and interpretations are unavoidable in any translations, it is legitimate to suggest that the ideologies of the missionaries might have influenced their translation process. In other words, the CUV that Chinese Christians are reading today reflects the translation context of the Western missionaries in the early twentieth century in China. A contextual Chinese reading

---

8. I also acknowledge that Chinese culture is not homogenous in itself, and the term "Chinese Christians" in this study encompasses Christians of ethnic Chinese background, whether located in China or overseas. In other words, this study does not claim to be representative of *all* Chinese Christians but is the contribution from *a* Chinese Christian to the possibilities of interpretations of the text. I identify myself as a Hong Kong born Chinese migrated to Australia. My interest in this topic is shaped by my cultural identity as an ethnic Chinese and by my religious identity as a Protestant Christian.

9. Starr, "Introduction," 3.

10. Starr, "Introduction," 3.

should therefore take into consideration this translation context, which is seldom acknowledged in previous discussions.

Incorporating the above factors, I propose that a contextual hermeneutics for Chinese Christians should be a "back-and-forth" exercise that involves the reading context, the translation context, and the ancient biblical context. Beginning with a reading that is sensitive to the Chinese context, it unveils the potential meaning of the text for readers within our culture. It is then necessary to examine how this "Chinese" reading relates to the ancient contexts of the biblical text. Using tools of biblical criticism, one may be able to recover the rhetorical message of the text for its ancient readers. Examination of the translation context may then shed light on the comparison between ancient biblical and Chinese contexts, allowing another "back-and-forth" maneuver in adjusting the reading potentials.

A contextual reading, in this sense, is not a static perception of the text limited to the group that shares the reading context. It is a dynamic process that may be adjusted in light of the analysis of the biblical and the translation contexts. This study is an attempt to demonstrate how this dynamic process may enrich understanding of a puzzling text, like Judges 19, beyond the Chinese context.

I begin by studying the context of early Republican China, which was the translation context of the CUV and a time when concubines were a social reality. Using primary literary sources to illustrate the life and status of concubines, I provide a reconstruction of a social and religious context that is hostile to concubines. I also identify the translation nuances of Judges 19 within the CUV, which collaboratively work to downplay the violence of the Levite and shift the blame toward his concubine. The narrative read in this context is then a warning to concubines to submit to the patriarchal system.

In the next step of the "back-and-forth" exercise, I employ various tools developed in biblical criticism to examine the text. First, I apply findings from comparative studies that look at the practice of concubinage within ancient Near Eastern cultures and explore the life and status of a concubine in the biblical context. This will clear away some confusion about the character of the concubine in Judges 19 and pave the way for studying the literary aspects of the text.

Next, I investigate the narratological artistry of Judges 19 and its impact on the rhetorical message of the text. By attending to the gaps and ambiguities in the narrative, it will demonstrate that, contrary to the Chinese reading that focuses on the concubine, the discourse is designed to draw the attention of readers to the Levite, his shocking personality and behaviors. The view of the narrator toward this character is then examined using point-of-view analysis, which suggests that the readers' sympathy is constantly being drawn away from the Levite. This establishes the Levite as the protagonist and demonstrates the implicit judgment upon this character embedded in the narrative.

The next chapter elaborates on this rhetorical purpose of Judges 19 through studying its use of intertexts. It will demonstrate that intertextual connections to Genesis 19 and 22; 1 Samuel 11; Deuteronomy 22; and 2 Samuel 13, collaboratively reflect motifs of hospitality, rape, and sacrifice. Each of the motifs, when compared to the intertexts, provokes negative evaluation of the Levite.

I then turn my attention to the ancient biblical context once again, this time focusing on the ideologies embedded in the text. I study the text from the perspective of hegemonic masculinity, demonstrating that the Levite is presented as a character who does not conform to the ideals of masculinity in the culture. This again provokes sentiment against him and further confirms the anti-Levite agenda of the text. This agenda is then studied through a political lens, which will demonstrate that the combination of pro-monarchic and anti-Levite ideologies in Judges 19 is suggestive of a political atmosphere that promotes the rule of the king and suppresses the influence of the country Levites. This is consistent with a historical setting of Josianic reform.[11]

The final chapter then brings together the reading context, translation context, and biblical context. As the findings from the investigations of the biblical text and its ancient Hebrew context end up conflicting with the CUV translation choices, I will suggest that an anti-concubinage agenda among Western missionaries, combined with the pressure to gain acceptance among Chinese authorities, rendered the translators less attentive to the anti-Levite rhetoric in the text. Instead, an anti-concubine influence was added to their translation. Through surveying recent Chinese commentaries on the narrative, I will demonstrate that this influence from the CUV continues to the present day, and it contributes to the neglect of the issue of violence against women in Chinese interpretations. This illustrates the tremendous power in the role of the translator and the need for more critical evaluation of translation.

This "contextual" interpretation of Judges 19 therefore challenges interpretations that justify violence against women and dismiss the issue as a "cultural matter." The violence in this text was not deemed acceptable even in patriarchal ancient Israel, and neither should it be acceptable in

---

11. This historical context is proposed by Gale A. Yee, "Ideological Criticism: Judges 17–21," 138–57.

any other cultures at any time. Taking this back to the Chinese reading context, it should be recognized that the apparent legitimization of oppression against women was the product of the translation context, and it did not stem from scriptural authority.

As a test case, this contextual Chinese reading of Judges 19 illustrates the potential of recovering the subversive message from the text through an interplay between the reading context and the biblical world.

Abbreviations

AB	Anchor Bible
ABRL	Anchor Bible Reference Library
AFER	*African Ecclesial Review*
AIL	Ancient Israel and Its Literature
ASV	American Standard Version
BibInt	*Biblical Interpretation*
BMW	Bible in the Modern World
BTB	*Biblical Theology Bulletin*
BZAW	Beihefte zur Zeitschrift für die alttestamentliche Wissenschaft
CBQ	*Catholic Biblical Quarterly*
CNV	Chinese New Version
CUV	Chinese Union Version
DCH	*Dictionary of Classical Hebrew*
Dtr	Deuteronomist
DtrH	Deuteronomistic History
DV	Delegates' Version
ERV	English Revised Version
ESV	English Standard Version
FCB	Feminist Companions to the Bible
JBL	*Journal of Biblical Literature*
JJS	*Journal of Jewish Studies*
JSOT	*Journal for the Study of the Old Testament*

JSOTSup	Journal for the Study of the Old Testament: Supplement Series
LHBOTS	Library of Hebrew Bible/Old Testamenet Series
LXX	Septuagint
MT	Masoretic Text
NAC	The New American Commentary
NCBC	The New Cambridge Bible Commentary
NICOT	New International Commentary on the Old Testament
NIV	New International Version
NKJV	New King James Version
NLV	New Life Version
NRSV	New Revised Standard Version
OTL	Old Testament Library
RCUV	Revised Chinese Union Version
SemeiaSt	Semeia Studies
TWOT	*Theological Wordbook of the Old Testament*
VT	*Vetus Testamentum*
VTSup	Vetus Testamentum Supplements
WBC	Word Biblical Commentary
WTJ	*Westminster Theological Journal*
ZAW	*Zeitschrift für die alttestamentliche Wissenschaft*

1

Reading Judges 19 in a World with Concubines

A Chinese Contextual Perspective

Introduction

JUDGES 19 HAS BEEN traditionally understood as a portrait of the extreme ruthlessness of the Israelites when they disobeyed God.[1] This discourse has attracted much interest from scholars in recent years and various reading potentials have been suggested: some have proposed that it is a pro-monarchic scheme;[2] others consider it part of a polemic against Saul and the Benjaminites;[3] still others follow a different direction and read in it the conflicts between systems of marriages.[4]

All these hermeneutical approaches, though having their own merits, do not appear to read from the perspective of the concubine. Phyllis Trible attempts to bridge this gap with her literary analysis in *Texts of Terror*. Focusing on the concubine, Trible's reading exposes the subtleties of male violence and power in the text. However, this reading does not take into account the social contexts of concubines nor the ideological worlds that include the cultural heritage of concubinage. In Trible's analysis, the only information regarding the life and status of concubines is a very brief summary: "a concubine has an inferior status that places her beneath other females. Legally and socially, she is not the equivalent of a wife but virtually a slave, secured by a man for his own purposes."[5] The significance of concubinage can hardly be demonstrated with such a simple description.

---

1. Boling, *Judges*, 277; Butler, *Judges*, 410–16.
2. Such as Yee, "Ideological Criticism," 138–57.
3. Amit, "Literature," 28–40.
4. Bal, *Death & Dissymmetry*, 80–93.
5. Trible, *Texts of Terror*, 66.

The neglect of the issue of concubinage is in fact common within Western biblical scholarship. Interpretations of Judges 19, along with those of other texts involving concubines in the Hebrew Bible, seldom investigate the practice of concubinage. Little is known about concubines in ancient Israel, as they have not attracted much interest in scholarship.[6] Yet the existence of concubinage is undeniable in the Hebrew Bible. The Hebrew term *pîlegeš*, translated as "concubine," appears in Gen 35:22, 36:12; 2 Sam 3:7; 1 Chr 1:32; Esth 2:14, just to name a few.[7] Even when the figure of the concubine is prominent, such as in Judges 19, commentators seldom focus on her identity as a concubine and its potential impact on the reading of the narrative.[8] This pattern of neglect may be related to the lack of a parallel in the Western social context. With the success of Christian teaching—promoting monogamy in Western culture—concubinage has long been considered something of the ancient past. Readers from this culture simply cannot relate to such a character.

The context of reading is very different in Asian countries, especially in China.[9] Concubinage has been part of the marriage system in Chinese culture since ancient times. It continued to be a widely accepted and legal social practice until 1950, when the government of the People's Republic of China finally issued a legal prohibition.[10] Even today, the term

---

6. The topic attracts only a single paragraph in *The Interpreter's Dictionary of the Bible*, Baab, "Concubine," 666. There has been little detailed scholarship on the topic and most refers to the work of Engelken, *Frauen im Alten Israel*, 74–126. The other exception is the unpublished dissertation of McComiskey, "Status of the Secondary Wife." Yet this has not drawn much attention from subsequent scholarship either.

7. A list of all occurrences can be found in Engelken, *Frauen im Alten Israel*, 119–22.

8. Many commentators acknowledge that her status is different from that of a wife but do not go further in articulating the difference and how this might impact the reading of the text. For example, Butler, *Judges*, 417–18; Soggin, *Judges*, 284. While Schneider attempts to study more closely the woman's identity, more questions than answers seem to be raised: Schneider, *Judges*, 248–49. Some almost ignore the character altogether, such as Boling, *Judges*, 271–79.

9. Here I refer to the reading context of "Cultural China," which is not limited to mainland China, but includes those in Taiwan, Hong Kong, overseas and diasporic Chinese over the world. For a helpful discussion on the fluidity and inclusiveness of the term, see Yeo, *Musing with Confucius and Paul*, 423–25.

10. Although the Republican (Guomindang) government claimed to support monogamy, it accepted concubines as co-habiting partners and declared that "concubinage is not marriage and hence not bigamy." Therefore, concubinage remained marginally legal during the Republican government. The Communist government introduced monogamy laws in its regions in the 1930s, yet it was not until 1950 that the People's Republic of China was established and concubinage was formally abolished by

"concubine" is neither a foreign nor ancient concept to Chinese readers, as it conjures up associations and images of concubinage, which are part of the cultural heritage.

When Christianity entered China again in the sixteenth century,[11] concubinage was a vivid social reality that confronted the European missionaries; the collision of values and cultures was unavoidable. The issue of concubinage became a focal point of discussion in dialogues between missionaries and locals during evangelism, and the condemning attitude of missionaries was reflected in their writings and Bible commentaries in Chinese. Texts from the Hebrew Bible relating to marriage and concubines attracted much attention in Chinese Christian circles. Following the teaching of missionaries, Chinese pastors and evangelists vigorously denied the legitimacy of concubinage and discouraged the practice among Chinese Christians. Yet there were also Chinese Christians who related the practice of concubinage in the Hebrew Bible to their own social situation. There is even a record of a certain Christian acquiring a concubine after reading the Genesis account of Abraham.[12] In both cases, it was clear that, to the early Chinese Christians, there was a common element between Chinese and ancient Israelite cultures, and the Chinese social context influenced their interpretations. It was particularly significant during the Republican era, as concubinage became a heated topic in politics, and many advocated for its abolishment as part of the New Culture Movement. Reading Judges 19 and other biblical texts involving concubines from the perspective of a Chinese, and particularly with the socio-political background of the early Republic, is not reading in an ideological vacuum. It is reading from within a cultural heritage of concubinage, in a world containing the very real existence of concubines.[13]

This chapter is an attempt to bring to life the often-neglected issue of concubinage and illustrate the reading potential of Judges 19 of the Chinese people living in the late Qing to early Republican China. For Chinese readers in this period, the early twentieth century, their interpretations involved a vigorous interaction between two sides: on one side was their

---

law. Zheng and Lu, *Minguo juan*, 7.

11. While there is evidence of Nestorian religious activities in China from the seventh century, it is more relevant to consider the re-entry of Christianity by the European missionaries in the sixteenth century here.

12. Li, "Siyang jiaowu suowen," 7–8.

13. This is, by no means, negligence on the part of other cultures that face the issue of polygamy and contribute to the reflection of relevant biblical texts. For instance, it remains a very real situation that confronts African churches, see Kiruki, "Polygamy," 119–47.

cultural heritage of concubinage and, on the other, was the anti-concubinage Christian teaching they received from Western missionaries who introduced Christianity to them and translated their Bible.[14] The following discussion first portrays the life and status of concubines in the late Qing and Republican China, focusing on the sociological and legal aspects that are relevant to the passage. It then explores the attitude of Western Christian missionaries on the matter of concubinage, and the way in which they influenced the reception among Chinese Christians of texts involving concubines. Judges 19 is then read with the awareness of such ideology and culture. I focus on the text in the CUV, as it was published in the same timeframe of the early twentieth century and remains the most influential translation of the Bible in Chinese to date.[15]

How would Judges 19 in the CUV provoke responses from readers with a cultural heritage of concubinage, or even, from concubines themselves? How might the cultural context influence the interpretation of the narrative? Through illustrating the reading potential of Chinese Christian readers, this chapter forms the starting point of a contextual study of the text and also sheds light on the understanding of the ancient Hebrew context, where concubines were part of society.

Concubinage in China

History of Concubinage in China

Concubinage was recorded in ancient Chinese history as early as the Shang dynasty (sixteenth to tenth centuries BCE).[16] It originated from slavery and formally became a part of the marriage system since the feudalistic lineage system required a segregation between the heirs of a "wife" and the heirs of "other female spouses."[17] The term *qie* (妾, concubine) is defined by *Hanyu Dacidian* (漢語大詞典, *Comprehensive Chinese Word Dictionary*) as

---

14. As Chloë Starr has aptly commented, the Chinese reader during the nineteenth and twentieth centuries did not only read from their own culture but was heavily influenced by the missionaries and their sending churches. Starr, *Reading Christian Scriptures in China*, 3.

15. The impact and popularity of the CUV is often deemed comparable to that of the King James Version in English-speaking churches. The thorough study of Chong Yau-yuk illustrates the dominance of the CUV in the Chinese churches; *Jidujiao shengjing zhongwen yiben quanwei xianxiang yanjiu*, 26–33.

16. Shi, *Naqie zongheng tan*, 15; Shang, "Zhongguo gudai shehui 'yifu yiqi zhi naqie zhi' bingcun yuanyin tanxi," 177.

17. Shi, *Naqie*, 19–21. See also Guo, *Qingdai juan*, 210.

"women whom a man marries apart from his wife in the old days."[18] Unlike mistresses, concubines were recognized as a part of the family with an ongoing marriage relationship with the husband.[19]

Various factors contributed to the continuation of concubinage through many centuries of Chinese history. The most prominent factor was the need for a male heir in ancestor worship. Ancestor worship was the heart of Chinese folk religions. The living were obliged to pay respect to their ancestors through ceremonial activities, through which the life and lineage of the family continued. Only the sons were deemed able to perform these duties. Not having a son would therefore terminate the family lineage and was regarded as the ultimate dishonor to ancestors. Concubinage provided extra opportunities to obtain male heirs apart from the single source of the wife, and this was the most glorified reason for maintaining the concubinage system throughout Chinese history.[20] However, as concubinage often took place in families with an existing male heir(s), this pointed to the fulfillment of male lust in a patriarchal society as being the ultimate reason for its existence.[21] Other factors acknowledged in influencing Chinese men to take concubines included compensation for arranged marriages and increased economic production through additional heirs.[22] As it was difficult to obtain divorce in practice (though theoretically possible by the husband's initiation),[23] concubinage was regarded as the logical means to fulfill these desires.

Women living in that patriarchal society were powerless to resist concubinage. *Nu Chieh* (女誡), the Chinese classic that was regarded as the "women's example" for centuries, advocated that the purpose of women receiving education was to learn the supreme authority of the male as well as the low status of the female; it emphasized that wives were to be submissive to their husbands.[24] In the Qing Dynasty, the government actively promoted Neo-Confucianism, which valued female chastity, filial

18. Luo, *Hanyu dacidian*, 2617, my translation.

19. Most concubines lived in the same household with the wife and rest of the family and were recognized as legal members of the family. Cheng, *Qing zhi minguo xuqie xisu zhi bianqian*, 3.

20. Shi, *Naqie*, 22–25. One can note here the obvious similarity to the need for an heir of Abraham through Hagar.

21. Cheng, *Qing zhi minguo*, 90–91.

22. Shi, *Naqie*, 23–37.

23. Though there were the "seven reasons for divorcing wives," which included childlessness, in practice, divorce was seldom approved by the court. Cheng, *Qing zhi minguo*, 86.

24. Chung, *Chinese Women in Christian Ministry*, 54.

piety, and obedience to and respect for elders; it further legitimated the submission of wives to their "superiors"—the husbands. Not only were they unable to oppose their husbands in taking concubines, they were even expected, if they were sonless, to encourage the husband to take one or more concubines.[25] Women who became concubines were mostly from impecunious families and were sold to relieve the financial burden of the family, or they had been maids or prostitutes and had come into the favor of the patriarch.[26] In any case, these females had little, if any, autonomy, and concubinage was their means of survival in society.

As concubines were acquired monetarily, and maintaining bigger families required greater financial means, concubinage was a symbol of prestige, wealth, and power. Generally, the number of concubines reflected the extent of wealth, and it was ultimately demonstrated in the emperor's palace.[27] Although concubinage was theoretically discouraged in some periods of history,[28] by the late Qing, it became so popular that even some farmers and soldiers who did not have much wealth were recorded as having concubines.[29] While it is difficult to identify the exact extent in a statistical sense,[30] it is no exaggeration to say that the phenomenon of concubinage was a widely accepted part of the marriage system (though not necessarily practiced by all) and firmly rooted in Chinese culture.

Lives of Concubines in the Late Qing to Republican China

This section focuses on three aspects of the lives of concubines in the late Qing to the early Republic: status within the family, social status, and legal status. While it is necessary to consider the living conditions of Chinese

---

25. Shi, *Naqie*, 66–75.

26. Guo, *Qingdai juan*, 211–15.

27. Guo, *Qingdai juan*, 212–15. This is again similar to the practice reflected in the Hebrew Bible.

28. From the Tang to Ming dynasties, some legal documents imposed restrictions—such as "only men older than forty without sons can acquire a concubine"—yet historians view these restrictions as mere formalities that did not have true impact on society. Cheng, *Qing zhi minguo*, 12.

29. Guo, *Qingdai juan*, 210–11.

30. In Cheng's statistical analysis of concubinage within the population of Republican China, it is demonstrated that it largely depends on the economic capacity of the region. In affluent areas such as Guangzhou, it is estimated that one tenth of families had concubines; for the upper class, the ratio might have increased to between one third and a half. Cheng, *Qing zhi minguo*, 290–97.

women in general, more emphasis is placed on comparing the status of concubines with that of wives.

Status Within the Family

The difference in status between wives and concubines in the Chinese family was strict and detailed. Concubines always had a lower status than wives, a status that was reflected in the different rituals from the beginning (the marriage ceremony) to the end (the funeral), as well as all facets of daily living.[31] Details as basic as the address to the husband made obvious the difference between wives and concubines in the family. In the Qing, only the wife was allowed to use the address *fu* (夫, husband), whereas the concubine needed to address the husband as *jiachang* (家長, head of the household).[32] Financially, the wife generally had control over the domestic finances, and the concubine relied on the mercy of the wife for her portion. If the patriarch favored the concubine over the wife, or if the wife were physically not well enough to manage the finances, the concubine might become the one in charge, but these were exceptional cases.[33]

The financial insecurity of the concubine was aggravated by the lack of protection over the marriage relationship. As she was purchased by money, she could easily be resold or expelled without any reason, unlike the wife who was protected by law to a certain extent so that divorce was not easily obtained.[34] At times, concubines were given to others as gifts in exchange for advantage in business or politics. Once a concubine was sold to the patriarch, her original family (if she had one) lost its right to her, and she was regarded as the property of the patriarch. If anything happened to her, her original family could hardly intervene, and most often they also did not have the social and political power to do so. This was a quite different situation from that of the wife, who often came from a family of higher social status and was protected by the power of her original family, as the husband would try to avoid lawsuits or arguments with them. As for the concubine, she would often have nowhere to go if expelled. Worse still, if she escaped from the family, anyone who sheltered her was punishable by law.[35] In this sense, a concubine was merely an object owned by the patriarch, and her fate was dependent on his favor. And his favor was never

31. Wang, *Xiaoqie shi*, 25.
32. Cheng, *Qing zhi minguo*, 22.
33. Cheng, *Qing zhi minguo*, 140.
34. Guo, *Qingdai juan*, 217–18.
35. Cheng, *Qing zhi minguo*, 130–34.

a guarantee, for she might lose it when he got tired of her or often when the next concubine came into the family. In a situation of such insecurity, she could only be even more submissive and try at all costs to please the patriarch in order to maintain her living.

Overall, the domestic environment that a concubine lived in was rather hostile. From the moment she entered the family, she became the enemy of the wife and of any concubines who came before her; she also was the enemy of their children, because if she bore a son, it would be a potential threat to their own inheritances. Often, due to her lowly family background, she was belittled by all, including maids and servants in the family.[36] The only way for a concubine to improve in status was to bear children. If she bore a son, her status in the family would be elevated, though not as much as the wife, but she would at least be more secure within the family. This was reflected in the system of *zupu* (族譜, genealogies). In Chinese culture, the status of a person in a family is reflected by being recorded in the *zupu*. Wives were a part of the *zupu*, but most *zupu* did not record the names of concubines unless they had borne children.[37] A childless concubine was therefore a nameless person, not recorded and not remembered by anyone.

Social Status

The social circles of most "virtuous" Chinese women in the late Qing and early Republican China were formed by female relatives and neighbours. The status of a concubine was lower than the wife in social interactions and was most readily recognized and made visible by their dress code. Throughout Chinese history, until the end of the Imperial era, the dress code was a means of differentiating status. Concubines were not allowed the same "grade" of clothing as wives, and by the Qing, it was a specific decree that concubines were not allowed to wear red dresses, which were reserved for wives.[38] The red dress then became a status marker illustrating the superiority of wives, and the marginal status of concubines was so obvious that they could not hide it in social settings.

A woman's social status was also determined by her family background. As concubines had a less prestigious family background than wives—either having been purchased from a poor family or having been maids or prostitutes—their social status was often marginal. It became even

36. For examples of the rivalries between wives and concubines, and between their children, see Cheng, *Qing zhi minguo*, 208–17.
37. Cheng, *Qing zhi minguo*, 167.
38. Shi, *Naqie*, 280.

worse by the time of Republican China when Chinese intellectuals began the New Cultural Movement in 1919. They critiqued Chinese customs for being "old" and advocated modernization according to Western values and practices, and concubinage was identified as one of the major symbols of the "old" culture. Concubines and the system of concubinage were then under severe attack in the propaganda of Chinese intellectuals.

Many articles were published in newspapers and magazines during that time to advocate for the abolition of concubinage in the Chinese marriage system. A survey of these articles shows that concubines are condemned in three main areas.[39]

1. Concubinage is harmful to the health and careers of men: concubinage leads to lechery, which is harmful to a man's health, and it also wastes their time and energy in entertaining the concubines, which could have been better used in developing their careers.[40]
2. Concubinage is harmful to the family in causing rivalries and scandals: "concubines are seldom understanding people and when they enter a family, they fight for the husbands' favor and gossip . . . they come from lowly backgrounds such as prostitutes and singers, with no morals and become adulteresses once they are not watched . . ."[41]
3. Concubinage is harmful to the strength of the nation: concubinage promotes a culture of lechery and luxury in society, and the heirs of polygamy are often physically weak and hence weaken the nation.[42]

Although different authors placed different emphases on these three issues, the overwhelming opinion in the media in Republican China was clearly one of rejection of concubinage and rejection of concubines.[43] The hostility against concubines came not only from men, but also from women's

39. The scope of articles surveyed in this study covers the period before and after the New Cultural Movement, 1910 to 1949, as it reflects the social phenomena that gave rise to the movement and continued thereafter.

40. Examples include Li, "Naqie yu zuoqie de bihai," 37–38; "Shuo naqie zhi hai," 80.

41. "Naqie zhi hai," 75, my translation. The damage that concubinage brings to the family was the most frequently used argument; see Tianjin funü gailiang huibao, "Lun naqie zhi feili jiqi yihai wuqiong," 38; Chang, "Naqie de zuie," 384.

42. Hao, "Feichu naqie zhi pianmian guan," 5; Qian, "Jinzhi naqie wenti zhi shangque," 97–98; Du, "Lun xuqie," 16–18.

43. Although some articles also mention the protection of the rights of women as reasons against concubinage, the focus is nonetheless on the harmfulness of the existence of concubines; see for example, Yu, "Ruhe feichu naqie zhidu," 49–55, which lists the harm that a concubine brings to the family as the primary reason in the argument.

voices in the media as well. One of the seven key issues emphasized by the League of Women's Rights in 1922–1923 was that "the criminal law should declare concubinage a form of bigamy."[44] And women writers, though a minority in the media, also critiqued the existence of concubines severely.[45] While some of these writers may have intended to protect women by discouraging them from entering concubinage, the impact of their writings was nevertheless demeaning to those who already were concubines.

Socially and politically, the early Republican era was the most hostile to concubines in Chinese history. Their characters were vilified as adulterous and seductive, harmful to the men, to the family, and even to the nation. At a time when the entire nation was being motivated to strengthen the country in order to counter the intrusion of foreign power, concubines were pictured as one cause of the weakness of the Chinese nation and therefore were despised by all. A few tried to oppose this propaganda by restating the need for continuing the family line through concubines,[46] yet anti-concubinage advocates proposed "adoption of sons of close relatives" as a means of continuation of family lines.[47] The value of the existence of concubines was so much degraded that the only contribution they had been making to the family—in producing heirs—was also nullified. Even those who supported their existence did not appreciate their value as persons but focused on the benefits to the patriarchal system.

Legal Status

As Judges 19 is a passage involving rape and murder, this section focuses on the status of concubines in the Chinese legal system as they relate to these areas. In the Qing legal system, a person's family status determined his/her legal status.[48] The Qing code offered more protection for men than women. This was illustrated in the obvious difference in sentencing murder cases between husbands and wives (or concubines). If a woman killed her husband, she was inevitably sentenced to death, yet if a man murdered his

---

44. Yao, *Chinese Women*, 128.

45. For example, in an article written by Wuming nüshi ("anonymous lady"), five reasons are listed with detailed descriptions to explain the damage concubines bring to the family and to the men, whereas the suffering of concubines themselves is glossed over in merely two sentences. Wuming nüshi, "Zhongguo naqie de wojian," 40–41.

46. For example, Gu Hongming, who promoted concubinage as a means of "stabilizing the society," uses "teapot and teacups" as a metaphor to justify the idea that a man should marry several women. Zheng and Lu, *Minguo juan*, 13.

47. Hao, "Feichu naqie," 4.

48. Cheng, *Qing zhi minguo*, 21.

wife (or concubine), the sentencing was often as light as exile.⁴⁹ The different statuses of wife and concubine also were reflected in the law. Rapes committed against wives were punished more severely than those against concubines, for though both were regarded as offending the property of another man, the fact that wives were considered more valuable than concubines was reflected in the sentencing.⁵⁰

Not only was the identity as wife or concubine important to a woman's legal status, her chastity also was regarded as playing a vital role. In Neo-Confucian Qing, chastity was at the heart of a woman's value. Phrases such as "it is a small matter to starve to death but a big matter to lose chastity"⁵¹ were deeply rooted in the culture and were so popular to the general public that they were accepted as golden rules without being challenged. A chaste woman, such as a widow who had not remarried, received respect from all, whereas an unchaste woman was regarded as having depleted her own value and was despised by everyone. Chastity concerned not only the virginity of a woman or her sexual faithfulness to her husband; it also included verbal or physical interactions with men. It was so much emphasized in the culture that some women even committed suicide after being verbally assaulted by men or having been touched by men on the hands. Those who did commit suicide were commended by society as being chaste.⁵²

This ingrained concept of chastity in the culture was reflected in the fact that the chastity of a woman was decisive in legal situations. If the adulterous lover of a woman killed her husband, she would be guilty and be sentenced to death even if she was not aware of the murder plot, since her lack of chastity led to the incident. If a man caught his adulterous wife/concubine with the adulterer and killed them, he was not guilty of murder as it was deemed "reasonable."⁵³ Even when the concubine was brutally murdered—as recorded in a case where a concubine who was found to be adulterous was beaten and then buried alive—the patriarch was only lightly sentenced with two years of exile and thirty blows of heavy bamboo.⁵⁴

Although female chastity was regarded as of great importance, the responsibility fell on women to protect their own chastity rather than on men to respect it. It was extremely difficult for women to prove rape under the Qing code; for rape to be established, they had to prove that they had resisted

49. Cheng, *Qing zhi minguo*, 26.
50. Cheng, *Qing zhi minguo*, 35–41.
51. "餓死事小, 失節事大," my translation.
52. Guo, *Qingdai juan*, 256–59.
53. Cheng, *Qing zhi minguo*, 23.
54. Guo, *Qingdai juan*, 219.

throughout the entire ordeal. If not, it was only "illicit intercourse by mutual consent," and the women themselves were subject to punishment.[55] As for those regarded as having lost their chastity, there was even less protection by law: "when a man, having witnessed an illicit affair, proceeded to force himself on the woman, the incident could not be regarded as rape, because the woman was already a fornicator."[56] When the victim was a concubine, her fate was even more miserable. Concubines had little legal protection over their lives and when they were condemned as adulterous, their lives were even more dispensable. In the Qing code, a man killing an "at-fault" concubine who was, for example, disrespectful to an elder member of the family, was only punishable by 100 blows of heavy bamboo, and it could be redeemed by monetary means.[57] As concubines were mostly sold to the patriarch, there was little connection with their original families, and often little concern was raised regarding their deaths. This, in effect, protected the patriarchs who were acting violently toward their concubines.

Overall, concubines in the late Qing to early Republican China did not merely have an inferior status to wives. They were objectified, had no freedom of self, and were barely protected by the law. They lived in insecurity and hostility and were rejected by their family and by society. Their character was cast in a dubious light, and the social prejudice against them was insurmountable. This social context has a significant impact when we consider the character of the concubine in Judges 19. In the next section, I examine the second influence on Chinese interpretation: Christianity and its attitude toward concubinage.

Christianity and Concubinage

Attitude of Foreign Missionaries

Since the entry of European Catholic missionaries to China in the sixteenth century, one of the points of conflict between Western and Chinese cultures was centered on the marriage system. Monogamy was the norm in Western countries, yet Chinese culture had long accepted concubinage as a legitimate part of its marriage system.[58] The conflict was so severe that

---

55. The woman needs to provide evidence, including: (1) witness, either an eyewitness or people who heard her cry for help; (2) bruises or lacerations on her body; (3) torn clothing. Ng, "Ideology and Sexuality," 58.

56. Ng, "Ideology and Sexuality," 58, quoting Xue, *Duli cunyi*, 1080.

57. Cheng, *Qing zhi minguo*, 46–47.

58. It is disputed whether the Chinese marriage system was truly "polygamy" as such, for some scholars argue that since concubines had a different legal and social status, they are not wives in the strict sense and the Chinese marriage system should

early missionaries identified concubinage as one of the major hurdles for Christianity taking root in China, and likewise for missionaries accepting Chinese believers into Christian faith.[59]

Confronted with what was seen by Western culture as an unethical, uncivilized, and absurd practice, missionaries critiqued the custom of concubinage severely. Pamphlets produced for evangelistic purposes included an explanation of the Ten Commandments, which specifically identified concubinage as committing adultery.[60] Not only did they openly reproach concubinage, but also they prohibited those who had concubines from becoming part of the Christian church through baptism. Several cases were recorded in which Matteo Ricci (1552–1610), the Jesuit priest and pioneer of the Jesuit mission to China, refused to perform baptism for men who had concubines.[61] This was particularly significant in demonstrating the firm stand of the church, as Ricci was considered sympathetic to Chinese culture and often more flexible in his mission tactics among missionaries.

Protestant missionaries began to come to China at the end of the nineteenth century, and they maintained the same reproving attitude toward concubinage. They published articles such as "One man should not take two wives" in *Globe Magazine*, an influential magazine founded by missionaries for Chinese intellectuals.[62] The rationale of the missionaries was mostly focused on the damage of concubinage to the family, and only some touched on the core of Chinese Confucian teaching: inequality between men and women.[63] For example, *Yin Jia Dong Dao*, written by Griffith John in Chinese novel format in the late Qing, narrated the conversion story of a Chinese man. Through the voice of this character, concubinage was criticized for its hidden assumption of inequality between men and women:

> If a man has three wives he is considered a good man, yet if a woman has three husbands she is considered evil. This is discrimination against women . . . God created one man and one woman, not one woman two men, nor one man two women . . .

---

be described as "monogamy with concubinage." Shang, "Zhongguo," 176–78. For simplicity of discussion, I will avoid the term "polygamy" and refer to the Chinese system of concubinage only.

59. Cheng, *Qing zhi minguo*, 137.

60. Chen, "Lun ming qing shiqi jidujiao dui zhongguo jiating guanxi de chongji," 110.

61. Chen, "Lun ming qing shiqi jidujiao dui zhongguo jiating guanxi de chongji," 108–11.

62. Chen and Gui, "Xixue dongjian yu zhongguo jindai hunyin biange sixiang de yanjin," 216.

63. Cheng, *Qing zhi minguo*, 337.

hence anyone believing in God, from the Emperor to the gentry and the plebeian, should observe monogamy.⁶⁴

Concubinage and Interpretation of the Bible

The attitude of missionaries against concubinage also was reflected in their commentaries and interpretations of the Bible. They addressed the issue at great length whenever they found the opportunity. In *Tianzhu shengjiao shilu*, written by Michele Ruggieri (1543–1607), the first Jesuit who entered China, the explanation of the sixth commandment (according to Catholic tradition) stood out among others in length:

> The sixth commandment: do not commit adultery. The lust of human beings is severe and hence the strict prohibition. God made men and women and used monogamy for the purpose of procreation. It is sinful for men to take concubines. Why? One woman should not take two men; shall then one man take two women? Man and woman unite in trust, and the union is lost when the trust is gone. And it brings about jealousy between wives and concubines, and conflicts between their heirs . . .⁶⁵

Compared with his one- or two-line explanations for each of the rest of the Decalogue, it is obvious that Ruggieri not only interpreted the commandment against adultery in the context of the social issue of Chinese concubinage, but also that it was a significant matter worth emphasizing in his teachings.

Similarly, in the commentary on the Decalogue written by English congregational missionary Walter Henry Medhurst (1796–1857),⁶⁶ the issue of concubinage was addressed specifically in the discussion of the commandment against adultery. Medhurst pinpointed the two major reasons the Chinese acquired concubines: wealth and the need for an heir. In response to the common Chinese concept that those who can afford concubines should be allowed to do so, he argued that, based on the creation of God, one man should be married to only one woman regardless of wealth. He also attributed the provision of an heir to the will of God, and therefore obtaining sons from concubines was against God's will. He challenged the Chinese traditional emphasis of heritage: "If a man dies without sons, he can pay tribute to God and go to heaven; what is there to complain about? But if a man takes a concubine and commits adultery, he defies human

---

64. John, *Yin Jia Dong Dao*, 7–8, my translation.

65. Ruggieri, "*Tianzhu shengjiao shilu*," 52, my translation. For more examples of missionary comments, see Cheng, *Qing zhi minguo*, 336–40.

66. Medhurst, "Shentian zhi shitiao jie zhuming," 17.

ethics and the law of God; he will go to hell and suffer in eternity."[67] It is apparent that Medhurst regarded concubinage as a cause of perdition for the Chinese, and the social convention behind the practice needed to be rectified in order to bring salvation to the nation.

Condemnations of concubinage not only were restricted to commentaries on the Decalogue. In *Abraham's Life,* written by James Legge on the life of the patriarch in the format of a Chinese novel, Legge commented on the action of Abraham in marrying Hagar: "monogamy is the creation plan of God for human beings, yet one man should not marry two women, just like one woman should not marry two men . . ."[68] Upon Hagar being expelled from the family, again Legge commented: "the son of the concubine and of the wife cannot be equal heirs; hence one man should only marry one wife. The son of the concubine is illegitimate before God, and not a proper heir."[69] And in the concluding comments, he again emphasized: "Isaac was borne by the wife and was the proper heir, and the son of a concubine counts for nothing. This is to show the fault of concubinage."[70]

These examples of missionary writings illustrate the importance of the issue to the Christian church in China during that time and the effort of missionaries in combating the practice. The overall impression toward concubines that Chinese Christians received was certainly one of disapproval and rejection.

Responses from the Chinese

The reproachful attitude of the missionaries toward concubinage was initially met with great resistance from the Chinese, especially from the gentry who were the major evangelistic target in the early phase of the China mission. This was not surprising, as the gentry were the wealthy people who were more able to afford concubines. Many rejected the gospel, since missionaries insisted that to become a Christian they needed to be completely cut off from their concubines. Although a few appreciated the moral value of monogamy, Christianity was unable to make any significant impact in the Imperial period. Even at times when missionaries developed a personal relationship with the emperor, "the request of the Catholic Church for monogamy remained an insurmountable boundary."[71]

---

67. Medhurst, "Shentian zhi shitiao jie zhuming," 62–63, my translation.
68. Legge, "Yabolahan jilüe," 63–64, my translation.
69. Legge, "Yabolahan jilüe," 71.
70. Legge, "Yabolahan jilüe," 78.
71. Cheng, *Qing zhi minguo,* 331–32.

The situation changed considerably by the late Qing and early Republican era. As China became more open to science and to ideologies such as democracy from the West, Chinese literati also were exposed to Western culture, which was considered more advanced in many ways. Monogamy was one such aspect, and it was promoted in the propaganda of the New Cultural Movement. Some Chinese slowly began to convert to Christianity, and Chinese Christians quoted biblical teachings in their arguments against concubinage.[72] Even Chinese writers who did not confess Christianity would refer to Western culture and ethics in support of their advocacy against concubinage.[73]

The negative message from missionaries about concubinage generally was replicated by Chinese Christians. It is interesting, however, that at times Chinese Christians understood the matter of concubinage in the Bible from a different angle. In a church newspaper dated 1926, a Chinese Christian was reported to have acquired a concubine after reading the Genesis account of Abraham, thinking that this could be the way that God would grant him an heir. This created many disturbances in his church, and he finally divorced the woman after much reprimand from fellow Christians.[74] Although an opposite example, this incident further illustrates that biblical texts involving concubines attracted intense attention by Chinese Christians during the late Qing and the Republican China. It is reasonable to infer that when the Chinese read biblical texts involving concubines, they would have been very much alert to their presence and would have associated the text with their social context. It is with such understanding that we turn to the reading potential of Judges 19.

Reading CUV Judges 19 in Republican China

Judges 19 is a gruesome tragedy, yet the identification of the victim may vary depending on the reader's context. To Western feminist readers, the concubine who received such brutal, inhuman treatment, unimaginable by contemporary Western moral standards, would indisputably be *the* victim in the story. The details of the narrative work are highlighted in arousing sympathy from readers toward the concubine.[75] To the Chinese reader in the early twentieth century—who had a cultural heritage of concubinage and lived in a social context of prejudices against concubines—identifying the concubine in the passage as victim might not have been easy. In fact,

---

72. Wei, "Gei naqiezhe yi dangtou yibang," 5–6; Wang, "Naqie yu lihun," 49–64.
73. Shan, "Zhongguo jinzhi naqie zhi fangfa," 103; Du, "Lun xuqie," 18–19.
74. Li, "Siyang," 7–8.
75. Such as Lapsley, *Whispering the Word*, 35–50; Trible, *Texts of Terror*, 65–87.

the Chinese cultural fixation on female chastity and submission to male power, compounded with the translational choices made by European missionaries in the CUV passage, may very well have painted quite an opposite picture for the Chinese reader.

In the following section, I highlight the particularities of the CUV in several translational issues and then discuss the impact these may have had on the Chinese readers.[76] This is then followed by a reading of the text in the social context of early Republican China.

Highlighting Details of Judges 19 in the CUV

The following table highlights the particularities of the translation of Judges 19 in the CUV in several verses that significantly impact the interpretation. The main frame of comparison is with the Hebrew MT and the English Revised Version (1885).[77] The NRSV (1989) is also noted here to compare a contemporary English version.

Hebrew Text (MT)	Chinese Union Version (CUV)	English Revised Version (ERV)	New Revised Standard Version (NRSV)
Verse 2 wtznh ʿlyw plgšw	妾行淫 (the concubine committed adultery)	And his concubine played the harlot against him	But his concubine became angry with him
Verse 25 wyḥzq hʾ yš bpylgšw wyṣʾ ʾ lyhm hḥwṣ wydʿ w ʾ wth wytʿ llw-bh kl-hlylh ʿd-hbqr	那人就把他的妾拉出去交給他們，他們便與他交合，終夜凌辱他 (The man pulled his concubine out to give to them; they had intercourse with her, humiliated her all night.)	so the man laid hold on his concubine, and brought her forth unto them; and they knew her, and abused her all the night until the morning.	So the man seized his concubine, and put her out to them. They wantonly raped her, and abused her all through the night until the morning.

76. Here I will focus on the discussion of the message conveyed by the CUV translation; issues about models of translation, word studies, and the accuracy of translations will be addressed in chapter 6.

77. The point of comparison was chosen because the record of meeting in the board of translation of the CUV resolved to adopt "the text that underlies the revised English version of the Old and New Testaments" as the translational basis. Zetzsche, *Bible in China*, 200.

Hebrew Text (MT)	Chinese Union Version (CUV)	English Revised Version (ERV)	New Revised Standard Version (NRSV)
Verse 29 wyqḥ ʾt-hmʾ klt wyḥzq bplgšw wyntḥh lʿ ṣmyh lšnym ʿ śr ntḥym	用刀將妾的屍身切成十二塊 (used a knife to cut the corpse of the concubine into twelve pieces)	he took a knife, and laid hold on his concubine, and divided her, limb by limb, into twelve pieces.	he took a knife, and grasping his concubine he cut her into twelve pieces, limb by limb.

Verse 2

The meaning of the verb *tznh* has been controversial in biblical scholarship. It has been understood as deriving from *znh*, "to be a prostitute," or "to commit fornication," yet some suggest that it could be derived from a root meaning "to be angry" in Akkadian.[78] Cynthia Edenburg argues that it is a unique occurrence of a homonym of *znh* meaning "being angry, wroth,"[79] and the LXX[A] also uses *ōrgisthē* (grew angry), which evidences the latter option. If it is understood in terms of the first option, then it is contradictory to the Deuteronomic law that prescribes the death sentence for adulterous women. It is also difficult to explain why the Levite would still want her back by speaking kindly to her. Therefore, scholars have either followed the LXX version[80] or tried to resolve the matter by proposing readings that do not imply physical adultery, such as a metaphorical expression that refers to the concubine rejecting her husband's authority.[81] For scholars who take an adulterous implication of the verb, it is still maintained that there is ambiguity in the phrase and some room for interpretation.[82] This allows Lapsley to comment that "perhaps such ambiguity serves a different function: to dissuade the reader from attempting moral evaluations so early in the story."[83] The ERV attempts to convey this ambiguity with "played the harlot," and although the noun

---

78. Butler, *Judges*, 418–19.

79. The reasons she provides include the interpretation in the Targum, the context of the narrative that the Levite and the father do not treat the concubine as an adulteress, and the use of *mem* in the prefix of the preposition when the verb expresses infidelity. Edenburg, *Dismembering*, 16–17n28.

80. Such as Soggin, *Judges*, 286; Boling, *Judges*, 273–74; see also NRSV, NIV.

81. Such as Niditch, *Judges*, 191–92; Exum, "Feminist Criticism," 83.

82. See Schneider, *Judges*, 250–52.

83. Lapsley, *Whispering the Word*, 38.

"harlot" inevitably carries negative connotations, the preceding verb "play" adds a flavor of uncertainty to the description.

The translation of the CUV, however, conveys a message in a totally opposite manner. By translating *tznh* as *xingyin* (行淫, "committed adultery"), there is no room for any other interpretation than that the concubine had been involved in an extra-marital, immoral sexual relationship. In the Chinese cultural context, where chastity was the paramount virtue of women, the labeling of a concubine as an adulteress is heavily value loaded. Therefore, to the Chinese reader, this verse does not merely set the scene by giving the reason the concubine was in her father's house. This verse in the CUV could instead steer the direction of the reading of the entire narrative and provoke vigorous value judgment by the readers against the concubine.

Verse 25

In translating the actions of the Levite against his concubine, the CUV does not translate the full force of the verb *ḥzq* ("seized") and uses a more neutral word *la* (拉, "pulled"). In comparison to the English translations, "laid hold" (ERV) or "seized" (NRSV) function to draw the attention of readers to the activities of the Levite. This in turn highlights his initiation of the matter, which is in stark contrast to the passivity of the concubine. As the verb *ḥzq* in the *hiphil* carries a sense of strong holding, vigorous action, and violence, the translation of the CUV largely reduces the force of his action. His aggressive deeds, in turn, appear much more value neutral to Chinese readers.

In the translation of the actions of the mob against the concubine, the CUV uses *jiaohe* (交合, "intercourse")—which is a gentle way of expressing sexual relationship without any implication of force or initiative—to translate the Hebrew euphemism for sexual intercourse *ydʿ*. While it is true that *ydʿ* does not imply whether the intercourse is voluntary or not, the next verb *ʿll* (abuse) is explicit in expressing the violence of the mob in forcing the concubine into it. Though there is no specific verb for rape in the Hebrew Bible,[84] the context of the verse here clearly refers to rape. As there are verbs in the Chinese language that denote rape, such as "*qiangjian*" (強奸, "rape"), the use of *jiaohe* in the Chinese translation may be seen as downplaying the violence of the mob.[85]

The combination of these translation choices in the CUV results in bringing down the violent tone of the scene as expressed in verse 25. It renders

---

84. Brenner, *Intercourse of Knowledge*, 136–37.

85. It is noted that the English versions contemporary to the CUV also use the euphemism "knew" to translate *ydʿ*, which is replaced by "raped" in the NRSV.

Chinese readers ignorant of the degree of the brutality toward the concubine that is implied in the Hebrew text. Yes, we understand that the Levite initiated her facing the mob, and she had intercourse with multiple men and was humiliated by them. But was she actively resistant to their actions, and had she been subjected to force? Who was ultimately responsible for this incident? The CUV does not seem to provide clear answers to these questions.

Verse 29

There are several places in the CUV translation of this verse that obviously deviate from the Hebrew text. First, the verb *ḥzq* that describes the movement of the Levite is omitted, simplifying his action as "used a knife to cut" instead of "he took a knife, and laid hold on his concubine," as in the ERV. This is the exact same verb that was downplayed in the translation of verse 25, and the reoccurrence can hardly be incidental. The omission takes away the focus from the action of the Levite and from his forceful grasp of the concubine conveyed by the meaning of *ḥzq*. Second, the CUV translates *lʿ ṣmyh* "to the bones" as "*shi shen*" (屍身, "corpse"), which loses the visual effect of the details of the gruesome dismemberment scene. To cut a human body into twelve pieces would no doubt involve cutting down to the bone—how else could it be dissected? Hence, the purpose of providing this piece of detail in the MT is clearly to visualize the dismemberment and intensify the sense of horror to readers. Compared to the ERV and NRSV that both translate "limb by limb," this effect is lost in the CUV when the detail is obscured. Third, while the Hebrew text is notably silent about whether the concubine was alive or dead at the scene, the use of "*shi shen*" in the CUV renders her undoubtedly dead before the Levite put his knife on her.[86] These deviations in the translation of the CUV accumulate to portray the scene of dismemberment in plain, value-neutral language, masking it almost as a post-mortem dissection. The ultimate effect is one that downplays the brutality of the Levite and reduces the horrifying rhetorical effect upon readers.

Having noted these particularities of the CUV of Judges 19, we now integrate them with the socio-political and cultural context in Republican China.

---

86. Although the LXX has "for she was dead" in the preceding verse and takes the action of the Levite in verse 29 on a dead body, it is clear that the Hebrew text is silent on this matter.

Reading CUV Judges 19 from the Social Context of Republican China

Interpretative Framework

The first phrase "in those days, when there was no king in Israel" in Judges 19:1, which forms an *inclusio* with 21:25 and recurs in 17:6 and 18:1, has been identified as providing the framework for understanding the narrative—that the morality of the Israelites was appallingly low at the time when there was no king.[87] To CUV readers in the early twentieth century, this phrase might bring to mind quite different connotations. At the end of the corrupted and frail Qing, the newly formed Republican government represented advancement, democracy, and new hope. Having "no king," instead of connoting chaos and disorder, was a sign of new order, liberation, and civilization. Even without associating this biblical narrative with their contemporary political events, the connection between lawlessness and "no king" was not as direct and apparent.

What would have been more apparent and alarming to the Chinese was the character "concubine" introduced at the end of verse one. As previously noted, the issue of concubinage had been at the heart of the cultural clash between missionaries and local Chinese since the introduction of Christianity into China. If the issue of monogamy in other passages had been prominent in interpretations, surely this narrative here, with a concubine as a main character, would have attracted attention from Chinese readers. If extensive moral lessons about concubinage had been drawn from the Abraham account, Chinese readers reading Judges 19 would expect the Bible to have something to say about the ethics of concubinage in this narrative too. In a Chinese devotional article published in 1934, the title for the reflection on Judges 19 was "A Levite Marrying a Woman as Concubine," and drew moral lessons from the fact that the Levite had a concubine:

> Reading this chapter allows us to see how morally corrupted was the people of Israel . . . The reason for moral corruption is their faith, and the priests were the ones upholding the faith of the people. Levites were the chosen priesthood. In this chapter we see at the very beginning a Levite married a woman as concubine . . . this Levite, marrying an adulterous woman as concubine, how much was the corruption of the priesthood . . .[88]

---

87. Lapsley, *Whispering the Word*, 37.
88. Chen, "Lingxiu rixin," 68, my translation.

The reflection continued further to draw the application that leaders should be morally upright and completely ignored the treatment of the concubine in the narrative. There was not even one word commenting on the brutal actions of the Levite or the mob. It is striking that the author did not seem to see the inhuman treatment of the Levite toward his concubine as a sign of moral corruption. Nor was the horrific gang rape by the mob worth mentioning at all. Rather, what was highlighted as immoral was the fact that a Levite took an adulterous woman as his concubine.

This reflection clearly illustrates that in the socio-political and cultural climate of the early Republican era, the Chinese reading of the passage was fixated on the issue of concubinage. This fixation from the very beginning of the narrative is then further encouraged by the second verse that depicts the concubine as having committed adultery. As chastity determined the value of a woman in the social context, any woman who committed adultery was despised by everyone in her neighbourhood and her family—including her own parents. She shamed her own family by her unchaste actions and did not deserve to live any longer. This was even worse if she were a concubine. There was no legal protection over her life at all. She was at the disposal of her patriarch, whom she had sinned against. No sympathy would be given to her by anyone regardless of what happened thereafter.

This context is vital in the interpretation of the entire narrative. For as much as scholars have tried to demonstrate that the narrator meant to arouse sympathy from readers through the poetics of the story, this sympathy may be difficult to achieve in the reading from the CUV. Any sympathy would have been taken away by the first impression that she was not a chaste woman. Having given the label of unchaste woman to the concubine at the beginning of the narrative, any literary effort thereafter to draw readers closer to her would have been nullified and interpreted otherwise.

One of the most problematic interpretative issues that scholars have wrestled in this passage is the lack of moral judgment in the narrative, either from the characters or the narrator. To Chinese readers of the CUV, this was not so much an issue. The value-loaded image of the adulterous concubine already provided a severe moral judgment at the very beginning of the story, and it became their interpretative framework for the rest of the narrative. Moreover, to early Republican readers, this adulterous concubine represented an echo of the demeaning images of concubines in their media. Already it was promoted in newspapers and propaganda that concubines were destructive to families and promiscuous; and, look, concubines were adulterous even in the Bible! In an article against concubinage from a Chinese Christian journal in 1942, "the Bethlehem woman who committed adultery against her husband in Judges 19" was listed as one of the examples from the Bible supporting the argument that concubines tend to be adulterous and they destroy the family.[89] Indeed, this nameless concubine in Judges 19 was then no longer an individual who happened to be promiscuous; she represented her "category" of women—she was a typical, adulterous concubine and what happened to her would have implications for the rest of her kind.

With this framework of interpretation, we continue to read the rest of the passage.

The Fate of an Unchaste Concubine

While it was bad enough in the Chinese mind that a concubine would commit adultery, the next detail in the narrative pushes her even further away from their approval: this adulterous concubine left her husband. The virtues of women in Neo-Confucianism were all about chastity and submission to male authority, and this woman defied both. As a concubine, she did not have any freedom of movement and was not allowed to leave the patriarch's household without his approval. The CUV clearly expresses that she initiated this action, which implies that she escaped from his house. For this action alone, she was punishable by law. And even worse, she went back to her own father. How much shame would she have brought to her family? It was shameful for any Chinese woman to leave her husband and return to her parents, let alone a woman who was married as a concubine and committed adultery. She could even have put her father in danger, for anyone who sheltered an escaped concubine could be prosecuted. Furthermore, she lived in her father's house for four months; this was a sure sign that she demonstrated no repentance at all. If she had any sense of morality, she would have regretted her action and shown her remorse by committing suicide. To live shamelessly in her father's house for four months further illustrated to Chinese readers her promiscuous character: it was probably not an accident that she committed adultery, as if she was somehow seduced by the adulterer, for she showed no remorse nor made any attempt at compensation.

At this point, Chinese readers would be appalled at the character of the concubine and would expect that she be punished in some way: it was only right she received some consequence for her actions.

Therefore, verse 3 would come as a surprise to the Chinese reader—for the husband did not grab her and beat her up, as one would expect; instead, he went to ask her to come home by speaking kindly to her! The action of the Levite was so unexpected that it might give readers a positive impression of his character. How benevolent was this man! He did not count the wrongs of

---

89. Wang, "Naqie yu lihun," 58–59, my translation.

the concubine and was even coming in person to receive her home. Not only was he taking the trouble to make the trip, he was forgiving enough to say kind words to her. An adulterous concubine certainly did not deserve this kind treatment, and no wonder her father was so happy to see the Levite: he was willing to accept his daughter back. This was way beyond his expectation. The extended hospitality scene in verses 4–9 was therefore no surprise, for the father would try his best to express his bountiful gratitude. Everything was just too good to be true, and there could be a sense of doubt in the action of the Levite: was he truly so benevolent that he did not mind that his concubine committed adultery? Could he be in love with her so much that he could ignore all social expectations and gossiping from others? This hint of doubt might even pave the way for the later events.

In verse 10, the insistence of the Levite to leave would then be read by most Chinese readers as a gesture of patriarchal authority, which was not to be questioned. After all, he was the owner of the concubine, and he had every right to decide when he was to leave. As he had already made a positive impression with readers by his extraordinary kindness to the concubine, it was easy to gloss over any doubts about his decision-making. Rather, the details of the narration would foreshadow that something significant was soon going to happen.

The pace and suspense of the narrative continues to build with the description of the old man accepting the group to his house. Finally, in verse 22, the mob appears. The response of the house-owner to the mob in verse 23 has provoked discussion in biblical scholarship about his rationale in offering the two women.[90] Yet, to a Chinese reader, the attention would be drawn to another detail in his conversation, namely the virginity of his daughter. It was in such stark contrast to the unchaste concubine that one could not miss it: certainly it was more worthwhile to protect the virgin daughter than the unchaste concubine. To juxtapose the two was simply inviting a preference to sacrifice the concubine. After all, according to the law, it was much less serious an offense for an unchaste woman to be gang raped than a chaste virgin.

Therefore, when the concubine was pulled out of the door, it might seem a reasonable choice, for it would have been absurd to send the virgin out. As the CUV removed the emphasis on the force of the Levite in verse 25, and described it in a neutral and matter-of-fact manner, it did not provoke value judgment against the Levite as readily as the Hebrew

---

90. For example, Block suggests that his sense of duty in hospitality supersedes his obligation to his own daughter, "Echo Narrative Technique," 334. Lasine takes an opposite view and comments that it is an inversion of the hospitality of Lot in comparison to Genesis 19; "Guest and Host," 39.

text would have. The actions of the mob also were downplayed by using less severe terms to describe their activity ("intercourse" instead of "rape"); the violence was taken away by the CUV translation and, again, did not promote sympathy toward the concubine. In fact, to readers, this ordeal could have been taken as a fulfilment of the long-awaited punishment. As a concubine, she was an object that belonged to the patriarch, and he had the right to give her away to anyone at any time as he pleased. Now that she had committed adultery, and was insubmissive to him, he had even more reason to evict her from his protection. He had already been kind enough to take her back, yet he had no obligation to shelter her any longer. Whatever happened to her after she stepped out of the door was not the fault of the Levite, but the consequence of her own actions.

Hence, when one reads in verse 26 that she comes back and falls at the door, the focus might not be on how weak she is, but on the fact that she actually comes back. Why is she alive at all? For any traditional Chinese woman facing gang rape, the right thing to do was to resist until death. If she remains alive, it casts doubt on whether the mob was actually forceful or whether she has somehow willingly complied. Either way, it does not encourage sympathy toward the concubine. Not only is she alive, she even comes back to the Levite. By pulling her out to the mob, it signifies that he had evicted her from his protection, and her life and death did not matter to him anymore. She could not have expected any help from him. Moreover, now that she has been "humiliated" by a group of men, she has become even more unchaste and shameful. It is almost incomprehensible for him to take her back again. Therefore, when verses 27–28 depict the Levite telling her to get up and go, it is a kindness in him to lay eyes on her at all. She is so undeserving that he could leave her behind to die.

Perhaps the only action done to the concubine in the narrative that truly shocked Chinese readers is her dismemberment in verse 29. However, as the CUV has already downplayed the force of the Levite and also pronounces her dead at that point, the attention of Chinese readers would be diverted from the brutality of the action to its implications. In Chinese culture, it was of vital importance that a person died with a whole body. It was considered a great misfortune if anyone died with body parts missing. Death without a whole body was often associated with criminals being beheaded or dismembered, which were more severe punishments than death by poisoning or hanging. To die without a whole body was hence a great dishonor that anyone would want to avoid. Therefore, verse 29, instead of causing horror and sympathy, might bring to mind connotations of shame and dishonor. The action of the Levite might even be interpreted as demonstrating that the concubine has disgraced herself so much that she has lost any value as a woman. Instead of provoking value judgment upon the one who dismembered her body, the CUV translation, together with the Chinese culture, provokes a value judgment upon the dismembered body itself.

Reading the CUV translation of Judges 19, the concubine is not so much a pitiful victim drawing sympathy from readers. Rather, she is portrayed as a shameless, adulterous woman who brings the misfortune upon herself. The Levite, on the other hand, had done more than what is expected of him. In a socio-political climate advocating abolition of concubinage, and with the priority given by European missionaries to promoting monogamy, this narrative may well have served as a warning to all Chinese Christians. To the men, it confirmed that concubines were promiscuous in nature and, therefore, do not take concubines; to the women, especially the concubines, it was a warning to maintain their chastity. Unchaste behaviour led to severe consequences, including gang rape and even death without a whole body. This was a narrative that showed no mercy to concubines and echoed contemporary prejudices they received in their social world. In this sense, this translation could have reinforced patriarchal values and oppression toward Chinese women.

Conclusion

To the Chinese reader, the story of the concubine in Judges 19 came to life when situated within the socio-political and cultural context of early Republican China. She was an object belonging to the patriarch, her living depended on his favor, and she had to submit to him in every way. When she did not, dire consequences followed. She was not protected legally, and she was despised by all. Throughout her life, she was objectified, demonized, and rejected. Even if a Chinese concubine was fortunate enough to hear the gospel, she found condemnation of women of her kind in the Bible. The following monologue recorded by Jesuit missionary Louis le Comte reflects the desperation of concubines trapped between Chinese culture and Christianity:

> I belong to an official who bought me. If I leave his house, he has legal authority to seize me back, and beat me like punishing slaves. If I am lucky enough to escape from his search, where can I find a safe shelter? My parents who sold me dare not take me, and I will inevitably fall into the hands of another man, and he will still put me into situations I want to avoid. Therefore I should stay in my current home, but how to resist a violent person who only sees me through his lust? And his lust is protected

by the laws of the empire . . . command me what I can do, but do not refuse to baptise me.[91]

Such hopelessness and despair could well have been the voice of the concubine in Judges 19. The question remains, was this indeed the message of the scriptural passage? Was the narrative written as a warning to the women, especially to the concubines, in ancient Israelite society, or was it somehow misinterpreted and mistranslated in the Chinese context? This will be explored in the following chapters.

---

91. Cheng, *Qing zhi minguo*, 331, my translation. Although Louis le Comte was a figure in the seventeenth to the eighteenth centuries, this monologue well illustrates the situation of Chinese concubines and hence I am borrowing it across time. In fact, their lives and status did not improve much from then to the Republican era, if it did not worsen.

Reading the *Pîlegeš* (Concubine) in Judges 19 in the Historical Context

Introduction

THE *PÎLEGEŠ* (CONCUBINE) IN Judges 19 is the only female character in the narrative. Though portrayed without any speech, she is the persona on whom the entire story centers. Understanding this character hence plays a significant role in the interpretation of the text. However, the representation of her exact identity as a concubine is much disputed in contemporary biblical scholarship, ranging from "a spoiled wife"[1] to "virtually a slave."[2] This illustrates that there are certain hurdles, or even confusion, in the reading of this character.

At the heart of the issue is the question "what is a *pîlegeš*?" Most English versions of the Bible translate *pîlegeš* as "concubine." Given the lack of a parallel in today's society, especially in the West, there is a gap that readers and commentators need to bridge in order to understand her social identity.[3] What did it mean to be a concubine in ancient Israel? What were her marital, social, and legal statuses? Answers to these questions are important for the interpretation of the narrative.

It is therefore necessary to seek understanding of concubinage in the historical context of ancient Israel. The primary source of investigation is, of course, the Hebrew Bible, yet extra-biblical materials in the ancient Near East may also be helpful. According to proponents of the comparative method, or the contextual approach, as it is sometimes called, the Hebrew Bible is a product of its time and hence is susceptible to influences from its nearby cultures. It is therefore potentially beneficial to consult literary and

---

1. Louis M. Epstein considers her running away in verse 2 as a narrative description of a spoiled wife. "Institution of Concubinage," 167.

2. Trible, *Texts of Terror*, 66.

3. In fact, even in societies with the practice of concubinage or the living memory of concubines such as China, there could be differences in the practice as compared to that of ancient Israel.

historical sources from the ancient Near East in order to understand the practice of concubinage found in biblical texts. This chapter adopts this approach, brings together the findings of studies on the issue, and examines the subsequent implications for the interpretation of the narrative.[4]

In order to identify the issues to be clarified, I begin with a survey of the perception of the concubine in Judges 19 in current biblical scholarship, paying particular attention to points where opinions diverge. I then examine the practice of concubinage within the Hebrew Bible, focusing on the issues raised in the previous section. This is followed by an analysis of relevant studies based on ancient Near Eastern sources and their significance for the interpretation of Judges 19. This chapter demonstrates that the comparative approach is beneficial in clearing away certain difficulties in the understanding of the identity of a *pîlegeš* yet is insufficient for resolving all the questions concerning this character in the interpretation of the narrative.

The Concubine of Judges 19 in Biblical Scholarship

This section aims to identify the issues puzzling current biblical scholarship concerning the concubine in Judges 19. It surveys various perceptions of her identity and illustrates the diversity and ambiguity in the discussions. In order to sketch the big picture, it examines contemporary English commentaries and also feminist publications, as the latter tend to take a closer look at the concubine. It demonstrates that there are two major points of confusion among scholars: the terminology used in addressing the *pîlegeš* and her marital status. These bring ambiguities to the perception of her social and legal status, and in turn have an impact on the interpretation of the narrative.

Terminologies Used in the Designation of the *Pîlegeš*

A survey of scholarship on the use of terminologies designating the *pîlegeš* shows that there is not much consensus. Most English versions of the Bible, such as the NKJV, NIV, NRSV, ASV and ESV, translate *pîlegeš* in Judges 19 as "concubine." However, an exception can be found in the New Life Version (NLV). The NLV translates *pîlegeš* as "wife" in 19:1, and "woman" in the rest of the occurrences in 19:9, 10, 24, 25, 27, 29. As both "wife" and "woman"

---

4. Due to the limitation of the scope of this chapter, I draw upon the findings of studies that examine primary sources without going into the details of each source *per se*.

correspond to ʾ*šh* in Hebrew, it appears that the NLV translators do not recognize *pîlegeš* as a category distinct from ʾ*šh*.⁵

A similar sense of ambiguity also is observed among commentators. While many recent commentators translate *pîlegeš* in Judges 19 as "concubine,"⁶ in their comments on the text, some replace the term with alternative designations: Butler uses "secondary wife,"⁷ Soggin and Niditch both use "wife."⁸ These designations lead to confusion as to the author's understanding of the identity of the *pîlegeš*: is a concubine the same as a wife? What is the difference between a concubine and a wife in the Hebrew Bible?

The terminologies used to designate the *pîlegeš* are notably more divergent among feminist scholars. Though some follow the tradition and refer to her as "concubine,"⁹ others use terms such as "secondary wife" and "concubine wife" interchangeably without much clarification.¹⁰ For other authors, the term "concubine" is utterly rejected. Both Mieke Bal and Tammi J. Schneider consider the English word "concubine" as implying cohabitation without a marriage bond, which is inappropriate in the case of Judges 19. Bal sees her as a legal wife in a patrilocal marriage system and coins the name "Beth" for her instead,¹¹ whereas Schneider seems to have given up on translating the term and uses the transliteration *pîlegeš*.¹² Cheryl Exum also rejects the word "concubine," as it "gives the impression that she is less valued, and probably more expendable than a legitimate wife,"¹³ and uses "Bath-sheber," with the meaning "daughter of breaking," as her designation for the woman.

---

5. This may be explained by the purpose of the NLV in providing an easy-to-read version with limited vocabularies (see Gerber, "English Translations of Scripture," 16), and possibly the distinction between *pîlegeš* and ʾ*šh* is not deemed significant enough to the translators to warrant another word. However, this nonetheless demonstrates the ambiguity of the identity of the concubine to the translators in this instance.

6. See Butler, *Judges*, 405; Webb, *Book of Judges*, 454; Soggin, *Judges*, 283; Boling, *Judges*, 271; Niditch, *Judges*, 185; Block, *Judges*, 536–37; Matthews, *Judges and Ruth*, 178.

7. Butler, *Judges*, 419, 421, 427.

8. Soggin, *Judges*, 279–80; Niditch, *Judges*, 194.

9. See Trible, *Texts of Terror*, 66; Ackerman, *Warrior*, 235.

10. Jones-Warsaw, "Toward a Womanist Hermeneutic," 174–77.

11. Bal, *Death & Dissymmetry*, 81.

12. Schneider, *Judges*, 248.

13. Exum, *Fragmented Women*, 170. The connotation is also recognized by John McKenzie, who notes that concubine "is a misleading term, because it denotes an illegitimate union"; *World of the Judges*, 164.

The diversity of terminologies used to designate the *pîlegeš* in Judges 19 illustrates that there is no consensus on her identity. Was she a concubine, a wife, a concubine wife, a secondary wife, or some combination of the above? Were these categories somehow interchangeable in the ancient Hebrew marriage system? The various positions adopted by the different authors point to more ambiguity than understanding in this regard. If she is not to be called a "concubine," as Bal, Exum and Schneider contend, neither the coining of names for her as "Beth" and "Bath-sheber," nor the use of the transliteration *pîlegeš* seem to be beneficial in helping the modern reader understand her social identity. In fact, their strategies of replacing the difficult term "concubine" with other even less familiar terms may bring new questions rather than clarification.

Marital Status of the *Pîlegeš*

The root of the problem in designating the *pîlegeš* is, as this section demonstrates, largely related to the divergent perceptions of her marital status. Here I first survey the opinions of scholars on the marital status of the *pîlegeš* in Judges 19 and then discuss the implications for the reading of the text.

Scholarly Opinions

While many commentators agree that the *pîlegeš* is married to the Levite, the ways that they perceive this marital union have differing nuances. Some emphasize the legality of the union by acknowledging her as "a legitimate wife, but of second rank"[14] or "legal wife of secondary rank."[15] Other scholars attempt to provide more details of this union: Matthews asserts that "her status is a secondary wife (i.e., one without a dowry)";[16] and Niditch makes inferences from the accounts of concubinage in Genesis, suggesting that concubines in the Hebrew Bible are often acquired for additional fertility for the husbands, with "social obligation and contract of some kind" implicit in the marriage bond.[17] There is, however, no further explanation of this vague concept of social obligation and contract. It is not clear from these

---

14. Soggin, *Judges*, 159.
15. Exum, *Fragmented Women*, 177.
16. Matthews, *Judges*, 180. However, he gives no account of such interpretation, and neither is there any explanation of how being a wife without a dowry affects the marital contract or her status within the marriage.
17. Niditch, *Judges*, 191.

comments exactly how the concubine is different from the wife in terms of her status, both within and outside the family.

Bal, on the other hand, argues for a totally different understanding of the marital status of the *pîlegeš*. She contends that the meaning of *pîlegeš* is a wife "in the older kind of marriage in which the wife stays in her father's house,"[18] and this "patrilocal marriage" is a marital union among nomads where the husband visits the wife at irregular intervals. Bal suggests that the *pîlegeš* in Judges 19 comes from a tradition of patrilocal marriage, whereas the Levite is from the tradition of virilocal marriage, in which the wife moves to the clan of the husband. The narrative is then interpreted as a power struggle between the two marriage systems.[19]

A few scholars appear to be more skeptical of the marital status of the *pîlegeš* in Judges 19. In highlighting the concubine as the victim of violence in the text, Trible comments that "legally and socially, she is not the equivalent of a wife but is virtually a slave, secured by a man for his own purposes."[20] She then designates the Levite as the concubine's "master,"[21] and it is unclear whether Trible considers this type of relationship to resemble marital union at all. Webb's view also is rather ambiguous on the issue. He addresses the concubine as the Levite's "partner," and the use of the term "son-in-law" in verse 4 is interpreted as her father's "full acceptance of his daughter's relationship with the Levite as formal and approved."[22] It is not explicit whether this "relationship" is considered legal marriage as such.

Schneider, on the other hand, is most explicit among the commentators in rejecting the married status of the *pîlegeš*. She argues that the references to *pîlegeš* in biblical stories do not explicitly state the marital status of the women, and it is unknown in Judges 19 if there are any marital arrangements between the two.[23] While Schneider acknowledges that the term could refer to secondary wives in certain societies, this meaning in the text is rejected, for there is no evidence of a primary wife in the narrative.[24] She

---

18. This form of marriage may not last for a lifetime, and it may not be monogamous. Bal, *Death & Dissymmetry*, 84.

19. Bal, *Death & Dissymmetry*, 86–89. This interpretation, however, has not gained much support. Exum, for example, contends that it does not fit most biblical occurrences of the term *pîlegeš*; *Fragmented Women*, 177n13.

20. Trible, *Texts of Terror*, 66.

21. Trible, *Texts of Terror*, 67.

22. Webb, *Book of Judges*, 456–57.

23. Schneider, *Judges*, 247.

24. Schneider, *Judges*, 248–49. However, whether a primary wife is mentioned in the narrative is totally irrelevant to the status of the *pîlegeš*. The primary wife may simply be neglected by the narrator for she does not contribute to the flow of the narrative.

also challenges the understanding of the terms that seem to imply a marital relationship in the text. She argues that ʾyš (man) in verse 3 should be translated "man" instead of "husband,"[25] and casts doubt on the translations of "father-in-law" and "son-in-law" for ḥōtēn and ḥātān in verses 4–5.[26] Instead of indicating a marital union, these terms in the narrative are interpreted as being "used intentionally to show how problematic these relationships were, especially at this time of Israel's history."[27]

Ackerman tries to strike a middle ground by proposing two types of pîlegeš in the Hebrew Bible, each with different marital statuses. The first type is "married to a man as a secondary wife," whereas the second type is "a woman who was unmarried but in a mistress-type relationship with a man."[28] Based on the use of titles, including "husband" and "father-in-law" in Judges 19, this pîlegeš is then classified as the first type of married concubine.[29]

This survey of scholarship on the marital status of the pîlegeš illustrates that it is very much an issue in dispute. All combinations of possibilities are attested among scholars: married; not married; both married and not married; and undecided. The diversity of opinions creates issues in the interpretation of Judges 19, as will be discussed in the next section.

---

25. While it is true that ʾyš could be translated both "man" and "husband," the reasoning of Schneider here seems somewhat circular. She presumes that pîlegeš in verses 1–2 does not imply marital union and so ʾyš in verse 3 cannot mean husband, for the narrative has not given him a wife. Then the designation ʾyš cannot be seen as a clue to their marital union.

26. Schneider, *Judges*, 255–56.

27. Schneider, *Judges*, 256. This argument assumes that "father-in-law" and "son-in-law" are inappropriate terms for describing men connected in relationship by means of a pîlegeš, yet Schneider has not demonstrated any evidence to support such an interpretation.

28. Ackerman, *Warrior*, 236. Her evidence for the second type of concubine is based on the categorization of "wives and concubines" in the list of women dwelling in the harem of kings such as David and Solomon. She understands these lists as excluding concubines from the "actual wives," therefore implying that these concubines are unmarried (*Warrior*, 250–51). Such an interpretation assumes that "wives" are the only title for legally-married women in ancient Israel, and hence when "wives" and "concubines" are put in juxtaposition, it designates a distinction in marital status. While the lists do imply a difference between wives and concubines, the juxtaposition does not necessarily refer to marital status, and hence the argument for this "second type of *pîlegeš*" is questionable.

29. Ackerman, *Warrior*, 236.

Implications of the Marital Status of Pîlegeš

The marital status of the *pîlegeš* in Judges 19 has relevance to the interpretation of the narrative in several aspects. This is illustrated below with examples from scholarship.

INTERPRETATION OF VERSE 2

The marital status of the concubine plays a significant role in how her actions in verse 2 are perceived. For those who advocate a married status, the interpretation of physical adultery poses a contradiction with the Deuteronomic laws, which prescribe death sentences to adulterous wives. Although the laws do not refer to the *pîlegeš per se*, if they are considered married to the husband, then the laws concerning wives may equally apply to concubines. This apparent illogicality prompts authors to propose alternative understandings. For example, Boling considers the action of the *pîlegeš* in returning to her father's house a gesture similar to divorce, and "as the Israelite laws do not allow for divorce by the wife, she became an adulteress by walking out on him."[30] The verb *znh* is therefore understood metaphorically in that she is considered unfaithful by initiating a separation. However, to Schneider who does not recognize the *pîlegeš* as being married to the Levite, the issue of verse 2 is then not so much of a problem. She contends that "there are no rules in the MT governing what is considered adultery or unlawful procedures for a *pîlegeš* because it is not a state that the laws recognize or regulate."[31] It is therefore "irrelevant" to her whether *znh* should be interpreted as physical fornication.[32] This contrast in interpretations demonstrates that the marital status of a *pîlegeš* is key to the understanding of the narrative.

---

30. Boling, *Judges*, 274.
31. Schneider, *Judges*, 251.
32. Schneider seems to be pointing to a loophole in the laws in that they do not regulate the behavior of a *pîlegeš*. While it may well be true that one cannot assume all laws concerning a wife were equally applicable to a *pîlegeš*, it is questionable whether this indicates a total ignorance of the laws concerning women of this status. After all, it is an identity that clearly exists in the biblical accounts, and it is hard to imagine that there is no legal concern regarding their behaviors.

Interpretation of the Gibeah Incident

The marital status of the *pîlegeš* is also significant in the interpretation of the Gibeah incident in verses 22–26. It is manifested on two levels—first in the hospitality of the Ephraimite and second in the rape by the mob.

During the stay of the group at Gibeah, the Ephraimite offers both the *pîlegeš* and his virgin daughter to the mob (verse 24). This raises questions of whether the host has an obligation to protect the *pîlegeš* and whether he has the right to offer her to the mob. The relationship of the *pîlegeš* to the Levite therefore plays a role in the interpretation. If she is married to the Levite, there seems to be a stronger obligation of hospitality from the Ephraimite to include her in his protection. This is demonstrated in Matthews's discussion: "women are legal extensions of their husbands and thus would come under the same protections guaranteed to their husbands—as long as their husbands identified them as such."[33] The concubine is therefore considered as having a similar—if not equal—social status as a wife in terms of protection by the host in the culture. In other words, if she is not married to the Levite she may not be granted the same level of protection. This illustrates that the marital status of the concubine has implications for her social status and influences how others in society may perceive her.

The relationship between the *pîlegeš* and the Levite also is important in the interpretation of the gang rape, since it influences how the violence might be viewed in the historical context. As the laws on adultery in Deuteronomy 22:23–29 illustrate, the severity of the penalty for rape is very much related to the marital status of the woman. If she is married, the man who offends her should be put to death, according to verses 25–27. If she has not been betrothed, verses 28–29 prescribe a monetary fine payable to her father, and the offender is to marry her for life.[34] Without getting into the notorious argument of whether the Deuteronomic laws were enacted in reality, it nonetheless reflects an attitude toward the matter of rape that is dependent on the marital status of the woman. It is therefore important to understand whether the *pîlegeš* is considered married to the Levite in the eyes of the ancient readers. However, this aspect of significance in the text has not been generally recognized. Few address the issue of how the rape might have been perceived in the culture of ancient Israel, and none seem to consider the marital status of the woman in their discussion.[35]

33. Matthews, *Judges*, 187.

34. It has been noticed that the prescription in Exodus 22:15–16 is apparently different from that in Deuteronomy 22:28–29. However, Carolyn Pressler argues that the two are variants of the same principle; see Pressler, *View of Women*, 35–41.

35. Ken Stone attempts to read the incident from the perspective of the

These examples illustrate that the marital status of the concubine has implications for her social and legal statuses, which in turn impacts how the narrative of Judges 19 may be interpreted. There is much diversity of views on these issues, and little information is known on the practice of concubinage in ancient Israel, apart from some general and vague concepts such as "a concubine has lower status than the wife." What did it actually mean to a woman to be a *pîlegeš* and how would it have affected her life? Did the status of a concubine make her legally more vulnerable? Would her actions, or the actions done to her in the text, have been viewed differently in her historical context if she were a wife? It is evident that a more thorough consideration of the practice of concubinage in the historical context of the text is required.

Concubinage: A Comparative/Contextual Approach

Comparative study of the Hebrew Bible emerged as a result of the advances in the discovery and deciphering of ancient Near Eastern texts over the past two centuries. It is grounded in the recognition that the Hebrew Bible is a product of its time and culture, which renders it susceptible to influences from nearby regions. It is therefore potentially fruitful to compare and contrast literary and historical sources from the ancient Near East to the biblical corpus. The goal is to situate the biblical text in its historical context, hence the alternative name "contextual approach" advocated by William Hallo and K. Lawson Younger.[36] Various models and approaches have since been proposed. Scholars' attitudes toward the methodology have ranged from "parallelomania," drawing parallels excessively with too many postulations, to "parallel-onoia," avoiding parallel readings so much that the cultural influences are totally neglected.[37] In more recent decades, scholars are recommending an intermediate attitude, which recognizes the benefits of comparisons and yet exercises the method with caution.

This intermediate approach is demonstrated in an article by Shemaryahu Talmon that addresses the principles and problems of the comparative method. In particular, it emphasizes the importance of studying

---

Mediterranean culture of honor and shame, arguing that the rape of the woman is a way to shame the man to whom she belongs. However, he considers the insult as applying to all women of the household of the man and does not differentiate between whether she is married to the man or whether she is a wife or a concubine. It would be beneficial to explore this further. Stone, "Gender and Homosexuality," 98–101.

36. Hallo and Younger, *Context of Scripture*, xxv.

37. For an overview of the various methods, see Hays, *Hidden Riches*, 22–36.

inner-biblical parallels prior to making comparisons with extra-biblical materials: "In the evaluation of a societal phenomenon, attention should be paid to its function in the developing structure of the Israelite body politic before one engages in the comparisons of parallel phenomena in other societies."[38] In other words, in the reconstruction of the historical context of biblical texts, priority is given to the tradition as established and attested in the Hebrew Bible, and extra-biblical resources are subsequently used for contrasts and comparisons to the Hebrew practice. The sources used for comparison should also be weighted according to their temporal and geographical affinity with ancient Israel. This avoids isolating individual texts from the biblical tradition, as well as setting up connections between texts that are too far apart for legitimate comparisons.

Talmon's approach provides a platform for utilizing ancient Near Eastern resources without venturing too far from the specific context of historical Israel. This forms the framework here for examining the practice of concubinage in ancient Israel. In order to gather information on the primary context, I first focus on the texts in the Hebrew Bible that relate to concubines, then consult studies that examine customs in the ancient Near Eastern sources.

Concubinage in the Hebrew Bible

In studying the practice of concubinage in the Hebrew Bible, there are two issues that complicate the exercise and need to be addressed first. One is the reluctance to acknowledge the existence of concubinage, and the other relates to the Hebrew terms for concubines.

The Reluctance to Acknowledge Concubinage

The practice of polygamy, or more precisely polygyny, is undeniable in the Hebrew Bible. Not only is it evident in narratives such as the Genesis accounts of the patriarchs and the name lists of the wives and concubines of kings such as David and Solomon, Deuteronomic laws such as Deuteronomy 21:15–17 also assume the situation of multiple wives. However, there has been little attention paid to the topic of concubinage itself, and the practice does not seem to be sufficiently considered even in studies on families and marriage systems in ancient Israel.[39]

38. Talmon, "'Comparative Method,'" 356.
39. For example, in the investigation of families in First Temple Israel, although Blenkinsopp acknowledges that "polygamous union occurred throughout most of

On some occasions, one can even observe a deliberate toning down of the historicity of polygyny in biblical Israel. For example, writing in the nineteenth century, Sereno Dwight dismisses the persistence of the polygamous situations in Genesis by describing the relationship between Hagar and Abraham as "temporary intercourse with a bondwoman; and ceased as soon as Hagar had conceived."[40] A similar attitude also is observed in recent scholarship in *Flame of Yahweh: Sexuality in the Old Testament* by Richard Davidson. His conclusion to the discussion on the phenomenon of concubinage is that the practice is rare in ancient Israel and should be condemned.[41] The attitudes of Dwight and Davidson show that the agenda of these authors has somewhat distorted their interpretation of the practice of polygyny in the Hebrew Bible. In upholding monogamy as the divine will, they try to minimize and push aside the existence of polygyny in ancient Israel. These sorts of attitudes may have contributed to a general lack of attention from scholars on the issue of concubinage.

Hebrew Terms for Concubines

The study of concubinage in the Hebrew Bible has also been complicated by the different Hebrew words used to describe women in the household who have sexual relationships with the master. Apart from *pîlegeš*, some scholars consider *'mh* (handmaid) and *špḥh* (maidservant) as representing the same category of women and include all three terms in their discussion of the practice of concubinage in ancient Israel; hence the complication.

For example, Neufeld's study in the 1940s, which is often cited by later scholars,[42] considers the use of the three terms *pîlegeš*, *'mh* and *špḥh* in the biblical texts as denoting women who "served the same purpose, all were acquired in the same way, all were female attendants and formed part of the household."[43] Hence he regards all three Hebrew terms as the "biblical

---

the biblical period," he does not seem to consider in any depth what it means to the marriage system. He even calls the Levite's concubine his "girlfriend" in his passing remark on the narrative, which shows either disinterest or imprecision concerning her identity as a concubine. Blenkinsopp, "Family in First Temple Israel," 58, 77.

40. Dwight, *Hebrew Wife*, 5–7. Interestingly, this is along the same line of argument as the missionaries in China at about the same time.

41. Davidson, *Flame of Yahweh*, 206–11. He even suggests that David, a man after God's own heart, may have returned to monogamy at a later stage of his life with Bathsheba, 206–7. Obviously, the evidence in the text to support such a claim is weak, and the comment stems from the agenda of the author in rejecting polygamy.

42. For example, McComiskey, "Status of the Secondary Wife," 92.

43. Neufeld, *Ancient Hebrew Marriage Laws*, 121–22.

names for a concubine," and that the difference in the terms is only a philological one: *'mh* and *špḥh* originate from female servants while *pîlegeš* does not seem to be associated with the household. He infers, from Genesis 35:22; Judges 18:1–2; 2 Samuel 15:16; and 20:3, that *pîlegeš* "seems to be associated with greater laxity of morals" and then postulates that "it is not unlikely that originally she was nothing more than a prostitute."[44] A *pîlegeš*, according to Neufeld, has the same legal status as *'mh* and *špḥh* but she may only be accepted temporarily for the sole purpose of bearing children. He concluded that "the concubine is not married by her master, and her status differed very slightly from that of a slave."[45]

There are several problems with Neufeld's argument. First, the interpretation of *'mh* and *špḥh* as "biblical names for a concubine" seems to indicate that all occurrences of these terms are referring to women who have sexual relationships with the master. This does not fit the context of some texts. On some occasions, such as Exodus 21:32; Leviticus 25:44; Deuteronomy 5:14, *'mh* is used in parallel with *'bd* (male servant), which suggests that *'mh* is to be understood as a counterpart, that is, a female servant. In fact, in some texts it is rather clear that concubinage is not implied, such as Exodus 2:5; 1 Samuel 1:11; and 2 Samuel 14:15.[46] Although it is true that the terms are also used to refer to certain female servants who are given to the master for childbearing, such as Hagar and Bilhah, it is possible that *'mh* and *špḥh* are used to indicate their identities as servants rather than sexual partners of the masters.

Second, the examples that Neufeld uses to suggest that a *pîlegeš* has a greater laxity in morality are problematic. The fact that Absalom has intercourse with the *pîlegešîm* (plural form of *pîlegeš*) of David does not necessarily mean the women willingly participated; it is inconceivable that being left alone in the palace they were able to resist the force of Absalom. It is more likely that the women were targeted and raped due to the implication of such actions, that is, the usurping of power over the man with whom they were associated.[47] Moreover, although the etymology of *pîlegeš* remains uncertain, the suggestions proposed by scholars thus far do not point to any

---

44. Neufeld, *Ancient Hebrew Marriage Laws*, 123.

45. Neufeld, *Ancient Hebrew Marriage Laws*, 124.

46. Carolyn Pressler argues for the general meaning of "bondswoman" for *'mh* in "Wives and Daughters," 157–58.

47. Karen Engelken also considers the action of David leaving the women behind to be a test for Absalom rather than an expectation of them to defend the palace; *Frauen*, 79.

association with moral laxity or prostitution.[48] The connection of prostitutes with *pîlegeš* is therefore rather questionable.

Third, the transient nature of the relationship between the master and the *pîlegeš* that Neufeld proposed also creates a problem in understanding their appearance in genealogies (such as Gen 22:24, 36:12; 2 Sam 5:13; 2 Chr 11:21). It is difficult to explain why the *pîlegeš* is mentioned and put in juxtaposition with wives, if she was not considered a permanent member of the household. Also, the inclusion of *pîlegeš* in the list for kings instead of ' *mh* or *šphh* also seems to indicate that *pîlegeš* is in a different and higher category.

Considering these problems with Neufeld's view, Epstein's discussion provides a better understanding of the terms regarding concubinage in the Hebrew Bible. He considers *pîlegeš* as a category of freeborn or freed women who are "secondary wives" distinguished in status from the wives. Only women called *pîlegeš* are the concubines of the master. He may also have sexual relationships with the slaves, either his own slaves or those belonging to the wife, and they are called slave-wives, ' *mh* or *šphh*, who are distinguished from and are lower in status than the concubines.[49] The difference between *pîlegeš* and ' *mh* or *šphh* is then a difference in the identity of the woman in being free or enslaved. It therefore has significant legal implications, and Epstein contends that "the slave-wife and the concubine, while next to each other in social rank, were extremely far from each other in legal position."[50] The distinction between *pîlegeš* and ' *mh* or *šphh* in the Hebrew Bible, according to Epstein, is clear and the terms are not interchangeable.[51]

Epstein's stand offers a more unambiguous perspective in examining the practice of concubinage in ancient Israel as it identifies *pîlegeš* as a specific

---

48. Engelken also gives a summary in *Theological Dictionary of the Old Testament* of the various proposals of the etymology of *pîlegeš* by scholars and considers the existing explanations unsatisfactory. "*Pîlegeš*," 549.

49. Epstein, "Institution of Concubinage," 157–8. Similarly, Engelken recognizes that the *pîlegeš* is not a slave and she has a higher position than the ' *mh* and *šphh*, Engelken, *Frauen*, 124.

50. However, "when the master freed his slave-wife and yet retained her in his harem, she became a concubine by law"; Epstein, "Institution of Concubinage," 363. The study of an inscription from the tomb at the Royal Steward also led Rabin to confirm that the *pîlegeš* had a legal status that the ' *mh* did not have. Rabin, "Origin of the Hebrew Word *Pîlegeš*," 363.

51. He offers a convincing explanation of the only instance of apparent confusion, that of Bilhah, who was both designated as *šphh* or ' *mh* (Gen 30:3–4) and *pîlegeš* (Gen 35:22): Bilhah belonged to Rachel and hence was a slave-wife as long as she lived, and when she died she became a *pîlegeš*, concubine, as she remained in the household. Epstein, "Institution of Concubinage," 160–61.

category of women in the household. As the Levite's concubine in Judges 19 is clearly referred to as *pîlegeš* in the narrative, the discussion below primarily focuses on biblical texts that involve the term *pîlegeš*.

Concubinage in Biblical Texts Involving Pileges

The term *pîlegeš* occurs thirty-seven times in the Hebrew Bible.[52] The only publication so far that has provided a comprehensive analysis of all its occurrences is the reworked dissertation of Karen Engelken: *Frauen im Alten Israel: eine begriffsgeschichtliche und sozialrechtliche Studie zur Stellung der Frau im Alten Testament*. The discussion here first summarizes her observations and then applies them to the text of Judges 19.

Engelken devotes one chapter to examining the phenomenon of polygamy in the Hebrew Bible and incorporates all the passages that depict polygamy with and without the word *pîlegeš*. She then divides the texts involving *pîlegeš* into genealogies and narratives and includes a detailed description of each of the occurrences. Her study yields some findings that are relevant to the current study:

1. Regarding polygyny: the Hebrew Bible takes polygyny as an existing custom and does not regard it negatively. Only marriage with two sisters is later prohibited in Leviticus 18:18.[53] As multiple wives are possible within the ancient Israelite household, polygyny does not necessarily involve *pîlegeš*.

2. Regarding the status of concubines: *pîlegeš* denotes a marriage relationship with lesser rights than the wife, and hence is translated "Nebenfrau," auxiliary-wife.[54] She is not a slave, unlike ʾ*mh* or *špḥh*; she is subordinate to the chief wife (or wives). She is often not mentioned by name in genealogies, compared to the chief wives whose names are usually mentioned.[55] It is also conceivable that she does not become a member of her husband's family to the same degree as the chief wife and thus retains a certain level of independence, which may allow her to live apart from the house of the man.[56]

3. Regarding reasons for concubinage (for the women): the Hebrew Bible does not specify whether a dowry or bridal payment is involved

---

52. Engelken, "*Pîlegeš*," 549.
53. Engelken, *Frauen*, 124.
54. Engelken, *Frauen*, 124.
55. Engelken, *Frauen*, 122.
56. Engelken, *Frauen*, 124.

in marrying a concubine; therefore, it is difficult to determine if concubinage was a means of marriage for those who were financially deprived. However, there must be a reason for the women to renounce the rights within marriage and choose to become concubines instead of wives. It is noticed that there is a high proportion of concubines with non-Israelite origins, which may indicate that foreign women have a lower social status in marriage.[57]

4. Regarding reasons for concubinage (for the men): it is often emphasized in the Hebrew Bible that concubines are acquired for the reason of progeny. However, Engelken also considers polygyny as a means for the men to legitimize sexual relationships with multiple women. As prostitution and adultery are negatively viewed in the traditions, it may have been a way to circumvent the rigid codes of ethics.[58]

5. Regarding "*beena* marriage": the description of Gideon's *pîlegeš* in Judges 8:31 is considered resembling "*beena* marriage," yet evidence for the practice elsewhere in the Hebrew Bible is not sufficient. It should be considered an exception rather than the norm for a *pîlegeš*.[59]

6. Regarding adulterous intercourse with concubines: Engelken notices from both the case of Absalom and Reuben that adulterous intercourse with concubines is seen as an attack upon the authority of the husband.[60] It appears that the focus of such action is on the usurpation of power rather than on the violation of the marriage bond through adultery.

Implications for the Pîlegeš *in Judges 19*

The observations of Engelken bring certain insights and clarifications to the dispute among scholars on the concept of concubinage in ancient Israel. First, there are clear distinctions between a wife and a *pîlegeš*. As multiple wives are accepted in ancient Hebrew culture, the existence of a *pîlegeš* is not the mere consequence of marrying more than one woman. The *pîlegeš* should be considered as a separate category, having a lower status than the wife. While translating *pîlegeš* as "concubine," "auxiliary-wife"

---

57. Engelken, *Frauen*, 122, 125.

58. Engelken, *Frauen*, 125.

59. Engelken, *Frauen*, 94. This is the "patrilocal" marriage system Bal reads in Judges 19; *Death & Dissymmetry*, 84.

60. Engelken, *Frauen*, 79, 101.

or "secondary wife" simply pertains to the preference of the commentator, the designation should never be confused with "wife," which should be preserved for the chief wife (or chief wives). The practice of scholars, such as Soggin and Niditch, in calling the *pîlegeš* in Judges 19 the wife of the Levite is therefore misleading and should be avoided.

Second, a *pîlegeš* is legally married to the husband. Engelken does not recognize any differentiation in the Hebrew Bible of "two types of concubine," one married and one not married, as proposed by Ackerman; neither is there evidence of a concubine being in a mistress-type relationship, as suggested by Schneider. The evidence of *beena* marriage is also insufficient for this mode of marriage to be considered in the case of the Levite's concubine. She is socially and legally recognized as a married woman in her historical cultural context.

Third, Engelken's comment concerning the dwelling of a concubine seems to point toward the possibility that she is less attached to the husband's family, rendering perhaps the action of the concubine in returning to her father's home somewhat acceptable to the culture. If that is the case, the accusation that the concubine acts like a harlot by running away is a rather unexpected condemnation, and it may give more weight to the interpretation of the verb *znh* in verse 2 that the concubine became angry with her husband.

There are, however, also issues raised in Engelken's discussion that are worth further investigation when applied to the understanding of Judges 19. While the lower status of the concubine compared to the wife is clear, it is uncertain how this status difference is manifested. Would the lower status of the concubine render her less protected in terms of hospitality? Would she be more susceptible to become a victim of rape than a wife? What would be the social implications of the rape of a concubine? Was there any stigma associated with the identity of a concubine? These are questions relevant to the understanding of the portrayal of the concubine in Judges 19, yet the study of Engelken has not sufficiently addressed these issues.

The limitations of Engelken's studies may be partly attributed to the lack of information in the Hebrew Bible itself. After all, concubinage is not frequently mentioned in the biblical tradition, and a significant portion of the occurrences of *pîlegeš* is situated in the genealogies from which limited information can be gathered. Moreover, the absence of the term *pîlegeš* in the legal codes renders postulations from interpreters almost unavoidable. These factors impose certain constraints upon the study of the practice of concubinage in ancient Israel based solely on the Hebrew Bible. This takes us in the next section to extra-biblical sources.

Comparing Concubinage in the Hebrew Bible with Extra-biblical Resources

A survey of existing comparative studies of concubinage in the ancient Near East reveals that it is rather difficult to extract information about the *pîlegeš*, mainly for two reasons. First is the lack of attention from scholarship. Only three studies can been identified that attempt the task of comparing concubinage in ancient Near Eastern sources with the Hebrew practice, including Epstein in the 1930s, Neufeld in the 1940s, and McComiskey in the 1960s. The second reason is the muddling of terms. As mentioned earlier, Neufeld does not differentiate between *pîlegeš* and *'mh* or *špḥh*, leading to the confusion of the status of each. It is even more complicated in the work of McComiskey, who uses the terms "concubine," "slave-wife" and "secondary wife" in both biblical and extra-biblical sources without delineating the differences.[61] It is virtually impossible to tease out specific information from his study for the discussion of the *pîlegeš*. In view of the difficulties, the following focuses on the study of Epstein, who devotes his attention to the *pîlegeš*, and uses the findings from Neufeld and McComiskey for supplementary purposes.

Marriages of Concubines

While not much is known about the marriage ceremony in ancient Israel, Epstein makes inferences from Assyrian laws and proposes a differential treatment in the ceremonies for concubines and wives. As the Assyrian laws prescribe that a concubine not go through the veiling ceremony at the wedding (though she is to be veiled when she appears on the street), he postulates that such practices might be similar among the Hebrews.[62] He suggests that a formal marriage ceremony, such as that for wives, is lacking in the marital unions of concubines, and that the marriage formula used in wedding ceremonies for wives such as "she is my wife and I am her husband" would also be missing for concubines even if there were a ceremony.[63]

Epstein notes that in Babylonian sources, the gifts in legitimate marriages, *mohar* or *mattan*, are not found in concubine marriages. The former is the purchase price given to the bride's parents, the latter the nuptial gift from the husband to the bride herself. He considers *mohar* and *mattan*, as being implied for marriages in the Hebrew Bible for wives and yet would be unusual

---

61. For example, McComiskey, "Status of the Secondary Wife," 98–101.
62. Epstein, "Institution of Concubinage," 165–66.
63. Epstein, "Institution of Concubinage," 165.

for concubines. He also contends that a contract is absent in the case of a concubine marriage.[64] However, Epstein also observes in the Code of Hammurabi that a dowry is obligatory even in the case of concubine brides, and he suggests that a similar practice may have existed among the Israelites for those concubines who came from better families. The evidence is therefore inconclusive concerning whether a concubine had a dowry.

The findings of McComiskey differ somewhat from those of Epstein. He surveys ancient Near Eastern legal sources on marriage and finds that the marriage contract is often seen as the evidence of a legal marital union. While there is no direct evidence of a marriage contract for concubines, he suggests from the Code of Hammurabi that "it was highly probable that it [a marriage contract] is necessary to validate marriage to a concubine."[65] Noticing the similarities between Sarah's giving of Hagar and the Nuzi legal practice of a wife's initiative in finding a concubine for the husband, he then proposes that the wife's consent may constitute a contractual agreement for the marriage of concubines in ancient Israel.[66] Although the example of Hagar is a case for ' *mh*, it might be inferred that the consent of a wife would also be necessary for a *pîlegeš*.

While the interpretation of sources may differ somewhat between scholars, the observations above nonetheless indicate that concubinage was not an uncommon practice in the ancient Near East, and it was generally recognized as a legal marital union. Some sort of differentiation in marriage terms and ceremony between wives and concubines also was common in the different cultures. As the marriage ceremony was a social event that announced the union, this suggests that the distinction between wives and concubines was an important one. It was necessary in these cultures that a woman's identity as a wife/concubine was made known to others without confusion. In other words, the identity of a concubine was bound by the way the marriage ceremony and contractual agreement were carried out. While it is uncertain whether the practices in Assyria and Babylonia reflected the exact customs in Israel, these observations at least suggest that a similar perception might have been shared by the various cultures.

Social Status of the Concubines

It had been generally recognized that the status of the concubine was inferior to the wife in the family. Epstein explicates the illustration of this inferiority

---

64. Epstein, "Institution of Concubinage," 162–63.
65. McComiskey, "Status of the Secondary Wife," 28.
66. McComiskey, "Status of the Secondary Wife," 50.

by drawing comparisons from the Hammurabi records where one concubine was obliged to wash the feet of her matron, to carry her chair into the temple, to be her companion in joy or in sorrow, and to grind flower and bake bread for her.[67] It seems that the lower status of concubines compared to wives rendered them responsible for duties of the household as well as for serving the wives. However, considering concubinage was a phenomenon more prominent in the wealthy households, Epstein also comments that concubines would have had a higher level of economic stability compared to some other women in society. The duties of concubines in the household would then depend on the economy of the individual family.[68]

On the other hand, the social status of a person might also have related to the family of origin. Epstein suggests that concubines might have come from average households of modest parents. She might also have been a daughter of a concubine, a captive-wife[69] or slave-wife, where she would rank socially lower than her sisters born from wives. He also observes that a greater number of concubines are foreign women, although Hebrew concubines are also found in the biblical texts.[70] This would imply that a certain level of class distinction existed in Hebrew society, and that it was a significant matter to consider in matchmaking. This might also provide another reason for the co-existence of concubinage and polygamy in ancient Israel—that the social class of some women rendered them inadequate to be wives and they needed to settle in the position of concubines.

McComiskey observes in Sumerian laws and the Code of Hammurabi that the status of the first wife is protected above the concubines.[71] He considers the ancient Israelite wife had a similarly high status in that she superintended the home. Taking Hagar as a paradigm, he considers "the security of the concubine in the home is always in jeopardy because of the primary wife who could at any time request her dismissal."[72] Exodus 21:7–11 is then regarded as a later development in the social protection of slave-wives/concubines for maintenance and marital companionship.[73] Neufeld, on the other

---

67. Epstein, "Institution of Concubinage," 168.

68. Epstein, "Institution of Concubinage," 157.

69. The status of the captive wife, in Epstein's view, is not sufficiently described in the Hebrew Bible. He considers it somewhere between a concubine and a slave-wife; Epstein, "Institution of Concubinage," 160–61.

70. Epstein, "Institution of Concubinage," 160. This is similar to Engelken's view, *Frauen*, 122.

71. McComiskey, "Status of the Secondary Wife," 77–78.

72. McComiskey, "Status of the Secondary Wife," 93–94.

73. McComiskey, "Status of the Secondary Wife," 96. Epstein also considers that the protection offered to slave-wives in Exodus 21 would at least equally apply to

hand, is more optimistic about the status of the concubine. He also emphasizes the inferior position of the concubines and asserts that "a certain stigma attached to concubines who were always subservient to the wife as their mistress." However, he regards that there is a certain level of domestic security for the concubines: "there was . . . a feeling common to the Semitic world that it was iniquitous to sell concubines, especially when they had borne children. It is safe, therefore, to assume that the custom was the same in Israel." The case of Hagar is then perceived as an exception.[74] It can be assumed that if the slave-wives were protected to a certain extent in the household, then the concubines would be treated the same, if not better.

Bringing together observations from various studies, it is apparent that the social status of the concubine was visibly and significantly lower than the wife. She might already have had a low social status from her family of origin, and when she married to be a concubine, she had to remain subservient to the wife/wives of her husband at all times. There was certain protection over her livelihood and security in the household, but not much information is known in this regard.

Legal Status of Concubines

On certain legal issues, some scholars consider that the concubine was treated similarly to the wife. It is generally agreed that the restrictions on concubines were the same as on the wife in matters concerning fidelity to the marriage.[75] Epstein draws from examples in the Code of Hammurabi and Assyrian laws to suggest that the concubine was expected to be treated similarly to the wife in matters of divorce and adultery. Applying a similar concept to the Hebrew practice suggests that the offence of adultery would lead to capital punishment for both the man and the woman as stated in Deuteronomy 22:22, regardless of whether she was a wife or a concubine. However, as the term *pîlegeš* does not appear in legal codes in the Hebrew Bible, there remains some doubt on the matter.

In issues such as widowhood and inheritance, the concubine was considered as having a different legal position from the wives. Epstein observes that the concubine belonged to the successor of the estate upon the death of the master, which was different from the wives, who were not to be taken

---

concubines; "Institution of Concubinage," 168.

74. Neufeld, *Ancient Hebrew Marriage Laws*, 124.

75. Neufeld, *Ancient Hebrew Marriage Laws*, 125; Epstein, "Institution of Concubinage," 174.

by the son or the successor.⁷⁶ There could also have been a development in the practice, in that she could remain in the house of her master's heirs, subject to their authority (2 Sam 3:7; 1 Kgs 2:17). She was probably entitled to exercise her option to leave with her personal belongings.⁷⁷

Concerning the rights of inheritance of the sons of concubines, it is apparent in ancient Israel that sons of concubines could become an heir to the estate if there were no other sons from the wife. It is also logical, as there would be no point in acquiring a concubine for the sake of procreation if the son of the concubine could not become an heir to the estate. Similar practices have been observed in Assyrian laws and the Code of Hammurabi.⁷⁸ It may then be inferred that bearing sons could be a means of increasing the security and status of concubines.

Other issues concerning the legal status of a concubine have also been considered. In the Code of Hammurabi, since a concubine is legally a free person; she has full ownership of her properties. She may also do business transactions within the limits given to married women.⁷⁹ The legal rights of concubines in financial management are, however, not explicit in the Hebrew Bible. It is therefore uncertain whether the Hebrew concubines enjoyed a similar legal status.

It is evident from the above that, compared to the law codes in the ancient Near Eastern cultures, little is known about the legal status and rights of concubines in ancient Israel. Indeed, when the legal rights of Israelite women in general remain obscure to us, it is hard to expect a more detailed picture of the concubines. However, it is significant to recognize that the absence of the term *pîlegeš* in the laws does not necessarily imply a total indifference in customary laws. It is possible that the laws concerning wives might have been used to cover the concubines in some situations such as infidelity; in other situations, such as inheritance, the laws might have necessitated a differential treatment from the wives.

Overall, the ancient Near Eastern sources are helpful in revealing some aspects of the practice of concubinage across cultures. However, as the sources used for comparative studies by scholars so far heavily rely on law codes such as the Code of Hammurabi and Assyrian laws, one should also note that the absence of laws specifically referring to concubines in the Hebrew

---

76. Epstein, "Institution of Concubinage," 157.

77. Neufeld, *Ancient Hebrew Marriage Laws*, 125; Epstein, "Institution of Concubinage," 174.

78. Although the Code of Hammurabi requires an act of adoption by the father of the sons of concubines; McComiskey, "Status of the Secondary Wife," 65–67.

79. Epstein, "Institution of Concubinage," 169.

Bible in fact poses difficulties for comparison. In most cases, the comparison is made between law codes of the ancient Near East and narratives in the Bible, and the inherent difference in the genres may obscure the evaluation. With this caution in mind, the implications of findings in this section are considered in the interpretation of Judges 19.

Implications for the Interpretation of Judges 19

On the Status and Identity of the Concubine

The status of the *pîlegeš* in Judges 19 has been a confusing matter for some scholars, as they are concerned with the absence of a wife of the Levite in the narrative. However, as the ancient Near Eastern sources suggest, the identity of a concubine is determined by the way the ceremony and marital contract is carried out. When the text calls her a *pîlegeš*, she is married as a concubine and is bound by social expectations on her, regardless of how many wives the Levite has. The absence of a wife in the narrative is in fact irrelevant.

Both biblical tradition and ancient Near Eastern studies point toward the inferior social status of the concubine's family of origin. This provides a background understanding of the household of the concubine's father, suggesting that he is possibly economically deprived. This would mean that his hospitality toward the Levite is not a display of wealth, as some have imagined,[80] but rather an action that might be over and beyond what he could afford. The detailed description of his hospitality in the narrative would have left a strong impression in the minds of the ancient audiences, which then acted as a stark contrast to what occurred to the group in Gibeah. However, the motivation of the father in doing so is left to the imagination of readers—it could be that he is to be seen as a very kind man, or that he cares for his daughter and hence is very keen for her marriage crisis to be resolved, or even, in the long run, that he simply cannot afford another mouth to feed.

On the Interpretation of Verse 2

As both biblical and extra-biblical sources confirm the married status of the concubine, it can be safely assumed that fidelity to the marriage would be expected of her. The possibility of illicit sex in verse 2 should be evaluated in light of the reactions of both the Levite and his father-in-law, who do not react in ways expected for physical adultery within a marriage relationship.

80. Webb, *Book of Judges*, 461.

However, as there is no evidence in the studies as to how the action of a concubine returning to her father's home would be perceived in the historical context, it is difficult to determine whether a metaphorical understanding of *znh* is a reasonable reading. We do not know what is implied in the ancient Hebrew culture when she initiates departure from the husband's household—whether it would be seen as a gesture of divorce or merely an expression of dissatisfaction in the marriage relationship, or whether she would be regarded as equivalent to being a harlot. The ancient Near Eastern sources examined do not seem to address the issue, and the passing comment from Engelken on the possible flexibility of the lodging of the concubines also cannot be conclusive in the matter. Therefore, it is difficult to assess the rhetorical force implied in the narrative through comparative studies.

On the Gibeah Incident

Both biblical texts on *pîlegeš* and extra-biblical sources confirm the married status of the concubine and apply legal views of matters of adultery similarly to wives and concubines. It is apparent, then, that the rape of the concubine would be seen by the ancient audience as adultery against the Levite and condemned by the laws. However, not much information has been gathered from either within or outside biblical traditions regarding rape by non-family members of concubines as opposed to full wives. We do not know whether there would have been any difference if she were a wife, and whether she is considered more susceptible to such violation due to her identity as a concubine.

Overall, it is evident that extra-biblical sources have a certain measure of value, although limited, for understanding the historical context of concubinage in Judges 19.

Conclusion

The comparative approach adopted in this chapter is helpful for clarifying certain issues in the understanding of the practice of concubinage in ancient Israel. It clears up the confusion concerning the marital status of the concubine and provides some insights into her social and legal status. A concubine in ancient Israel was legally married to the husband with the prospect of a long-term relationship. She had a lower status than the wives and yet a higher status than slaves, although she might have been instructed to perform household duties. In terms of physical fidelity, there was no difference in the expectations of wives and concubines. These contribute to the understanding of the *pîlegeš* portrayed in Judges 19.

There are, however, also limitations in this approach. Given the scarcity of the sources available, both within and outside the Hebrew Bible, there are still key issues in the interpretation of the text that remain unresolved. What is the rhetorical effect intended in the narrative, particularly in verse 2 and in the Gibeah incident? Is the narrator drawing sympathy from the audience for the concubine or condemning her as a harlot deserving retribution? These are important issues to consider in the reading of the text, and the attempt to situate the concubine in her historical context using the comparative approach is insufficient to answer these questions. It is necessary, then, to resort to other reading methodologies in order to resolve these problems.

3

Reading Judges 19 as a Narrative

Gaps, Ambiguities, and Point-of-View

Introduction

THE RECOGNITION OF THE applicability of the tools of literary criticism to biblical narratives began especially with the publication of Erich Auerbach's *Mimesis* in 1953.[1] The increasing interest among biblical scholars in the next decades led to the rise of narrative criticism in the 1980s. The legitimacy and necessity of reading biblical narratives from the lens of their narrative artistry have now been generally acknowledged. The passage under discussion, Judges 19, clearly exhibits literary features belonging to the genre of a narrative.[2] It is therefore essential to consider the poetics of the text and the subsequent impacts of the appreciation of these features to its interpretation.

Several studies have previously attended to various literary aspects of Judges 19, but there is not yet a thorough examination explicitly using methodologies developed in narratology. This chapter demonstrates the benefits of the tools of narrative criticism—namely the concept of ambiguity and point-of-view studies[3]—to the reading of the text and show how they enable readers to uncover the rhetorical intent of the narrator.[4]

This chapter begins with an overview of narrative criticism and an evaluation of previous efforts by scholars in regard to Judges 19. This demonstrates that the narrative artistry of the text has not been systematically

---

1. Liang, *Shengjing xushi yishu yanjiu*, 33–34.

2. For a discussion of the definition of narrative, see Moore, "Biblical Narrative Analysis," 27

3. In order to connote that "point of view study" is a specific narrative tool distinct from the general meaning of "point of view," I hyphenate the term here.

4. While it is more precise to phrase this as the intent of the implied author, according to the conventions of narratology, the distinction is considered irrelevant in most discussions of biblical narratives; see Ska, *"Our Fathers Have Told Us,"* 42. Hence the terminology adopted here.

explored. This contributes to the perception of an apparently equivocal attitude on the part of the narrator toward the actions of the Levite. The next section studies the points of ambiguity in the narrative using the techniques developed by Meir Sternberg. It contends that these gaps and ambiguities reflect a narrative design: in one way or the other, they draw the attention of readers to the Levite and his shocking personality and behaviors. The view of the narrator toward this character is then examined in the next section using the techniques of point-of-view studies by Gary Yamasaki. A point-of-view analysis suggests that readers' sympathy is drawn away from the Levite, and the narrative functions to highlight his cruelty.

Narrative Criticism

Overview

Narrative criticism is the study of biblical narratives using theories developed in narratology. The term arose in the 1980s; it was initially applied to studies on the New Testament and soon extended to the reading of the Hebrew Bible. The development of narrative criticism has been influenced by classical narratology, Russian formalism, and French structuralism, as well as New Criticism of the Anglo-American literary school. Narrative criticism emphasizes the autonomy and self-referentiality of the text, as opposed to the kind of historical criticism (which dominated biblical scholarship for almost two centuries previously), that explores the historical world of the text and investigates its source, form, and redaction. Narrative criticism focuses primarily on the text itself. It generally treats the biblical narratives as artistically unified wholes, and the center of examination is hence the final product of the text.[5]

Stephen Moore provides a succinct summary of the areas of concern in narrative criticism: "it typically appropriated narratology to analyze plot, characterization, point of view (or narrative perspective), narrative settings, temporal dynamics, and other stock features of biblical narrative."[6] Various scholars have written on the methodologies of investigating these literary features and have given examples on how the interpretations of the biblical texts may be enhanced, including Robert Alter,[7] Shimon Bar-Efrat,[8] Adele

---

5. Moore, "Biblical Narrative," 33.
6. Moore, "Biblical Narrative," 29.
7. Alter, *The Art of Biblical Narrative*.
8. Bar-Efrat, *Narrative Art in the Bible*.

Berlin,[9] and Meir Sternberg.[10] Though the style and focus of these works may differ, a common thread among them is that these literary features are considered techniques used by the narrator for the purpose of communication. A close analysis of the use of these devices in a narrative opens the door to the understanding of its rhetorical intentions.

This creates immense potential for the interpretation of biblical narratives, as the analysis of the poetics in the text extends beyond appreciation of its aesthetic values to the evaluation of the rhetorical purpose of the discourse. This is significant, as readers of the sacred Scripture often look beyond the happenings, that is, the story of the discourse, and question the communicative purpose of such narration within the biblical corpus. This inclination may be most pronounced in readers' attempts to uncover the narrator's ethical evaluation of the events and characters in the texts. The narratives, however, are often lacking in explicit comments and didactic instructions, with the narrator appearing almost equivocal at times toward the story. Reading the texts with narrative criticism then provides a means for readers to unmask this apparent equivocality of the narrator. Judges 19 is one such narrative that lacks explicit ethical evaluation, and reading the text using tools of narrative criticism has the potential to uncover the moral perspective of the narrator toward the story.

Narrative Criticism and Judges 19

Previous Scholarship

There have been several attempts among scholars to adopt a literary approach to the reading of Judges 19. Mieke Bal, renowned Dutch narratologist, was the first to illustrate such potential in *Death & Dissymmetry*, in which she reads the discourse in the light of a conflict between patrilocal and matrilocal marriages. She provides a detailed analysis of the first three verses of the passage and contends that a situation of matrilocal marriage in the family of the concubine may resolve the tensions in the text.[11] However, as the subtitle of the book suggests, Bal's feminist critique of the political coherence in the Book of Judges dominates her interpretation, and the literary aspects of the passage are used almost as subsidiary features supporting her ideological claims.

---

9. Berlin, *Poetics and Interpretation of Biblical Narrative*.
10. Sternberg, *The Poetics of Biblical Narrative*.
11. Bal, *Death & Dissymmetry*, 80–93.

In *Texts of Terror*, Phyllis Trible, on the other hand, provides a reading of Judges 19 that is primarily focused on literary analysis of the passage. She examines the text according to the scenes of the narrative, and in some parts of her study utilizes tools of narratology such as analysis of the development of the plot.[12] However, as the focus of her interpretation is on how these literary features illustrate the gendered interaction and relationships between the characters (including male to male, male to female), the cumulative force of the narrative devices is not thoroughly explored in its own terms. Fokkelman comments that her study is "a curious combination of good stylistic analysis and wrong value judgment," and the first reason he gives for this opinion is that "she confuses his (the narrator's) reticent art of storytelling as his point of view."[13] This suggests that the narrative artistry of the text has yet to be thoroughly examined, and the lack of such appreciation contributes to misconceptions concerning the view of the narrator.

More recently, Jacqueline Lapsley has recognized the apparent equivocal attitude of the narrator and undertakes the task of "attending closely to the narrator's voice" in the story.[14] Though she aims to study the way empathy from the reader is manipulated by the narrator, the approach she adopts does not utilize the full potential of investigating the rhetorical effect provided in narrative criticism. While the point of view of the narrator has been recognized in narratology as an important means for the expression of ethical evaluation, the only element throughout Lapsley's study that explicitly discusses the manipulation of the narrator's viewpoint is in the comment on the use of *hinnēh* in v27.[15] The rest of her interpretation of the chapter comes from attending to the subtle literary hints in the text, such as the repetition of the use of the word "heart," as clues to the narrator's perspective.[16] While some of her observations make valid points, a systematic analysis on the narratological maneuvering of the point-of-view throughout the passage is lacking, which significantly weakens her argument. As scholars have recognized, the expression of point-of-view is not a single incident in a certain verse, but an activity continuing throughout the entire discourse.[17] The art of the narrator's manipulation of the reader's

---

12. For example, she divides the development of the plot in 19:27–28 into "Resolve, Interruption, and Resumption"; Trible, *Texts of Terror*, 78.

13. Fokkelman, "Structural Remarks on Judges 9 and 19," 40 n16.

14. Lapsley, *Whispering the Word*, 36.

15. Lapsley, *Whispering the Word*, 47–48.

16. Lapsley does not differentiate the narrator's "point of view" in the strict narratological sense but takes it as a more general meaning, as in the attitude of the narrator.

17. For example, the discussion on the changes in the informational and

empathy cannot be substantially appreciated unless the technique is followed through from beginning to end.

Current Potential

The survey on previous scholarship in literary readings of Judges 19 illustrates that the ideologies of the critics often dominate their interpretations of the poetics in the text. While it is true that one can never be entirely objective in any reading, this does not render an assessment of the narratological functions of the text an impossible task. There remains room for attending to the narrative artistry, and the cumulative effect on the communicative functions of the text, before leaping to ideological interpretations.

In particular, the tools of narrative criticism in the reading have not been fully utilized in previous studies in at least two respects. First, the poetic use of ambiguities in the narrative *per se* have not been explored. How are these ambiguities presented in the text? What are their meaning potentials? What is impact of the accumulation of ambiguities? How may they affect the way the events and the characters are perceived? All these questions warrant a closer examination of the use of the ambiguities and ambivalences in the passage. As Sternberg provides an exhaustive analysis of the technique of gaps and ambiguities in biblical narratives,[18] the text of Judges 19 is explored in this chapter particularly in light of his findings.

Second, the silence of the narrator on the evildoings in the narrative is the main reason that many struggle to apprehend the rhetorical function of the text. Lapsley has rightly suggested that empathy arousal is a narratological means of evoking the readers' moral imagination, and the evaluative stance of the narrator may be discerned through an analysis of the devices that function to align the empathy of the readers.[19] The manipulation of point-of-view has been recognized in narratology as an important strategy in this regard, and scholars such as Boris Uspensky have developed theories explicating the functions and shifts in the point-of-view in a narrative.[20] The potential of applying these theories to biblical narratives has been demonstrated in the discussion of point-of-view (or particularly via

---

normative axis of point-of-view in Sternberg's discussion in the wooing of Rebekah follows the entire discourse, which makes a much more convincing argument; *Poetics of Biblical Narrative*, 132–53.

18. Sternberg, *Poetics of Biblical Narrative*, 187–321.
19. Lapsley, *Whispering the Word*, 35–38.
20. Uspensky, *A Poetics of Composition*.

focalization) by Berlin,[21] Fokkelman,[22] and Robert Funk;[23] Yamasaki has published two books that have convincingly established the value of the practice.[24] Lapsley's study has not considered these methodologies and hence, there is much potential to develop further in this direction. The second section of this chapter applies Yamasaki's approach to investigate the changes in point-of-view throughout Judges 19, attempting to illustrate the way the text is crafted to elicit readers' empathies.

It is anticipated that, by attending to both the ambiguities in the narrative and the point-of-view, a more comprehensive analysis of the rhetorical function of the text will be provided, revealing the stand of the narrator toward the characters of the story.

Gaps and Ambiguities in Narratives

Overview

Narratives are, by nature, highly selective of the information that they choose to expound, as no discourses can ever include every detail of every aspect of a story. This selectiveness is particularly significant in biblical narratives for two reasons. First, the succinct characteristic of the writing of the Bible limits the amount of information offered to readers, and many elements of the story that are not considered central to the communicative purpose of the narrative are often omitted.[25] Second, the generally presumed omniscience of the biblical narrator renders the lapse in detail *not* an issue due to limited knowledge on the narrator's part, but due to a deliberate choice made in withholding certain information. This writing tactic has been discussed by various scholars,[26] and Sternberg provides one of the most in-depth and comprehensive analyses over several chapters in *The Poetics of Biblical Narrative*.

Sternberg distinguishes between two kinds of omission, gaps and blanks: "the literary work consists of bits and fragments to be linked and pieced together in the process of reading: it establishes a system of gaps that must be

---

21. Berlin, *Poetics*, 43–52.
22. Fokkelman, *Reading Biblical Narrative*, 123–55.
23. Funk, *Poetics of Biblical Narrative*, 100–132.
24. Yamasaki, *Watching a Biblical Narrative*; *Perspective Criticism*.
25. For example, the description of the appearances of characters, which is fairly standard in fiction, is seldom included in the biblical narratives.
26. Such as the chapter "Narration and Knowledge" in Alter, *Art of Biblical Narrative*, 155–77; and the chapter, "The Unwritten" in Funk, *Poetics*, 285–301.

filled in."[27] This is not mere unmentioned information, as the narrator may choose to neglect details that are irrelevant to the plot, which Sternberg calls "blanks." Gaps are, on the contrary, omissions where relevant information is withheld for the sake of reading potential and interest, as the absence heightens the reader's sense of suspense. This may involve the omission of an event, motive, causal link, character trait, or plot structure.[28]

The filling of gaps may take place through simple linkages of elements in the plot, or it may be a sophisticated process involving conscious effort by readers. Readers take an active role in filling in the gaps and forming hypotheses during the reading, yet this does not render the process arbitrary. The text itself forms the criteria for the validity of hypotheses, and an "illegitimate gap-filling is one launched and sustained by the reader's subjective concerns (or dictated by more general preconceptions) rather than by the text's own norms and directives."[29]

The understanding of "gap-filling," Sternberg contends, should instead be guided by five factors: (1) the different materials pertaining to action, theme, structure and normativeness explicitly communicated by the text; (2) language and poetics; (3) the perceptual set established by the work's generic features;[30] (4) the special nature and laws and regularities of the world the narrative projects; (5) the basic assumptions derived from everyday life and its cultural conventions in the narrative.[31] Gap-filling is therefore an exercise in constructing an hypothesis that strives to organize the maximum number of these elements in the most cohesive manner.

Multiple hypotheses may be valid for the filling of a gap at one point of the narrative, which gives rise to possibilities and ambiguities. As the storytelling progresses, more information is provided that may render one hypothesis more likely than the other or even offer closure that invalidates all hypotheses but one. At times, however, there is no closure, and the gap remains permanent, and dual or multiple systems of gap-filling that are mutually exclusive may co-exist in the narrative.[32]

Sternberg regards gaps and ambiguities as a frequent and sophisticated literary technique in biblical narratives. Its artistry is displayed in various ways, including "the opening and timing of gaps, the processing of information and response, the interlinkage of the different levels, the

---

27. Sternberg, *Poetics of Biblical Narrative*, 187.
28. Sternberg, *Poetics of Biblical Narrative*, 236–37.
29. Sternberg, *Poetics of Biblical Narrative*, 189.
30. This refers to the expectations of readers in relation to the genre of the work.
31. Sternberg, *Poetics of Biblical Narrative*, 189–90.
32. Sternberg, *Poetics of Biblical Narrative*, 223.

play of hypotheses with sanctions against premature closure, the clues and models that guide interpretive procedure, the roles fulfilled by ambiguity."[33] All of these features may be manipulated to promote narrative interest through three effects, namely curiosity, suspense, and surprise: "The rise of curiosity signifies that the past has been deformed; suspense entails a future opaque and open; surprise is a measure of false understanding and a call for a repatterning of what has gone before."[34] An analysis of the dynamics between the three throughout the narrative may then reveal the rhetorical purpose of the narrator.

In Sternberg's explication of his theory on gaps and ambiguities, the omission of the exact time and cause of death of the concubine in Judges 19 is used as an example of a gap that works to raise suspicion about both the Levite and the mob.[35] Though the rest of the narrative is not included in his analysis, this demonstrates the potential for reading the text in light of this methodology. This potential is now explored in the next section.

Narrative Gaps in Judges 19

Commentators have acknowledged that certain information is withheld at several crucial points in Judges 19, including the identity of the man who pulled the concubine out to the mob in verse 25 and the exact time of death of the concubine.[36] Moreover, the interpretation of *znh* in verse 2, as well as the extended hospitality between the father-in-law and the Levite in verses 5–9, also seems puzzling to readers. All these elements of elusiveness lead to divergent interpretations among scholars, as each attempts to fill in the gaps differently and reconstruct coherent readings of the story. Extensive efforts have been made to justify each choice of gap-filling, with some reasons more convincing than others, and yet the narrative gaps *per se* have not been thoroughly studied. The possibility of an ambiguity designed to enable the divergent and even conflicting interpretations of those gaps has not been considered. This section identifies each of the gaps and explores the possibilities of reconstruction, proposing that these gaps reflect the use of rhetorical devices in creating curiosity, suspense, and surprise for readers regarding the character of the Levite.

---

33. Sternberg, *Poetics of Biblical Narrative*, 231.
34. Sternberg, *Poetics of Biblical Narrative*, 263.
35. Sternberg, *Poetics of Biblical Narrative*, 238–40.
36. Cf. Boling, *Judges*, 276; Webb, *Book of Judges*, 428.

Ambiguity in Verses 2–3: Does He Know?

> 19:2–3 But his concubine played the harlot against him, and went away from him to her father's house at Bethlehem in Judah, and was there four whole months. Then her husband arose and went after her, to speak kindly to her and bring her back. (NKJV)[37]

The information provided in verse 2 and verse 3 stand in some kind of contradiction. If the concubine had "played the harlot" in the sense that she committed sexual infidelity, then it is very difficult to understand why the Levite would still want to bring her back, let alone speak tenderly to her. To do so would defy the Deuteronomic laws that demand the death sentence for women who commit adultery.[38] Scholars have also deemed it unreasonable for an offended husband to respond in such graciousness, which leads to various attempts to harmonize the incongruity: some opt for a metaphorical understanding of *znh* and propose that it refers to her action in leaving the household of the Levite,[39] and others take the LXX version and translate "became angry with" and try to smooth out the incongruity by characterizing it as a domestic conflict.[40] However, as Mieke Bal has observed, these harmonizations are in fact imposing the commentators' own moral values, experiences, and worldviews upon the text in determining what is "possible" and "impossible."[41] As it seems impossible to have the Levite responding with such kindness and forgiveness toward a concubine who has been sexually unfaithful, then what happened must have been something other than physical infidelity.

Instead of trying to harmonize the two verses, a narratological approach can leave this standing as a gap, at least for a time. The suggestion that the concubine "plays the harlot" and the Levite responds with kindness could be understood as a narrative incongruity, which Sternberg calls "juxtaposition-turned-opposition." This is where "the narrative juxtaposes two pieces of reality that bear on the same context but fail to harmonize either as variants of a situation or as phases in an action," and this

---

37. The English translation here is taken from the NKJV, as this version demonstrates very well the nuances of the use of ambiguity in these two verses.

38. Deuteronomy 22:22. Though one may argue about the applicability of the Deuteronomic laws to the social world depicted in Judges 19, this law still reflects a worldview in which adultery was regarded as a deadly sin.

39. Such as Matthews, *Judges and Ruth*, 419.

40. For example, Boling, *Judges*, 271; Edenburg, *Dismembering*, 145–46. This is also reflected in the NRSV.

41. Bal, *Death & Dissymmetry*, 82–83.

contributes to the grounding and foregrounding of gaps.[42] The text here then presents a narrative gap, as the reaction of the Levite does not appear consistent with the action of the concubine. It calls for the reader's effort in bridging the gap in order to understand the story, but there is no need for an immediate resolution of the puzzle.

One of the first things to consider is the relative reliability of the two pieces of information in opposition. As Sternberg observes, in incongruities within biblical narratives there is sometimes a difference in the level of information reliability. Descriptions that come from the narrator often have higher authority than the speeches, in that the characters may not be telling the whole truth and the omniscient narrator is more reliable.[43] In this case, however, both verse 2 and verse 3 are provided by the narrator; they should therefore be seen as having equal credibility and hence together form a *non sequitur*. In other words, as per the description of the reliable narrator, the concubine did "play the harlot;" and the Levite did want to win her back by speaking to her heart. The fact that the inner thoughts of the Levite are provided by the narrator further confirms the deliberate use of the *non sequitur*, as readers may otherwise suppose the Levite had gone after the concubine for revenge or compensation.

This *non sequitur* then prompts readers to ask: How could the Levite respond in such a way? A logical possibility would be: Perhaps he didn't know about the unfaithfulness of his concubine? This piece of information is only known to readers by the revelation of the narrator, and there is no indication in the narrative itself whether the Levite was aware of it or not. The omniscient narrator partially discloses to readers the inner mind of the Levite in his intention to speak kind words to the concubine yet does not clarify that he was aware of sexual unfaithfulness. It is quite possible that the concubine neither discussed nor informed him of her departure, or else he could have stopped her from leaving. The Levite may not have been aware of the reason for her leaving, when he has waited long enough and perhaps has heard that she has gone back to her father, he decides to seek reconciliation and bring her back home with kind words. This reconstruction assumes an imbalance between the information known to the readers and that of the Levite and provides a reasonable explanation for the situation while adhering to the surface meaning of the text.

Another possible interpretation of the *non sequitur* is that the Levite does know about his concubine's unfaithfulness and yet he is extraordinarily gracious, and he loves her so much that he is willing to take the initiative in

---

42. Sternberg, *Poetics of Biblical Narrative*, 243–44.
43. Sternberg, *Poetics of Biblical Narrative*, 244–46.

seeking her with kind words. Although this seems quite an unusual explanation, it is not without its support in the text. The detail of "four months" at the end of verse 2, as Schneider has suggested, may work as a hint that the Levite waits long enough to ensure the concubine is not pregnant before bringing her back.[44] This may prompt readers to wonder: Perhaps he knew after all, and yet his love for her overcame all feelings of anger and humiliation? Perhaps there *is* such an exceptionally loving man in this world? This hypothesis also coheres with the surface meaning of the text, but is contrary to the first hypothesis, as it assumes equal information known to the readers and to the Levite. There is not yet closure to this gap at this point in time, as further clues are lacking in the narrative so far.

The first reconstruction renders the Levite ignorant of his concubine's motivations, whereas the second reconstruction pictures him as a person of remarkable love and forgiveness. The two hypotheses are mutually exclusive, as they are dependent on the assumption that either the "he knows" or "he doesn't know." The narrative gap therefore brings the focus of readers to this character, which will steer the direction of the reading for the rest of the narrative. In order to validate/invalidate these hypotheses, readers will be looking for clues about the personality traits of the Levite.

As verses 2–3 do not seem to provide sufficient information to favor either of the reconstructions over the other, an ambiguous tension is created, maintaining both hypotheses at this point, which in turn arouses the interest of readers. This serves a twofold function.[45] On the one hand, curiosity is raised, in that readers want to know about the past: Is the Levite aware of the unfaithfulness of his concubine? On the other hand, suspense is also generated by the same ambiguity: Will he find out? And what will he do if he finds out? Or is he indeed an extraordinarily loving man? These questions will motivate the reading interest for the rest of the narrative.

It is therefore evident that verses 2–3 play a significant role at the beginning of the narrative.[46] Not only do they provide background information necessary for the discourse, but also they open a narrative gap,

---

44. Schneider, *Judges*, 253.

45. Sternberg identifies three reading interests that may be promoted by narrative gaps, namely curiosity, suspense, and surprise. Curiosity and suspense differ in terms of the time frame: curiosity refers to the information withheld that has already happened in the timeline of the narrative, and suspense refers to the unknown of the future; Sternberg, *Poetics of Biblical Narrative*, 263.

46. Contrary to Wong, who asserts that "the information given in 19:2–3 really seems altogether superfluous, so much so that one suspects its presence in the narrative is solely for the purpose of providing a more complete plot parallel with the Samson episode in 15:1–7"; Wong, *Compositional Strategy*, 108.

which contains essential information for the understanding of the rest of the plot.[47] Furthermore, they form the basis of a reading strategy focusing on the character of the Levite, which will progressively develop him as the protagonist through the rest of the narrative.

Ambiguity in Verses 5–8: Why Is He Silently Staying On?

> 19:5 On the fourth day they got up early in the morning, and he prepared to go; but the girl's father said to his son-in-law, "Fortify yourself with a bit of food, and after that you may go." 6 So the two men sat and ate and drank together; and the girl's father said to the man, "Why not spend the night and enjoy yourself?" 7 When the man got up to go, his father-in-law kept urging him until he spent the night there again. 8 On the fifth day he got up early in the morning to leave; and the girl's father said, "Fortify yourself." So they lingered until the day declined, and the two of them ate and drank.

The second ambiguity in the passage is found in verses 5–8, where the Levite stays in his father-in-law's house beyond the customary period of hospitality of three days.[48] This is a breach of cultural convention and points to an information gap that stimulates readers to seek an explanation. Readers would therefore ponder the reason for the extended stay.

The change of pace in this scene calls for further consideration of the narrative gap presented. The preceding verse (verse 4) covers a time period of three days with a summary: "His father-in-law, the girl's father, made him stay, and he remained with him three days; so they ate and drank, and he stayed there." In verses 5–8, however, the pace of the narrative significantly slows down and provides a detailed description of the interaction between the father and the son-in-law over the next two days, where the father-in-law repeatedly urges the Levite to stay and enjoy more food. The speech of the father-in-law is recorded three times in verses 5, 6 and 8; yet the Levite is notably silent throughout the account.[49] This brings to readers' attention the father-in-law's exceeding hospitality and the Levite's silent compliance.

---

47. Sternberg considers the centrality of a narrative gap as proportional to the havoc it plays with the intelligibility of the plot; *Poetics of Biblical Narrative*, 248. In this case, the gap in verses 2–3 is a key to the entire plot and hence plays a significant role.

48. For a discussion on the custom of hospitality in the Hebrew Bible, see Hobbs, "Hospitality," 3–30.

49. Although the father-in-law urges the Levite to stay the fourth time in verse 9, it is not considered here, as this does not result in the silent compliance of the Levite.

The repetition of the speech of the father-in-law renders the silence of the Levite even more remarkable and unusual. Conversation is naturally two-way, and to record a conversation between two people where the dialogue is merely one-way indicates something is missing; it is not only once, or twice, but three times! It is hardly a coincidence but a narratological means of withholding information on the speech and thoughts of the Levite, thereby inviting readers to fill in the gap: Did he say anything in response? If not, why is he silently staying on?

Putting the reasons for the exceeding hospitality of the father-in-law aside, there are two possibilities regarding the Levite's response: either he is unwilling to stay but subjects himself to the will of his father-in-law; or it is his own wish to stay longer than the customary practice. The portrait of the Levite in this scene is entirely passive, almost to the extent of being a puppet following the instructions of his father-in-law. This seems to provide grounds for the first hypothesis—that he is simply complying with the wish of his father-in-law—which adds to the portrait of his character a gentle temperament, in that he avoids tension with others by all means. He may even be timid in expressing his own views, hence the complete silence throughout the scene. This would appear consistent with the second hypothesis from the previous gap in verses 2–3, that he is an extraordinarily loving person in accommodating the unfaithfulness of the concubine. The character of the Levite, from a combination of these two hypotheses, is then remarkably noble and gentle.

There are, however, also grounds for supporting a second reconstruction to the gap, in that it is the Levite's own wish to stay on. The motif of enjoying food recurs throughout the scene, both in the form of bread in verse 5 and in the action of eating in verse 6 and verse 8. Though eating and drinking are inevitably part of hospitality, to repeatedly mention this motif seems to highlight the importance of the element of food enjoyment for the delay. It is possible, then, that the Levite is indulging in the food provided by his father-in-law and that he also wishes to stay on for longer. This would cast a negative light on his character, depicting him as a gluttonous man taking advantage of the kindness of others. The silent compliance, in this case, becomes an act of pretense, concealing his greed. This image is less consistent with the overly loving figure proposed in the second hypothesis from verses 2–3, and hence adds more weight to the first hypothesis that he is not aware of the unfaithfulness of his concubine.

As the text again does not provide sufficient information to favor either of the reconstructions over the other, both hypotheses should be maintained for the time being. This adds complexity to the character of the Levite, as the two opposite portraits from the reconstructions become further apart:

either he is such a good man that he is constantly bending himself to the wishes of others; or he is a selfish man with no respect for the conventions of the culture. These conflicting images effectively raise curiosity from readers, as they ponder what kind of person he really is.

Ambiguity in Verse 25: Who Pulled the Concubine Out?

> 19:25 But the men would not listen to him. So the man seized his concubine, and put her out to them. They wantonly raped her, and abused her all through the night until the morning. And as the dawn began to break, they let her go.

After the Levite and his group finally depart on the fifth day, they arrive at Gibeah where an old man takes them in for the night. The climax of the story begins at verse 22, as the mob from the city come pounding at the door, requesting the Levite be brought out for homosexual intercourse. The old man offers his virgin daughter, together with the concubine, and is rejected, yet in verse 25 there comes a sudden turn: the concubine is taken out to the mob and subsequently gang raped. However, the text is intriguingly ambiguous concerning the person who pulls her out, referring to him as "the man." Is it the old man, the master of the household, or is it the Levite? The identity of "the man" plays a vital role in the dramatic progression of the narrative, as it has a profound impact on how the character of the Levite is perceived. The equivocal expression hence opens a gap in the narrative that demands to be filled in by readers.[50]

Following on from the old man's offer in verse 24, it is plausible that "the man" is referring to the old man himself, who takes the liberty of being the host and shoves the concubine into the mob.[51] If this is the case, then either his action is too fast for the Levite to react, or being such a subservient character, the Levite is unable to resist the aggression in order to protect his beloved concubine. This hypothesis is consistent with the passive, gentle portrait of the character of the Levite from the previous gaps and, being seen as powerless in protecting the one he loves, confirms further his timid character. This vulnerable image of the Levite may elicit empathy from readers, as again and again he seems to be overpowered by people around him

---

50. Embry suggests that "the verse may be intentionally ambiguous so as to implicate both the old man and the Levite," yet he does not explicate further the potential functions of such intentional ambiguity; Embry, "Narrative Loss," 291n16.

51. Some scholars consider that this possibility cannot be excluded on textual grounds, though the reference to the Levite is more probable; see Boling, *Judges*, 276.

in the narrative: first by the unfaithful concubine, then by his father-in-law, and now by even the host, who is merely a new acquaintance.

On the other hand, the text also allows for an alternative hypothesis. As the old man's proposal is already rejected by the mob at the beginning of verse 25, he might have given up on the negotiation. "The man," in this case, is the Levite who sees that the old man has seemingly failed to stop the attack; now the Levite perceives the impending threat against himself and responds by pulling his concubine out as a substitute.[52] The following phrase, at his concubine, is consistent with this interpretation in that they are then both referring to same person.

This reconstruction then portrays the Levite in a completely opposite manner than in the first hypothesis. It renders him an egocentric character, who has absolutely no mercy toward his own concubine and instinctively thrusts her out in order to save himself. This then challenges the reconstruction of a loving, gentle, and submissive figure from previous narrative gaps, and those who have subscribed such an image may begin to wonder: Perhaps he is not such a kind man after all? Perhaps he is indeed selfish and greedy, as implied in his overstaying in the father-in-law's house? Perhaps he seeks reconciliation with the concubine only because he does not know about her unfaithfulness? This becomes a turning point in the narrative and prompts readers to reevaluate the previous hypotheses in a new light. Those who have been more inclined to accept a negative image of the Levite would, conversely, consider this piece of new information as a further confirmation of his vice. The brief "gap" in the identity of "the man" hence heightens the tension of the reconstructions from the previous narrative gaps and promotes the dramatic progression of the discourse.

As the evidence in the text for the identity of "this man" is seemingly resolved, the characterization of the Levite plunges further into ambiguity. Readers may still have good will in their minds, hoping, perhaps, "this man" is not the Levite? Pondering the two hypotheses, suspense is created, as readers are eager to know what may happen next. Will the loving husband, though timid, look for the concubine and save her from danger? Or will he prove himself to be the horrible person that readers fear, and act in even more drastic ways?

---

52. This view is attested to in the majority of commentators. For example, see Webb, *Book of Judges*, 468; Schneider, *Judges*, 262; Trible, *Texts of Terror*, 76.

Ambiguity in Verses 27–29: Is She Alive?

> 19:27 In the morning her master got up, opened the doors of the house, and when he went out to go on his way, there was his concubine lying at the door of the house, with her hands on the threshold. 28 "Get up," he said to her, "we are going." But there was no answer. Then he put her on the donkey; and the man set out for his home. 29 When he had entered his house, he took a knife, and grasping his concubine he cut her into twelve pieces, limb by limb, and sent her throughout all the territory of Israel.

The exact cause and exact time of death of the concubine are left ambiguous in verses 27–29. Is she dead by the time the Levite sees her (verse 27), and hence there is no reply to his command? Or did she die on the way home (verse 28)? Or, perhaps, is she still alive when the Levite seizes her body once again and thrusts the knife into her (verse 29)? Sternberg aptly identifies this as a narrative gap that leads to different judgments upon the participants.[53] If the concubine dies at the doorway, it would imply that the abuse of the mob is the direct cause of her death and hence invite judgment against their brutality; if she is alive until the Levite dismembers her, then this is an accusation against him for his horrific behavior devoid of any human conscience. As the text does not provide any closure, Sternberg contends that this forms a permanent elision and forces mutually exclusive readings, thereby blackening both parties at the same time.[54]

While Sternberg's observation seems reasonable on its own, if the previous gaps are also considered, the narrator is clearly focused on the Levite, and not the mob. Read in conjunction with the previous gaps—that jostle between positive and negative images of the Levite—this scene comes as a total shock to those readers who held onto any glimmer of hope concerning his good character. Not only does he not rush to save her from the mob, as those who hoped for the best might have imagined, but the fate of his concubine does not seem to bother him and nor stop him from having a good night's sleep. The brief commands "get up" and "we are going," when he sees her at the doorstep the next morning, reveal no trace of affection, and cast serious doubts upon the hypothesis that he is an exceptionally loving husband. If he loves her enough to tolerate her betrayal, he would not respond to her injuries with such callousness.

---

53. Sternberg, *Poetics of Biblical Narrative*, 239–40. While this ambiguity of the time and cause of death of the concubine has been recognized by many, few have investigated the narratological purpose for this obscurity.

54. Sternberg, *Poetics of Biblical Narrative*, 240.

Then, at last, when the Levite grasps the body of the concubine and mercilessly divides it into twelve pieces, the gentle and timid figure from previous gaps is utterly shattered. A person capable of such brutal mutilation to a fellow human being, even if she were already dead, could hardly be a tender, loving person. It is, of course, even more horrifying if readers ponder the possibility that she is still alive at the scene. It certainly creates surprise in the reading, as it would be totally unexpected from the foreground of the plot. For those who are more inclined toward having a negative image of the Levite from previous hypotheses, this scene still presents a horrifying climax to the narrative. It is one thing to be greedy or even self-centered, but quite a different thing to violently dismember a person who was once intimately related to oneself. The actions of the Levite come as a shocking surprise, which propels the adverse portrait to a point beyond imagination.

In this way, these verses present a closure to the previous narrative gaps. They effectively invalidate the image of a loving husband who is exceptionally gracious; his pursuit of the concubine was likely due to ignorance of her unfaithfulness. He probably did not submit himself to the will of his father-in-law in order to avoid tension; rather, he enjoyed the food and did not care about the social convention. If he were capable of dismembering the body of the concubine, then it is not surprising at all that he pulled her out to the mob in order to save his own life. The ruthless character of the Levite is revealed through this progressive revelation in the narrative, and it invites judgment on his behavior, as the final outcome presents a sharp contrast to the previous expectation of the readers. The more positive the image created by previous hypotheses, the greater the irony presented now. The rival hypotheses therefore converge at this point to condemn the Levite. Interestingly, however, while this scene closes the gap on previous ambiguities, readers still do not know whether the concubine is alive when the Levite sets the knife upon her. This continues to prompt readers to ponder the character of this Levite and continues to condemn his behaviors.

Combined Function of the Ambiguities

The potential reconstructions of the ambiguities regarding the persona of the Levite in Judges 19 have now been thoroughly demonstrated. Instead of opting for particular hypotheses as each new "gap" is encountered, this discussion has focused on the interactions of the hypotheses and the resultant rhetorical impacts on readers. It is clear that the ambiguities are not casual omissions; rather, they are crafted artistically at key points of the narrative to focus attention on the character of the Levite. The filling of the gaps requires conscious effort from readers, and as they engage in such activity, they are constantly confronted by the different hypotheses, rendering the portrait of the Levite more and more vivid, precisely because the earlier ambiguities have created so much tension.

As literature is a time-art where "the textual continuum is apprehended in a temporal continuum and things unfold sequentially,"[55] readers are also encouraged to reconsider the hypotheses as the narrative progresses and new information or new gaps are presented. Such reading back and forth works to validate or invalidate the previous hypotheses. This interplay between the narrative gaps again demonstrates the artistry of the rhetorical device, and it propels the plot toward the climax, where a closure of previous gaps is reached at the end.

While there are no explicit judgments from the narrator, an even more dramatic and powerful condemnation is developed through the progression of narrative gaps. This implicit judgment involves the active participation of readers and hence is effective in its rhetorical communication. Sternberg's comment on the David and Bathsheba episode also makes a fitting summary of Judges 19: "[t]he suppression of essentials, the narrator's pseudo-objectivity, and the tone rendering the horror as if it were an everyday matter: all these create an extreme ironic discordance between the tale's mode of presentation and the action itself, as reconstructed and evaluated by the reader."[56] In other words, the withholding of information that creates gaps and ambiguities in the narrative embeds a sophisticated play of poetics and requires careful unpacking by readers.

Are there further clues in the narrative that reinforce this interpretation? Apart from using the technique of ambiguities, how has the narrator manipulated readers' evaluation of the Levite? This is explored in the next section.

Point-of-View Study

Overview

The concept of point-of-view has attracted significant attention in literary criticism since the beginning of the twentieth century. Contrary to possible uses of the term that include the opinion or knowledge of a character, our concern here is particularly with the focalization of the narrator. It is "the positioning of the teller of a story vis-à-vis the elements in the story, whether

---

55. Sternberg, *Poetics of Biblical Narrative*, 199–200.
56. Sternberg, *Poetics of Biblical Narrative*, 192.

they be persons or objects, or even ideas."[57] Berlin explains the idea with the analogy of a camera: "The director (read 'narrator') positions the camera (read 'establishes the point-of-view') from which you view the action. There are two aspects to this positioning, both of which can have a profound impact on the narratee's (and the reader's) response to the story: angle and distance."[58] A desired rhetorical effect is then achieved through manipulating the angle and distance from which the story is told by the narrator.

This analogy is helpful in offering a basic understanding of the technique, yet, as Yamasaki points out, it limits the operation of point-of-view to a spatial orientation, which is overly simplistic in the case of narratives.[59] Literature expresses itself in texts, not visual images as in films, and the story is communicated through the creation of images in the minds of readers as they read. Apart from a spatial orientation, there are also other means of manipulating the textual elements in the construction of these images, all of which contribute to the establishment of the point-of-view in the discourse.[60]

Literary critics such as Boris Uspensky, Gérard Genette, and Seymour Chatman have composed detailed analyses of the manipulation of point-of-view in fictions.[61] Though utilizing different terminologies, such as "focalization" (Genette) and "point-of-view" (Uspensky and Chatman), the foci of their studies are alike in the investigation of the operations and effects of the technique in literature. The study by Uspensky provides the most comprehensive conceptualization, considering the function of point-of-view in five planes: spatial, temporal, psychological, phraseological, and ideological.[62] These are revealed through a detailed analysis of the language in the text, and the combination of the points of view from different planes then either concur or diverge to produce various rhetorical effects.[63]

Several biblical scholars have attempted to utilize the concept of point-of-view in the reading of the narratives in the Hebrew Bible. For example,

---

57. This is Yamasaki's expansion on the oft-cited definition of point-of-view by literary critic Percy Lubbock as "the relation in which the narrator stands to the story," *Watching*, 3–4.

58. Berlin, *Poetics*, 44.

59. Yamasaki, *Watching*, 4.

60. Yamasaki, *Watching*, 4–5.

61. Uspensky, *Poetics of Composition*; Genette, *Narrative Discourse*; Chatman, *Story and Discourse*. For a review of the work of these critics as well as the historical development of point-of-view studies in literary criticism, see Yamasaki, *Watching*, 11–41.

62. Uspensky, *Poetics of Composition*, 6.

63. Yamasaki, *Watching*, 30–3.

Berlin incorporates the theories of both Chatman and Uspensky in her paper, "Point of View in Biblical Narrative,"[64] and Bar-Efrat also offers a thorough coverage of the dynamics of point-of-view in biblical narratives in his monograph, *Narrative Art in the Bible*.[65] Yet it is Yamasaki who has most extensively and systematically examined the concept of point-of-view and developed Uspensky's theory to apply it to reading biblical narratives. The following provides a summary of Yamasaki's methodology; this approach is then applied to the reading of Judges 19.

Yamasaki's Methodology for Analyzing Point-of-View

While the interest of literary critics in point-of-view is oriented toward its poetics and hence focused on the evaluation of its effectiveness, Yamasaki's methodology for analyzing point-of-view in biblical narratives seeks to investigate its functions in interpretation.[66] The basic assumption is that the narrators of biblical narratives do not merely record an event, but "they want to ensure their readers come away from these stories with particular evaluative stances on the events experienced."[67]

Scholars have identified numerous methods used in this rhetorical purpose. Explicit comments by the narrator are considered the most effective way to bring out value judgments.[68] However, in the many cases of biblical narratives where explicit comments are lacking, evaluative guidance may be found in other textual elements, and point-of-view is one such element.[69] By manipulating the point-of-view in the text, readers are either being led to "merge" with a given character, thereby experiencing the actions subjectively and empathizing with him/her; or they are being held at a distance from the character, hence reducing identification and empathy.[70] Uncovering the use of this technique then reveals the narrator's implicit

---

64. Berlin, "Point of View in Biblical Narrative," 71–113.

65. Although the concept of point-of-view is dispersed among various chapters, the depth of Bar-Efrat's consideration on the matter remains impressive. For a summary, see Yamasaki, *Watching*, 133–42.

66. Yamasaki, *Watching*, 41.

67. Yamasaki, *Perspective Criticism*, 6.

68. Sternberg lists fifteen tools used in the biblical art of persuasion, and narratorial evaluation of an agent or action is considered the highest authority; *Poetics of Biblical Narrative*, 476–77.

69. Yamasaki, *Perspective Criticism*, 1. Sternberg also acknowledges the use of "the play of perspectives" in the art of persuasion in biblical narratives; *Poetics of Biblical Narrative*, 478–79.

70. Yamasaki, *Perspective Criticism*, 10.

evaluation—for or against a particular character—and therefore provides a direction for the interpretation of the narrative.

Building upon Uspensky's theory, Yamasaki proposes a methodology for analyzing the textual indicators of point-of-view in six planes: the spatial, psychological, temporal, phraseological, and ideological planes (as per Uspensky), and, in addition, the informational plane. Each of these planes is introduced below according to the order of their significance for interpretation as perceived by Yamasaki.

The Spatial Plane

The analysis of point-of-view on the spatial plane concerns the physical proximity of readers to a given character. A variety of positions can be established by the narrator, such as "attachment to a particular character" where the narrator's description follows the actions and positions of the character; or "sequential survey" where the viewpoint moves sequentially from element to element in a scene or from place to place; or "bird's-eye view" in which an encompassing view of the scene is seen from a broad horizon;[71] or "silent scene" where the distance is close enough to observe actions but not sufficient to hear conversations.[72] The narrator may alternate between these positions in the flow of the discourse to manipulate the distance between readers and the character.

There are various factors that contribute to the establishment of these positions. For instance, the degree of detail concerning the outward appearance of a character provided by the narrator may indicate the positioning, for greater detail represents higher proximity.[73] The textual elements of the narrative also play a significant role in the spatial positioning. Based on the insights of linguist Susumo Kuno, Yamasaki identifies various syntactical elements that influence the distance in relation to a character: the order of noun phrases in a coordinate structure, possessive noun phrases, and the subject of a clause. A character who is presented by nouns that appear earlier in the sentence, by a possessive noun or pronoun, or by the subject of a clause, tends to draw readers closer to him/her.[74] By analyzing the syntax of the narrative, the spatial positioning relevant to a character may be discerned, which in turn influences the empathetic evaluation of the character. Yamasaki considers

---

71. Yamasaki, *Watching*, 30.
72. Yamasaki, *Perspective Criticism*, 33–34.
73. Yamasaki, *Watching*, 158.
74. Yamasaki, *Watching*, 159–63.

the spatial plane to be of primary significance in point-of-view studies, and priority should be given to its investigation.[75]

The Psychological Plane

The manipulation of point-of-view in the psychological plane relates to whether the narrator is establishing an inside view of the mind of a character or not. It may be achieved by expressions of emotion, reasoning, hearing, seeing[76] or thinking, which all contribute to the unveiling of the inner workings and perception of a particular character. The indicators of the psychological plane may be identified by *verba sentiendi*, the verbs of sense perception, such as "thought," "felt" and "sensed," and the use of *hinnēh* (behold) in Hebrew is also common in denoting a shift in the line of vision, which is a clue to perception. An alternative technique, namely "indefinite details of perception," is also used in manipulating the psychological plane of point-of-view. As biblical narrators are omniscient, providing imprecise details of a description may shift the point-of-view of readers from the narrator to the character who is perceiving the event. These expressions lead readers to a subjective experience of the character, hence bringing them to a psychological proximity.[77]

The analysis of the psychological plane of point-of-view therefore involves the identification of the presence of the inside view of the characters. However, it is not a straightforward maneuver. As the biblical narrators only occasionally provide glimpses into the inner lives of characters, the absence of such expression in a narrative does not necessarily indicate that a psychological distance is intended. This intention is more pronounced, however, in a situation where substantial external actions of a character are provided and yet are devoid of revelations of his/her inner thinking. The contrast of a detailed outward observation renders the lack of psychological details more obvious. In the same way, the presence of an isolated inside view does not necessarily indicate that readers are drawn into a position of proximity to a character. Instead, a cluster of inside views with multiple forays into a character's thoughts and feelings

---

75. However, it is also noted that spatial alignment alone may not necessarily lead to empathy if the readers remain oblivious to the thoughts and feelings of the character. It is when spatial alignment is coupled with sympathetic inside views of the character that a sense of identification is generated in readers. Yamasaki, *Watching*, 158.

76. Yamasaki makes an important distinction between "looking," which can be an entirely external observation of the action of the character, and "seeing," which refers to a vision of the character that is internal; *Perspective Criticism*, 42–45.

77. Yamasaki, *Perspective Criticism*, 35–53.

produces a more substantial experience of the inner life of a character. Nevertheless, Yamasaki considers the discernment of the psychological plane an essential component in point-of-view study.[78]

The Informational Plane

The informational plane of point-of-view is the only one among the six that does not build on Uspensky's theory but stems from the insights of the informational axis of point-of-view by Sternberg. It refers to the degree of information possessed by the reader in relation to the characters in a particular scene. When readers possess the same information as that of a given character, there is a convergence between the information database, and readers are prompted to experience the event in the same way as the character. This leads to empathy toward or approval of the actions of the character. On the other hand, if there is a discrepancy in the information database, it builds a divergence between the reader and the character, and hence a sense of distance is generated, which contributes to an adverse evaluation of the actions of the character.[79]

The analysis of the informational plane is relatively straightforward, as it involves proceeding through a passage and comparing the degree of information possessed by readers and the characters. The difference in information may be conveyed by direct narratorial comments that a character "does not know," or be in the form of additional information provided to readers as background. These provide readers with more information than the characters in the scene. In addition, the fracturing of chronology in a narrative may also bring about a divergence of information between readers and characters, as the outcome of events is foretold to readers before being experienced by the characters. These divergences, in turn, distance readers from the characters and are an important element in the crafting of the point-of-view in the narrative.[80]

The Temporal Plane

While the temporal dynamics in novels have received considerable attention in literary-critical circles, Yamasaki considers these to play a tangential

---

78. Yamasaki, *Perspective Criticism*, 48–53.
79. Yamasaki, *Perspective Criticism*, 54–55.
80. Yamasaki, *Perspective Criticism*, 56–68.

role for readers in the evaluation of biblical narratives.[81] There are three ways that the temporal plane of point-of-view may operate to alter the positioning of readers in relation to characters.

The first aspect is positioning in relation to timeline. Biblical narratives are primarily retrospective in nature, which creates within readers a sense of distance from the characters engaged in the events. The use of extended discourse as well as present-tense verbs in the narratives may provide a sense of proximity against this default state.[82] However, due to the imprecise nature of expressing time in Hebrew verbs, the role of verbs in temporal dynamics in the narratives of the Hebrew Bible is rather limited.[83]

The second aspect is the ordering of events in the timeline. The genre of story is generally sequential, and the use of flashback and flash-forward alters this chronological order. When considered in combination with the informational plane, these flashback and flash-forward devices form a divergence, which has the effect of distancing readers from the characters.[84]

The third aspect is pacing of events in the timeline, which is the relationship between narrative time and story time in a narrative text. Pacing is categorized into the elements of "summary," where the story time exceeds the narrative time; "scene," where the story time equals the narrative time; and "pause," where the narrative time exceeds the story time. Within summary, material is further divided into broad summary, moderate summary, and tight summary, according to the relative lapses of time of the events. In general, the slower the pace, the more details an observer is able to perceive, and the greater is the sense of proximity generated. However, the impact on the empathy of readers toward a character may also be subject to other factors, such as the involvement of other characters in the scene, and hence the analysis of pacing is considered of limited value.[85]

Overall, Yamasaki considers the temporal plane of point-of-view as relevant for uncovering narratorial evaluation of characters, yet its contribution is not as direct as the previously mentioned planes.

The Phraseological Plane

The phraseological plane involves the differentiation of points-of-view through the use of speech characteristics. The examples given by both

81. Yamasaki, *Perspective Criticism*, 69.
82. Yamasaki, *Perspective Criticism*, 69–73.
83. Bar-Efrat, *Narrative Art*, 144.
84. Yamasaki, *Perspective Criticism*, 74–77.
85. Yamasaki, *Perspective Criticism*, 83–87.

Uspensky and Yamasaki focus on the relational designation of characters: a given character may be addressed or referenced by different characters with different designations, and each designation represents a "speech characteristic." When the narrator incorporates one of the designations into the narratorial voice, a shift in point-of-view is effected from that of the narrator to the character. This results in the reader's experiencing of the subsequent material from the point-of-view of the character.[86] Yamasaki contends that this plane of point-of-view is least developed among biblical scholars, and its significance to the evaluative interpretation of texts is the least among the five planes developed by Uspensky.[87]

The Ideological Plane

The ideological plane of point-of-view refers to the ideological stance of the narrator or characters as reflected in a narrative. It is distinguished from the ideology functioning at the level of the entire narrative, which Yamasaki terms the "macro-level" of ideology. The ideological plane of point-of-view concerns the "micro-level" of ideology, which is the personal stance of the narrator or character toward a particular issue or action at any point in the narrative.[88] The ideology of the narrator may be conveyed through explicit commentary or through expression by reliable characters; whereas the ideology of a character may be communicated to readers by direct speech, actions of the character, or by narratorial description. The analysis of the ideological plane of point-of-view therefore involves studying the dynamics of the shifts between the ideological stances of the characters and of the narrator.[89]

However, Yamasaki also contends that, as the biblical narrator's ideological view often dominates the discourse, there is less room for the dynamics between the ideological views of different characters in the narratives. Readers are therefore often led to merge with the point-of-view of the narrator instead of the characters, rendering the ideological plane the least critical among the six in studying point-of-view in biblical narratives.[90]

---

86. Yamasaki, *Watching*, 31–32; *Perspective Criticism*, 93–95.
87. Yamasaki, *Perspective Criticism*, 91.
88. Yamasaki, *Perspective Criticism*, 98–101.
89. Yamasaki, *Watching*, 173–80.
90. Yamasaki, *Watching*, 180; *Perspective Criticism*, 98.

Concurrence/Nonconcurrence of Planes

The above discussion of point-of-view dynamics in the various planes describes the ways that readers may be drawn to merge with, or be distanced from, a particular character. Yamasaki names this character the "point of view character," who is a key figure in the narrative. This is also the character whom the narrator implicitly evaluates through the dynamics of the various planes. I here use the term "protagonist" to refer to this character, as it is more generally recognized. The next step in the analysis is to put together the findings from each of the planes. A "concurrence of planes" means that the dynamics of different planes function in the same direction of merging (or distancing) of the protagonist. In general, devices on two or three planes are sufficient for the purpose.[91] When concurrence results in a merging with the protagonist, readers experience the event from the perspective of the character and hence develop a sense of identification and empathy. On the contrary, when concurrence results in a distancing from the protagonist, this leads to a negative evaluation of the character.[92]

A "nonconcurrence between planes" occurs when point-of-view dynamics from different planes work in opposing directions. This creates in readers a sense of distance from the protagonist and in turn results in a negative evaluation on the character.[93] Yamasaki's methodology provides a way of discerning the hints provided in biblical narratives for evaluating the protagonist. By attending to each of the six planes of point-of-view, and combining the findings from the planes, the crafting of the discourse in manipulating the distance between the reader and the character is revealed. This is particularly beneficial for the interpretation of narratives in which explicit evaluative comments on characters and events are absent.

Point-of-View Study in Judges 19

Judges 19 presents a story of a horrific gang rape and dismemberment of a concubine, and yet it is apparently devoid of any direct comments from the narrator concerning these brutal actions. This has caused many perplexities among commentators, and feminist scholars have often condemned the patriarchal ideology reflected in this apparent objectivity. However, a closer study of the narrative may reveal that the narrator is not as value neutral as it appears on the surface. As Fokkelman points

---

91. Yamasaki, *Perspective Criticism*, 106.
92. Yamasaki, *Perspective Criticism*, 110–11.
93. Yamasaki, *Perspective Criticism*, 112.

out, by naming the men in Gibeah in verse 22 "men of Belial," a term that connotes a destructivity resulting from a total disregard of God and his commandments, the narrator gives a framework for value judgment of the mob and its behaviors.[94] Though the gang rape itself does not seem to be condemned by direct comment from the narrator, this framework is sufficient for readers as a guide for their evaluation.

The sense of ambivalence in the narrative is therefore more directed to the character of the Levite, and point-of-view study may be used to discern implicit evaluative guidance from the narrator. While Yamasaki uses Judges 19:1-21 as one of the examples in his study,[95] his discussion is rather brief and does not cover the entire narrative. The following expands on Yamasaki's observation and offers a more thorough investigation of the various planes.

The Spatial Plane

Yamasaki reads Judges 19:1–21 as effecting an overall spatial proximity for the Levite: "Verse 1 of this passage places the readers in proximity to a certain Levite . . . In verse 2, the readers are removed from the presence of this Levite as they are led to follow his concubine . . . But after this, the readers are positioned back at the Levite's side, and are maintained in that position of proximity for the next twenty verse . . ."[96] While his observations on verse 1 and verse 2 are correct, in that the Levite and the concubine respectively occupy the position of the subject in these verses, his comment on spatial positioning in the rest of the narrative is overly simplistic.

A closer reading of textual indicators in the narrative offers quite a different picture. From verse 3 to verse 9, the subject of the clause and the possessive pronoun frequently switches between the concubine, her father, and the Levite. In verse 3, 'b hn' rh (father of the young woman) gives prominence to the concubine; and in verses 4–9, the same designation, and ḥtnw, his father-in-law, are used alternatively indicating that the Levite does not continuously possess syntactical prominence in the passage.[97] This is more akin

---

94. Fokkelman, *Reading Biblical Narrative*, 151–52.

95. Yamasaki, *Perspective Criticism*, 114.

96. Yamasaki, *Perspective Criticism*, 114.

97. Commentators have noticed the redundancy of using both "father of the young woman" and "his father-in-law." Contra Schneider, who doubts the legitimacy of such designations and suggests that this use is to show the complication of the relationship (*Judges*, 255–56). Here I propose that it could be a means of shifting the spatial proximity and avoiding attachment to any characters.

to the arrangement of a "sequential survey," where the readers are dissuaded from developing spatial proximity to any particular character.

The Levite occupies a more prominent syntactical role in verses 10–30, but there are several occasions that significantly interrupt this continuum. He is referred to as ʾ*dnyw*, his master, in verse 11 and verse 12; and again as ʾ*dwnyh*, her master, in verse 26 and verse 27. These possessive pronominal suffixes indicate the syntactical prominence of the servant and the concubine in the respective clauses. These interruptions, though brief, may temporarily distract readers from being merged with the Levite in the spatial plane.

Apart from textual elements, the degree of detail provided for a character is also a means for discerning spatial distance. Throughout the passage, the detail provided concerning the Levite is almost minimum: there is no description of his appearance, facial expressions, or fine movements; and it appears that he is being described from a distance. It is not until verse 29 that there is a sudden change in the degree of detail given: "When he had entered his house, he took a knife, and grasping his concubine he cut her into twelve pieces, limb by limb, and sent her throughout all the territory of Israel." By describing his actions with such precision, readers are abruptly drawn much closer to the character on the spatial plane at this particular moment. Putting together the findings from the linguistic elements, the diversion of the spatial proximity in verse 26 and verse 27 immediately before this dismemberment scene may render this sudden shift even more dramatic.

This analysis of the spatial plane of point-of-view reveals a less straightforward situation than that proposed by Yamasaki. As the Levite is the protagonist in the narrative, the plot inevitably follows the events surrounding him. However, this does not automatically lead readers to merge with this character in the spatial plane, as Yamasaki has assumed. A closer reading reveals that there is a progressive change in the spatial plane of point-of-view. It begins with a sequential survey, which dissuades readers from developing a spatial proximity with the Levite (and other characters), and this distance is maintained throughout the narrative until it abruptly changes at the dismemberment scene, where readers are brought to the closest spatial proximity to the protagonist through precise description of his actions.

The Psychological Plane

The psychological plane of point-of-view refers to the revelation of the inner minds of the characters. There are several instances in Judges 19 that are relevant to the analysis of the reader's understanding of the inner thinking of the Levite.

The purpose clause "to speak to her heart" in verse 3 is an expression of reasoning that reveals the motive of the Levite in going after the concubine. This should theoretically result in the reader's psychological proximity to the character, yet the movement is complicated by the narrative gap that these exact words create. As the previous section has demonstrated, this motive on the part of the Levite leads to an ambiguity in the reader's understanding of the Levite's psychological mind: Is he so loving to his concubine that he forgives her unfaithfulness, or is his action motivated by unawareness? With this piece of detail provided, readers have become more uncertain about the Levite's inner thinking, and instead of creating proximity, it brings a sense of distance. As Yamasaki has cautioned, a single revelation of the inner thinking does not necessarily result in psychological proximity, which is apparently the case here.

Yamasaki considers the use of the deictic-exclamatory *hinnēh* as a further device unveiling psychological perception. There are a number of usages of the term throughout the passage, including twice in verse 9, and once each in verses 16, 22, 24 and 27. However, Yamasaki's discussion does not consider the distinction between *hnh* (behold) and *whnh* (and behold). As Tamar Zewi has observed, *hnh* used in connection with the verb '*mr* ("to say") functions as introduction to direct speech and hence does not necessarily carry the connotation of visual perception as such. Instead, it is the use of *whnh* that might occur with verbs of sight and in related contexts indicating visual perception.[98] It is clear that the use of the term in verse 9 and verse 24 falls into the former category and hence is irrelevant in psychological plane analysis, whereas in verses 16, 22 and 27, it belongs to the latter category.

However, a closer reading of the text reveals that the use of *whnh* on these occasions does not automatically entail psychological proximity to the protagonist. In both verse 16 and verse 22, the visual perception does not belong to the Levite alone but to a group of characters: in verse 15 the group described includes the Levite, his concubine, and the servant, and hence the use of *whnh* in verse 16 may refer to the visual perception of any, or all, of the characters. Similarly, in verse 22, the old man and the Levite are portrayed as eating in the house when the mob comes, and the use of *whnh* here may likewise refer to the vision of either or both of these characters.

---

98. Zewi, "Particles," 21–38.

Therefore these occasions do not constitute a manipulation of the psychological plane of the protagonist.[99]

The only instance left to be considered then is verse 27. In this case, it is clear that *whnh* and the following clause align with the vision of the Levite. In addition, the description of the hands of the concubine on the door confirms that the phrase is intended to provide detail of the visual perception of the Levite. However, as other expressions of inner thoughts are lacking, it is uncertain whether *whnh* in this phrase functions to draw attention to the subject of the vision, and hence develop psychological proximity with him, or to draw attention to the object of the vision, in which case *whnh* functions as an exclamatory to raise awareness of what the Levite was seeing.

Apart from the devices discussed above, there are no other clues to the psychological perception of the protagonist in the passage. In fact, intriguingly, the narrator seems to be withholding any knowledge of his emotions from readers: he is noticeably silent in verses 5–8, rendering readers uncertain about his feelings toward the exceeding hospitality of the father-in-law. Despite being threatened with immense danger from the men in Gibeah, there is not one word on his emotions amidst the crisis. His emotional reaction to the gang-raped concubine is also lacking, resulting in much ambiguity concerning his attitude toward the events. And finally, his thoughts and motives for dismembering her are also absent in the description of the scene. The readers are therefore psychologically far removed from this protagonist, being excluded from his emotions and inner thoughts throughout the narrative.

The Informational Plane

The informational plane of point-of-view compares the level of information accessible to readers and to the characters. Although the narrator does not provide explicit commentary in Judges 19 that confirms the ignorance of characters, there is still potential for manipulation in the informational plane. As established in the previous section, there is an ambiguity in verses 2–3 that puts a question mark on whether the Levite was aware of the unfaithfulness of the concubine; this suggests a potential difference between the information possessed by the reader and the Levite. As the narrative progresses, the likelihood of this ignorance increases,

---

99. There are, of course, a number of uses of *whnh* that play different roles in different contexts. This analysis only aims to show the potential effect on the psychological plane without entering into the details of syntactical analysis.

for the alternative image of an exceptionally kind and forgiving husband diminishes with the advancement of the plot.

This potential difference in the information possessed by readers and the Levite is therefore sustained throughout the narrative, as readers constantly come back to review the assumption made at the beginning of the story. Each time readers revisit the ambiguity, the divergence of information becomes more tangible. This in turn develops a distance between readers and the Levite on the informational plane of point-of-view.

The Temporal Plane

Judges 19 presents a narrative retrospectively recorded in chronological sequence. There is no interruption of the positioning and order of events in relation to the timeline; hence the only aspect of the temporal plane of point-of-view beneficial for discussion is pacing.

An examination of the pacing of the narrative shows that both the beginning and the end of the narrative differ in pace compared to the rest of the discourse. The narrative from verse 1 to the first part of verse 3 covers a long period of time (at least four months), which categorizes it as a broad summary. The latter half of verse 3 through to verse 9 concerns a time period of several days, constituting a moderate summary. The rest of the narrative has quite consistent pacing: a tight summary up to verse 28, mingling conversations with actions that happen within a period of hours. Toward the end of the narrative, at verse 29, there is a pause and then the pace significantly slows down with a detailed description of the movements of the Levite: "he took a knife, laid hold of his concubine, and divided her into twelve pieces, limb by limb." This extended narrative time in taking the knife and seizing the concubine brings the attention of readers to this action and constitutes the climax of the narrative.[100]

As other characters are also involved in each of the tight summaries, these summaries do not result in any merging with characters in the temporal plane. Verse 29, on the other hand, may result in a merging with the character of the Levite, as it focuses on his actions. However, as Yamasaki contends, the temporal factor in point-of-view is often not a strong component and it needs to be read in conjunction with other planes in order to determine its impact on the movement of readers.

---

100. Bar-Efrat considers the extended narration time of the movement of Abraham in holding the knife over his son as constituting the climax of the story in Genesis 22:10; *Narrative Art*, 150. A similar situation is evident here in Judges 19:29.

The Phraseological Plane

The phraseological plane concerns the narrator's incorporation of speech characteristics distinctive of a character (such as personal addresses) into narratorial descriptions. The operation of this plane of point-of-view in Judges 19 is, however, rather negligible. There are no distinctive speech characteristics of the protagonist recognizable in the discourse. In terms of personal addresses, he is consistently referred to as *h' yš* ("the man"). Although he is referred to as *' dnyw* ("his master") in verses 11, 12, and again as *' dnywh* ("her master") in verses 26, 27, these are designations of relationship with other characters used in the context of their interaction. Unlike the examples given by Uspensky and Yamasaki, where designations that carry significant value connotations are used in narratorial descriptions, these do not represent a well-defined case of incorporation of speech characteristics.[101] Therefore, there is no apparent narratorial maneuvering of the phraseological plane of point-of-view in the narrative, which is consistent with its generally insignificant role in the view of Yamasaki.

The Ideological Plane

The ideological plane of point-of-view concerns the "micro-level" ideologies of characters and is often discerned through direct speech. A study of the speech of the Levite in Judges 19 reveals an interesting manipulation of the ideological plane.

From the beginning of the narrative, the Levite is noticeably silent until verse 11. In verse 12, he speaks for the first time in response to the suggestion of the servant to lodge in Jebus: "We will not turn aside here into a city of foreigners, who *are* not of the children of Israel; we will go on to Gibeah." His preference for Gibeah over Jebus in terms of lodging location is based on the ethnic composition of the people in the town, and the foreignness of the Jebusites is emphasized by the double address as "foreigners" and "not the children of Israel." This reflects a resistance to non-Israelites stemming from the ideology of the Levite, though there is no explanation provided for his reasoning. As this is the first conversation from the protagonist recorded, there is greater attention from the reader to its contents and to the ideology reflected.

---

101. Uspensky uses the shift in appellations of Napoleon ("Bonaparte" and "Napoleon") in *War and Peace* as an example of manipulation on the phraseological plane; *Poetics*, 27–32. Yamasaki uses the designation "Lord" in the Gospel of Luke as an illustration; *Perspective Criticism*, 94–95. Both examples provide obvious cases of the effect of the use of different designations.

This ideology then undergoes progressive challenges in the narrative. In verse 15, readers are told that when the group arrives in the town square of Gibeah, there is no one to take them in. This is an ominous sign of a lack of hospitality (as opposed to the common practice of the Israelites). The choice of Gibeah does not seem as promising as the Levite expected. And after an old man, who noticeably is an Ephraimite, finally takes them in for the night, in verse 22 the men from the city, "sons of Belial," come pounding at the door demanding homosexual intercourse with the Levite. The reality of the situation at Gibeah is in stark contrast to the expectations of the Levite, which completely falsifies his ideology: no matter what the reason is that made the Levite consider Gibeah a better place to be, the reality proves him wrong. As this reality is presented by the narrator, it is an indicator that the ideology of the Levite does not correspond to that of the narrator. This effectively distances readers from the Levite in the ideological plane of point-of-view. Therefore, as opposed to Yamasaki's contention that the ideological plane is often insignificant in biblical narratives, this passage offers an example where the ideology of the protagonist plays a noteworthy role.

Concurrence/Nonconcurrence of Planes

The above discussion demonstrates that the use of the technique of point-of-view is focused on the Levite (the protagonist) in the narrative. There is evidence of manipulation in five out of the six planes of point-of-view examined, except the phraseological plane, which is apparently not utilized by the narrator. The use of multiple planes attests that evaluative guidance is intended for actions of this character.

In bringing the effects of the various planes together, a general trend of detachment is primarily observed. It is particularly prominent on the psychological, informational, and ideological planes, which unanimously concur in order to draw readers away from the Levite. The functioning of the spatial and temporal planes, on the other hand, is slightly more sophisticated. There is a similar pattern on these two planes: a distancing is at work from the beginning of the narrative until verse 29, where a sudden shift of position closer to the character is evident. However, instead of merging readers with the Levite at this point, these planes work together to bring out the climax of the narrative: the attention of readers is drawn toward the Levite in spatial and temporal terms, which effectively magnifies his action of dismembering the concubine. As the psychological plane clearly puts readers at a distance, merging with the character is resisted. Quite conversely, the spatial and temporal positioning at the climax effects an even more prominent distancing, for the precisely described action of the Levite becomes even more unfathomable to readers.

This analysis demonstrates the cumulative effect of the various planes of point-of-view or focalization in the text that successfully keep readers at a distance from the Levite. This forms the basis for evaluative guidance from the narrator to view the Levite and his actions in a negative light: readers are not encouraged to identify or sympathize with him; instead, the manipulation of the point-of-view in the entire narrative functions to persuade readers to make an adverse judgment on this character.

Conclusion

This chapter has demonstrated the potential of reading Judges 19 with the tools of narrative criticism. The study of narrative gaps reveals a crafted poetics of the interplay of omitted details. This creates an enriching reading experience filled with curiosity, surprise, and suspense, as readers ponder the various hypotheses concerning the ambiguities; this also functions to draw attention toward the Levite. The final closure of the previous gaps in verse 29, though remaining an open gap itself, forcefully subverts any positive imagery of this man and casts a critical light upon his actions and character.

This interpretation finds resonance with the reading of the point-of-view of the narrative using Yamasaki's methodology. Three (the psychological, informational, and ideological) out of the six planes are found to draw sympathy away from the Levite, and the two other planes that draw readers closer to the character in effect magnify the absurdity and cruelty of his actions. The communicative function of this writing strategy is clearly to convey a negative evaluation of the character of the Levite and his behavior.

The discourse, read in this light, is no longer a value-neutral account of the gang rape and dismemberment of a female subjected to the patriarchy of her times. It is a critique of what happened in the story, persuading readers to reprimand such attitudes and actions, achieved through the numerous hints in the skillfully crafted narrative.

4

Reading Judges 19 Intertextually

Motifs of Hospitality, Rape, and Sacrifice

Introduction

Having explored the narratological tools used in Judges 19 and established the Levite as the protagonist of the narrative, I now turn to another form of literary criticism, namely intertextuality. Biblical scholars in recent decades have paid much attention to the interrelationship between texts, particularly in intertexts within the biblical corpus. As Benjamin Sommer contends, "the biblical authors themselves also comment on, explain, revise, argue with, and allude to texts written by their predecessors."[1] By attending to this interaction with intertexts, the meaning of the passage in view may be enriched and extended beyond the isolated text. Since the association of Judges 19 with intertexts in the Hebrew Bible is often recognized (especially in the case of Genesis 19), there is much potential for discerning the rhetorical effects of the narrative through bringing these intertexts into the reading. Numerous studies have attempted to do so, yet often the interpretive focus is on one or two intertexts, and seldom is the combined effect of the multiple intertexts considered.

This chapter is an attempt to discern the cumulative impact of the various intertexts on the interpretation of the narrative. Utilizing intertextual relationships established by various scholars, it demonstrates that the use of the intertexts may be categorized under three motifs, namely hospitality, rape, and sacrifice. Though the intersection of the study of motifs and intertextuality is not often recognized, there is in fact a common rationale behind the two: biblical texts do not stand alone but reside in a corpus of texts, and the understanding of any individual text may be influenced by

---

1. Sommer, *Prophet*, 2. Sommer favors the terms "influence" and "allusion" over "intertextuality" in describing intertextual relationships that focus on the author of the text, and the different use of terminologies by various scholars will be discussed later in this chapter. For now, "intertextuality" is used in the general sense referring to the study of the interrelationship between texts.

other texts within the canon. Both the study of motifs and the study of intertextuality are demonstrations of this influence.

According to Shemaryahu Talmon, the study of literary motifs in the Hebrew Bible concerns recurring themes that point to a deeper layer of meaning that is often relevant to the social context.[2] The analysis of motifs, in this sense, extends beyond the recurring literary components in intertextual interactions to the cultural contexts of the texts. This may shed light on the understanding of the rhetorical impact of the intertexts, as it provides a contextual scope through which the intertextuality may be interpreted. This chapter examines the three motifs in their cultural context and illustrates that they unanimously paint an adverse picture of the protagonist, the Levite. This anti-Levite rhetoric is consistent with the findings in the previous chapter and provides background information for the consideration of ideological aspects of the text in the next chapter.

Theories of Intertextuality and Motif

In this section, the concepts of intertextuality and motif are explored respectively. I first explore the definitions of the terms and their related theories in the field of literary studies, then discuss their applications in the Hebrew Bible. This demonstrates that there is an intrinsic connection between the two concepts, which in turn is used as the framework for the reading of Judges 19 in this chapter.

Intertextuality: Overview

The Concept of Intertextuality in Literary Studies

The recognition of the interrelationship between texts can be dated from Plato and Aristotle in ancient times.[3] Though it was not an entirely novel concept, the phenomenon began to gain popularity and attention among literary critics when the term "intertextuality" was coined by Julia Kristeva in 1965. Responding to the notion of a stable meaning, Kristeva combined the theories of Swiss linguist Ferdinand de Saussure and Russian literary theorist M. M. Bakhtin, arguing for an interrelationship of meanings between texts that is dependent upon the engagement of readers.[4]

2. Talmon, "'Desert Motif,'" 39.

3. For a brief survey of the concept of intertextual relationships at different stages of Western literary history, see Still and Worton, "Introduction," 2–15.

4. Allen, *Intertextuality*, 12–13.

The Saussurean definition of a sign as the combination of the signified and the signifier highlights the relational character of language. Signs are differential and non-referential in nature, with the possibility of a vast number of relations. Meaning is hence not an inherent property of a sign but depends upon the process of the combination and association within the differential system of language.[5] This reflects a notion of language in a generalized and abstract synchronic system.

Bakhtin, on the other hand, focuses on a word's existence within specific social situations and specific moments of utterance and reception.[6] He argues that the meaning of a word belongs to the linguistic interaction between specific individuals or groups within specific social contexts.[7] Text does not speak in a one-directional, simple monologue to the reader, rather, the creation and reception of words are conditioned by the presence of competing words in the discursive environment.[8] This dialogic character of utterances, where their meaning depends upon what has previously been said and also how those utterances will be understood by others, indicates the social and ideological nature of language. A word, in this sense, is not only relational because of its place within the abstract system of language, as per Saussure, but also, because of the nature of all language, viewed within concrete social situations.[9]

Kristeva develops her theory of intertextuality mindful of the Saussurean language theory and the Bakhtian dialogism of utterances in "The Bounded Text"[10] and "Word, Dialogue and Novel."[11] She extends the property of linguistic signs to the understanding of literary signs, as literary works are considered both as a selection of words from a language system as well as a choice of plots, images, ways of narrating, phrases and sentences from the literary tradition.[12] Meanings of literary works are then not only engaged in a web of relations of individual words, but also in a web of relations between various texts. Kristeva contends that a text is not originally created by authors from their own minds but constructed out of already existent discourses. A text is hence "a permutation of texts, an intertextuality in the space of a given text," in which "several utterances, taken from other

---

5. Allen, *Intertextuality*, 18–20.
6. Allen, *Intertextuality*, 20–21.
7. Allen, *Intertextuality*, 27.
8. Tull, "Intertextuality," 69.
9. Allen, *Intertextuality*, 29.
10. Kristeva, *Desire in Language*, 36–63.
11. Kristeva, *Desire in Language*, 64–91.
12. Allen, *Intertextuality*, 21.

texts, intersect and neutralize one another."[13] The definition of "text" also extends beyond the written word to include any form of communication understood in its context as a meaningful signifier.

By substituting "text" in her reiteration of Bakhtin's ideas, "Each word (text) is an intersection of word (text) where at least one other word (text) can be read,"[14] Kristeva extends her semiotic attention from language employed in specific social situations to text, to textuality and to their relations to ideological structures. She agrees with Bakhtin that texts cannot be separated from the larger cultural or social textuality out of which they are constructed.[15] Interpretation of texts therefore involves appreciation of the ideological structures and struggles in society embedded in the intertextual discourses. It is a dialogic and on-going process, in that meanings continue to reverberate in the text and to reflect the ideological tensions in the society.

Intertextual reading for Kristeva is therefore a dynamic conception of the "'literary word' as an intersection of textual surfaces rather than a point (a fixed meaning), and as a dialogue among several writings: that of the writer, the addressee (or the character), and the contemporary or earlier cultural context."[16] In other words, meaning is dynamically produced by readers rather than stably residing in the author.

Since Kristeva's introduction of the word "intertextuality," the term has been widely used in literary scholarship in the discussion of the interrelationship between texts, with vastly different, sometimes contradictory, methodologies, and assumptions. As Tull suggests, "the concept of intertextuality represents a battleground of differing emphases and claims, both linguistic and ideological . . . Few agree on how best to understand and use the term . . ."[17]

In order to avoid the reduction of intertextuality to the traditional notions of influence, source-study, and simple "context," Kristeva at a later stage drops "intertextuality" for a new term, "transposition."[18] Nevertheless, her supporters continue to defend the meaning of intertextuality as "originally" introduced by Kristeva and accuse those who do not adhere to this meaning as "abusing" the use of the term. However, in restricting

---

13. Allen, *Intertextuality*, 45, quoting Kristeva, *Desire in Language*, 36.
14. Kristeva, *Desire in Language*, 66.
15. Allen, *Intertextuality*, 45.
16. Allen, *Intertextuality*, 47–48, quoting Kristeva, *Desire in Language*, 65.
17. Tull, "Intertextuality," 59. This comment by Tull in 2000 continues to be true and is echoed by Miller in 2010. Miller, "Intertextuality," 283.
18. Allen, *Intertextuality*, 61–62, quoting Kristeva, *Revolution in Poetic Language*, 59–60.

the understanding of the term to the definition of Kristeva (though for the sake of precision in terminology), her apologists are in fact inadvertently demonstrating a notion of monologic discourse against its own dialogic theory.[19] Hence, others propose a more generalized use of the term inclusive of methodologies concerning influences and sources. The debate continues to the present day, and the diversity and tension are also reflected in the study of intertextuality within the biblical field.

The Study of Intertextuality in the Hebrew Bible

Since the 1960s, when the theory of intertextuality gained popularity in literary circles, biblical scholars have also begun to apply the concept explicitly to the study of the Hebrew Bible.[20] Various collections of essays discussing the theory and giving examples of its applications have been published, including *Reading Between Texts: Intertextuality and the Hebrew Bible* (1992) edited by Fewell; *Intertextuality and the Bible* (1995) edited by Aichele and Phillips; *The Quest for Context and Meaning: Studies in Biblical Intertextuality in Honor of James A. Sanders* (1997) edited by Evans and Talmon.

These collections of essays reflect a common understanding of the implications of Kristeva's theory to the interpretation of biblical texts, in that the reading of a text is no longer a closed system sufficient in itself. As meaning exists between a text and all the other texts that it refers and relates to, the search for the meanings of biblical texts then becomes an intertextual activity.[21] The application of this theory, however, has led to vastly different methodologies among biblical scholars.

In his overview of intertextuality in biblical scholarship, Miller classifies the different approaches into two broad camps: the "reader-oriented" approaches and the "author-oriented" approaches.[22] The first category refers to those who generally subscribe to Kristeva's definition of intertextuality, focusing on the connections between texts as perceived by the reader(s). It is a predominantly synchronic analysis of texts, where it "is irrelevant whether these texts were intentionally alluded to by the original author, or even available to

19. Tull, "Intertextuality," 72.

20. This is not to discount the presence of the practice of reading biblical texts along with other texts (either inside or outside the canon) throughout history, such as Rabbinic interpretations, which characteristically read biblical texts in light of one another. What is meant here is an explicit use of the term "intertextuality" as a methodological or theoretical assumption.

21. Allen, *Intertextuality*, 11.

22. For examples of scholars adhering to the two camps, see Miller, "Intertextuality," 288–91.

the author."[23] Meanings of a text incorporate endless possibilities in that the readers choose to bring together the text with intertexts.

The author-oriented approaches, on the other hand, focus on identifying the specific connections of intertexts that the author intends for readers to perceive in reading. It is a diachronic study that involves determining which text predates the others and, consequently, has influenced the others.[24] Meaning is defined by the author, and the task of readers is to discern the implicit allusions and explicit references as predetermined by the author, and thereby align themselves to the intended meaning. These author-oriented approaches can be viewed as an extension of the traditional historical approach, where dating of biblical texts and authorial intention are the main foci of attention. Scholars subscribing to these approaches are often engaged in delineating legitimate criteria of association between intertexts; lexical similarities such as shared vocabulary and phraseology, parallels based on content or motif, common genre, or shared structural features are often used.[25]

Sommer's influential study *A Prophet Reads Scripture: Allusion in Isaiah 40–66* is representative of this approach. He recognizes the use of intertextual associations by biblical authors and contends that it is an important perspective to consider when investigating the meaning of texts.[26] However, he allocates the term "intertextuality" to methodologies focusing on the text and the reader[27] and categorizes intertextual studies focusing on the author under the terms "allusion," "influence," "echo," and "exegesis."[28] These four categories are distinguished based on the different modes and purposes of interaction between the intertexts, and he argues that it is these categories that are relevant to the understanding of the intertexts in the Hebrew Bible.

It is obvious that scholars using these two different approaches of intertextuality have vastly different assumptions and preoccupations in biblical interpretation. Similar to literary critics who disagree upon the methodology of intertextuality, advocates of the two camps in biblical scholarship also have been defending their own positions and criticizing the other camp.

---

23. Miller, "Intertextuality," 284.

24. Miller, "Intertextuality," 284.

25. For a summary of the criteria as proposed by various scholars, see Miller, "Intertextuality," 294–98.

26. Sommer, *Prophet*, 2.

27. Sommer, *Prophet*, 7.

28. For a detailed discussion of the differentiation of the terms, see Sommer, *Prophet*, 10–18.

Those who adhere to Kristeva's definition of intertextuality insist that "intertextuality is a strictly synchronic discussion of wide-ranging intertextual relationships that necessarily precludes author-centered, diachronic studies."[29] To investigate intertextual connections within the biblical corpus searching for authorial intent and historical priorities therefore betrays the definition and should not be legitimately considered as "intertextuality." Alternative terms such as "inner-biblical exegesis" and "inner-biblical allusions" are proposed to refer to these author-oriented approaches in order to avoid confusion.[30] The more fundamental challenge to author-oriented approaches, however, lies in the uncertainty in reconstructing a reliable historical past and the multiplicities of speculations in the process.[31] The value of the findings of such reconstruction, and the subsequent claim of "author intended meaning," is then cast into doubt, for one cannot realistically get into the mind of an ancient author.

On the other hand, reader-oriented approaches are critiqued for minimizing the context in which biblical texts were produced. By focusing on the contemporary reader's associations of intertexts and subsequent control of meaning, the social and cultural contexts of the ancient texts are often pushed aside. This invites charges of eisegesis, and the fruitfulness of such outcomes for biblical studies is severely questioned.[32] Moreover, there is a lack of explicit methodology in reader-oriented approaches acting as guidelines, rendering *any* form of juxtaposition between *any* text an apparent candidate for intertextuality. However, when meaning is purely arbitrary and there is no limit to the possibilities of meanings in a text, it seems pointless to discuss any meaning at all.

The root of the diversity of approaches lies in the fact that "intertextuality" is a theory rather than a methodology, and hence there is significant room for various approaches to come under this hat. The basic assumptions of the theory, in terms of the interrelatedness of texts, are actually endorsed by both camps: the meaning of a text needs to be studied in conjunction with other texts that it relates to. However, as Miller has recognized, in any investigation of intertextuality, there needs to be a boundary.[33] One simply cannot

---

29. Meek, "Intertextuality," 283.

30. Meek, "Intertextuality," 305. The term "inner-biblical exegesis" was first proposed by Michael Fishbane in *Biblical Interpretation in Ancient Israel* (1985) and was later used by many. For a detailed discussion of the definitions and differences between "inner-biblical exegesis" and "inner-biblical allusion," see Meek, "Intertextuality," 284–90.

31. Meek, "Intertextuality," 304.

32. Meek, "Intertextuality," 304.

33. Meek, "Intertextuality," 289.

compare a text with the abundance of texts in the entire universe. The difference between the author-oriented and reader-oriented approaches, in fact, lies in the differences in the boundaries set. The author-oriented approaches set the boundary mostly within the canon of the Hebrew Bible (or texts contemporary to the biblical texts), whereas the reader-oriented approaches extend the boundary beyond this scope. In this sense, both approaches reflect applications of the theory, though in different dimensions.

As long as intertextuality remains a concept describing the interrelations between texts, and not an established methodology, it is bound to attract diverse approaches that may have conflicting assumptions. Rather than making a judgment on the "correctness" of the methodologies, the different use of the concept simply reflects different reading interests. Reader-oriented and author-oriented approaches apply the theory of intertextuality to serve different purposes and hence utilize different methodologies.

The reading interest in this chapter lies in the interpretation of Judges 19 through intertextuality with other passages in the Hebrew Bible. The boundary of the investigation is therefore primarily within this textual corpus. In this particular sense, it is author-oriented, as it searches for the intended rhetoric of the author in juxtaposing the intertexts, as well as its desired effect on readers.[34] However, it does not restrict itself in the search for literary sources and textual development. In order to incorporate considerations of the socio-cultural context, it also engages in the theories of "motif," which are discussed in the next section.

Motifs: Overview

The Concept of Motif in Literary Studies

The term "motif" in English was first used in the fields of art and music in the eighteenth–nineteenth centuries, and it was soon integrated into the language generally as a term indicating a recurrent theme or subject.[35] In the field of literary studies, it may either refer to a recurring element across different works, or one that recurs within a single work.[36] Scholars have since used the concept of motif to identify a broad range of textual elements including detail, metaphor, image, symbol, idea, and subject matter. There is no apparent

---

34. This is not to deny the potential of intertextuality in the reader-oriented approach, which has been demonstrated in Chapter 1 in the Chinese context.

35. Talmon, "'Desert Motif,'" 38.

36. An example of the use of motifs across different works is the study of folklore. Dan Ben-Amos provides a summary of the history and development of the usage of the concept in folklore studies in "Concept of Motif," 17–36.

consensus in the definition and nature of the term, and various methods have been used to incorporate the concept in literary criticism. To complicate the matter further, other terms such as "themes" are also used to describe a similar phenomenon, and "theme" is often used either interchangeably or complementarily with "motif" in articulating the concept.[37]

William Freedman provided a detailed analysis of the function of motif as a literary device in 1971.[38] Focusing on motifs employed within a single work, he defines motif as "a recurrent theme, character, or verbal pattern, but it may also be a family or associational cluster of literal or figurative references to a given class of concepts or objects . . . It is generally symbolic—that is, it can be seen to carry a meaning beyond the literal one immediately apparent."[39] Motifs can therefore be presented in different forms in a literary work, and the essence lies in the function that it plays in pointing to a meaning deeper than the superficial level. Freedman lists three ways that motifs contribute to the meaning of a literary work: cognitive, affective, and structural.[40] In the cognitive aspect, a motif can reveal something about the characters, setting, or theses and themes in a work. A motif may also function in the affective aspect, seeking to elicit certain emotive responses from readers. Structurally, the reappearance of a motif contributes to the flow and unity of the narrative.[41]

In studying motifs in a work, one does not stop at the stage of mere identification— the real question in interpretation is what the motif does to the communicative function of the text. It is hence important to explore beyond the literal text, to discover the connotations that the motif may carry. The literary value of motifs is that it enhances the complexity and the subtlety of expression of ideas in a work, which in turn add scope and depth to the reading experience.[42]

The Study of Motif in the Hebrew Bible

One of the first applications of the term "motif" in biblical studies was in a literary analysis of the book of Ruth in 1897.[43] It has since been used by biblical

37. Daemmrich, "Themes and Motifs," 566.
38. Freedman, "Literary Motif," 123–31.
39. Freedman, "Literary Motif," 127–28. He also proposes criteria for establishing the identification of a motif as well as assessing its efficacy (see 126–27).
40. Freedman, "Literary Motif," 125.
41. See also Morgan, "How Do Motifs," 200–201.
42. Freedman, "Literary Motif," 131.
43. Talmon, "'Desert Motif,'" 38. Talmon does not, however, provide a reference

scholars on various occasions with different methodologies, and there remain certain ambiguities in its formulation and definition.

Recently, Morgan attempted to clarify the definition of motifs in his application of the concept to biblical narratives, though some aspects of his arguments are debatable. Building on Freedman's foundation, he applies a more restricted definition for motif, particularly in delineating between motif and theme. He considers motif as a "discrete thing, image, or phrase that is repeated in a narrative," whereas the term "theme" refers to "a more generalized or abstract concept that is suggested by, among other things, motifs."[44] Morgan attempts to clarify the terms by detaching motifs from the ideological connotation that is embedded in the use of the device and allocating the symbolic function of motifs to themes. However, as Freedman emphasizes, the essence of a motif lies in the symbolic value that it adds to the interpretation of the narrative, and one then wonders if such demarcation by Morgan is practical: without pointing to a theme, would a motif still be a motif? And if a motif is bound to exist with a theme, then what is the practical value of differentiating the two? The intrinsic relationship between motifs and themes may then render such strict delineation unnecessary.

Moreover, following the definition of Freedman, Morgan's insistence on restricting the term "motif" to repetition within a single literary work creates problems when it is applied to the biblical texts. As the biblical corpus is composed of various works, and intertextual motifs do exist between different books of the Hebrew Bible, restricting the study of motifs to a single book (even if it is considered an individual work without the complexity of redaction layers) may then lead to incomplete understanding. Morgan attempts to combat this issue by recognizing motifs that exist within "literary traditions." When a motif is used across different works in a literary tradition, it is considered to be performing "diachronic" functions, and the reapplication of motifs in another work is then named "emplotment."[45] While Morgan's effort to clarify the concept of motifs is noteworthy, it is questionable whether a motif that performs a diachronic function can still be considered to be "within a single literary work." Again, such strict demarcation seems less than practical when applied to biblical studies, and it may be more beneficial to simply include the possibility of motifs being used in multiple literary works. The notion of motif in this study hence includes motifs across different literary works and does not make a distinction between motifs and themes.

---

for this study.

44. Morgan, "How Do Motifs," 198.
45. Morgan, "How Do Motifs," 204–5.

Nevertheless, the study of Morgan makes a significant contribution to the analysis of the function of motifs in biblical narratives. Contrary to those who reject the value of investigating authorial intention, he contends that the examination of biblical motifs may begin with the authorial audience in mind. "Whether it is possible or not to demonstrate the author's intentional construction of a motif, interpreters can still evaluate how an identified motif seeks to lead readers, progressively and cumulatively, to understand various elements of the narrative."[46] Using the text at hand, and/or other historical materials, interpreters can make plausible suggestions about the meaning and communicative function of a motif to the narrative. In order words, the interpretation of the rhetorical function of a motif does not rely on the demonstrable certainty of its diachronic use, which in reality can never be achieved. Nonetheless, the information gathered from attempting to address the context of the authorial audience remains beneficial, as it may recover potential ideological contentions embedded in the biblical narratives.

In contrast to Freedman and Morgan, Talmon favors a concept of motif that is found across different literary works.[47] The potential of the study of motifs in the Hebrew Bible is thoroughly explored in his collection of essays *Literary Motifs and Patterns in the Hebrew Bible*. In particular, he considers motifs an effective means for systematic conceptualization of abstract cognitions in the Hebrew Bible. As a large proportion of the Hebrew Bible is presented as narratives and events, it lacks a comprehensive and systematic formulation of ideas and thinking. Understanding of such concepts hence needs to be distilled, deduced, and integrated from narratological descriptions, and the study of motifs can bring together commonalities that recur in the biblical corpus in different contexts and forms. In this sense, motifs become "condensed literary signifiers of speculative thought," which are immensely helpful for discerning the rhetorical purpose of texts and narratives.[48]

Talmon's perspective on the tradition of biblical narratives not only includes the literary and religious realms, as per Morgan; he also puts specific emphasis on the connection of motifs to their social world. He contends that the heuristic value of motifs is "rooted in the fact that they arise out of existential conditions . . . they are deeply implanted in the collective experience and the synchronous and diachronous memories of the authors and the audience

---

46. Morgan, "How Do Motifs," 207.

47. For example, in his study of the barren wife motif, he includes texts from the books of Genesis, Judges, and 1 Samuel; Talmon, *Literary Motifs*, 159–70.

48. Talmon, *Literary Motifs*, 3–4.

to whom they address themselves."[49] In other words, a motif is something in the social context that the author and the readers share in the tradition, and the existence of a motif in a certain text is meant to arouse connotations from this shared cognition. These connotations are then incorporated into the reading of the text and shape the reader's reaction. The interpretation of biblical texts that contain motifs, therefore, extends beyond the superficial literal meaning confined in the particular text and conveys messages that refer to deeper concepts embedded in the social context.

In view of this functional aspect of motifs, Talmon provides the following definition for use in studying motifs in the Hebrew Bible:

> A literary motif is a representative complex theme that recurs within the framework of the Hebrew Bible in variable forms and connections. It is rooted in an actual situation of an anthropological or historical nature. In its secondary literary setting, a motif gives expression to ideas and experiences inherent in the original situation and is employed by the author to re-actualize in the audience the reactions of the participants in that original situation. The motif represents the essential meaning of the situation, not the situation itself. It is not a mere reiteration of the sensations involved, but rather a heightened and intensified representation of them.[50]

For Talmon, the analysis of a biblical motif therefore primarily involves intertextual considerations of the motif in different texts within the biblical corpus. In order to investigate further its social context, the scope of intertextual reference is then extended to literatures such as the Qumran scrolls, early rabbinic literature, and early Christian writings. As his concern is the specific connotation of a motif in the intellectual world reflected in the Hebrew writings, the boundary of his intertextual study of motif is the biblical canon and literatures intimately connected with the canon. He contends that studying biblical motifs in this manner will then aid in understanding the biblical author's ideas and thoughts, which in turn sheds light on the conceptual universe of the biblical world.[51]

Drawing insights from both Morgan and Talmon, the study of motifs in biblical narratives is both a diachronic and synchronic exercise. On the one hand, interpreters attempt to establish the connection between different texts that share the same motif within the biblical corpus, which inevitably carries a diachronic aspect as chronologic priority of traditions

---

49. Talmon, *Literary Motifs*, 4.
50. Talmon, "'Desert Motif,'" 39.
51. Talmon, *Literary Motifs*, 5–6.

is involved. On the other hand, the synchronic aspect of motif is considered through the way the meaning of the narrative is implied by the use of the motif within the literary, religious, and social traditions. It has become quite obvious in the discussion thus far that there are overlapping aspects between the concepts of motif and intertextuality, which are considered in further detail in the next section.

Intertextuality and Motif

It has been established in the discussion of the concept of intertextuality that the meaning of any text, including biblical narratives, does not stand alone, but is found within a network of connections with other texts. Although it is often used in reconstructing the chronological priority of texts, this should neither be perceived as the only concern of the study nor the end in itself. Identifying intertextual links should pave the way for further insights assisting interpretation of the text, as it reveals rhetorical intents of the author through references to other texts.

The study of motifs in the biblical corpus, on the other hand, is also an essentially intertextual activity. Motifs are identified through the recognition of intertextual associations within the canon, and this brings in the dimension of abstract conceptualization of the social world of the text including literary, religious, and cultural traditions. This goes beyond the superficial connection of the texts to the messages conveyed relating to the social conventions and ideologies in the context of the biblical world.

In this sense, the study of motifs can be viewed as an extension to the author-oriented approach of intertextuality. It helps to connect the findings of intertextual associations to the interpretation of the meanings of the text and to the understanding of the social world. In this regard, it is an echo of Bakthin and Kristeva in their emphasis on the influence of the social context to a text. On the other hand, an author-oriented approach of intertextuality may also have been seen as a foundation to the study of motifs. As motifs are meant to be recognized by readers, the intertextual linkages need to be strong enough not to be easily missed in the process of reading. A thorough investigation of author-oriented intertextuality then provides identification of motifs with a solid basis of interconnectedness between the relevant texts.

In other words, in cases of intertextuality where motifs can be established, there is potential for developing understanding of the authorial intents as well as the conceptualization of ideologies from the author's social world. The rest of this chapter is an attempt to demonstrate the potential of incorporating the concepts of both intertextuality and motif. It begins in the intertextual realm by demonstrating the relationship between Judges 19 and other texts in the Hebrew Bible and then extends to the study of the motifs that can be observed in these intertextual associations. It illustrates that such an exercise suggests an authorial intent in building these connections, which is thus relevant to the meaning and rhetorical purpose of the text.

It is essential to first review the scholarship that has previously contributed to the discussion of intertextuality and motif in Judges 19, before engaging in further examination of the use of the two concepts in this narrative.

Intertextuality in Judges 19

The literary connection of Judges 19 to other texts of the Hebrew Bible, especially in the case of Genesis 19, has long been recognized by commentators. Numerous studies have been published on the topic, and while the connections are generally accepted, the interpretations differ. The chronological priorities of the texts are disputed, and the explanations of the intended meaning of the connections have been even more diverse. In this section, I provide a summary of the discussions on the intertextual connections of the passage in recent scholarship and illustrate the need for further investigation on the cumulative effect of the intertexts.

The most comprehensive textual analysis to-date on the intertextuality of Judges 19 is found in *Dismembering the Whole: Composition and Purpose of Judges 19–21* by Cynthia Edenburg. She devotes an entire chapter of over 150 pages to the topic of intertextuality between Judges 19–21 and various texts in the Hebrew Bible, with over half of the examples from Judges 19. She establishes a set of six criteria of literary dependency, focusing on textual evidence in discerning author-intended direct textual links between texts.[52] These criteria are then applied to a comparison between Judges 19 and passages including Genesis 19, 1 Samuel 11, Deuteronomy 22, and 2 Samuel 13. As these passages, according to Edenburg, contain substantial textual associations with Judges 19, the focus of the review of scholarship below is on these four intertexts.[53]

---

52. The criteria include similarity of formulation, similarity of context and/of structure, transformation and reactualization of a common element, "ungrammatical" actualization of a common element, interaction between texts, and accumulative evidence. Edenburg, *Dismembering*, 171–73.

53. The associations with Genesis 22:10 that Edenburg considered "isolated parallels" will be incorporated in the discussion of motifs in the next section and not

While the textual analysis by Edenburg is extensive and convincing, there remains room to expand upon her discussion. As the focus of her book is on the dating and compositional history of the text, the intertextual features are investigated in order to support her theory that places the composition of the passage in the Babylonian or early Persian period. The major concern of her chapter on intertextuality is therefore on establishing the chronological sequence in the composition of the various texts, and the rhetorical purpose of each of the associations is not thoroughly considered. Nevertheless, her effort in establishing the various textual associations is monumental.

Unlike Edenburg, other scholars who study the intertextuality of Judges 19 usually focus on associations with a single intertext, and more attention is devoted to the meaning of the connection apart from literary influence and historical priority. The findings of these studies will be considered together with Edenburg's. For the purpose of clarity and order, I discuss a selection of publications that connect Judges 19 with each individual text separately, although at times a single study may include discussion of more than one intertextual relationship.

Genesis 19

Genesis 19 is the most extensively and thoroughly discussed intertext in relation to Judges 19. This textual association is often recognized in commentaries on Judges.[54] The following highlights relevant recent studies and follows the chronological order of the publications in order to demonstrate the development of the dialogue.

Susan Niditch brought the issue to academic attention with her article in 1982.[55] After highlighting the issues of hospitality, homosexual rape, the relationship between the Levite and his concubine, and holy war in Judges 19–20, she establishes that the theme of the narrative is community and unity within Israelite society. She then compares the text with Genesis 19 in an attempt to develop chronological priority. She contends that Judges 19 is more cohesive and comprehensive in terms of style, plot, theology, and

---

discussed here.

54. For example, Boling states that "a glance at Gen 19:9 will suffice to indicate why a literary relationship exists," in *Judges*, 279. Webb suggests that "the extensive verbal parallels between the present scene [of Judg 19:22–25] and that in Genesis 19:4–9 are obvious," *Book of Judges*, 467.

55. Niditch, "'Sodomite' Theme," 365–78.

integrality, and should therefore assume priority to the Genesis text.⁵⁶ The study of Niditch focuses on determining textual dependence, and it is her interpretation of the individual texts that shapes her understanding of the diachronic intertextual relationship.

Taking a synchronic approach and presupposing the priority of the Genesis text, Stuart Lasine focuses on the manner in which hospitality is presented by the characters in the two narratives. He contends that the "use of material from Genesis 19 allows the reader to contrast the situations at Gibeah and Sodom so that he can see how the old host inverts Lot's hospitality into inhospitality, and how the action of the Levite-guest is the inverse of the action taken by Lot's divine guests."⁵⁷ Combining an intertextual reading of 1 Samuel 11 with Judges 19–21 (which is discussed later), he proposes that the communicative purpose of the intertextual linkages is to "condemn the Levite by means of the subtle use of irony and absurd humor."⁵⁸ The study of Lasine thereby exemplifies how a synchronic intertextual approach may shed light on the authorial intent of the narrative in Judges 19.

Although also subscribing to the priority of Genesis 19, Daniel I. Block sees the rhetorical function of the intertext in a very different manner. He begins by providing a detailed analysis of the parallels between Genesis 19 and Judges 19 in terms of progression of the plot and linguistic features including vocabulary and syntax.⁵⁹ The similarities of the intertexts support his identification of the use of an "echo narrative technique" in Judges 19 that employs the preexistent account in Genesis 19 to shape the reader's understanding of the new situation.⁶⁰ He argues that the event in Sodom serves as a model of the corrupted city of Canaan, and the Gibeah narrative is patterned after this account in order to illustrate that the Israelites have become "canaanized."⁶¹ In other words, Block places the focus of intertextual comparison on the Sodomites in Genesis 19 and the men of Gibeah in Judges 19.

---

56. Niditch, "'Sodomite' Theme," 378. Though she also acknowledges that it is almost impossible to reach a definitive conclusion on the relationship between the two passages, the priority of Judges 19 has not been generally accepted by scholarship.

57. Lasine, "Guest and Host," 37.

58. Lasine, "Guest and Host," 38.

59. Block, "Echo Narrative," 326–33.

60. He defines echo narrative technique as "a story-teller's deliberate employment of preexistent accounts or segments thereof to shape the recounting of a new event"; Block, "Echo narrative," 325. Though using different terminologies, the study of Block is also a synchronic intertextual reading between the two narratives.

61. Block, "Echo narrative," 337–40.

Victor Matthews's study of the two intertexts includes both the focus of hospitality of Lasine and the censure of the lawlessness of the society of Block, yet he takes a different approach and uses findings of anthropological research to support his argument.[62] He establishes a "protocol of hospitality" and juxtaposes each of the narratives with this protocol, illustrating that "the writer(s) of Genesis 19 and Judges 19 has (have) deliberately created scenes in which the code of conduct is systematically violated. This may be part of a deliberate theme contrasting the 'flawed,' but valiant ancestor with towns and their inhabitants whose violations of custom justify their destruction."[63] Assuming the priority of the Genesis text, he also proposes that the Gibeah incident presents a worsened scenario compared to Sodom, in that all customs are ignored or corrupted. This in turn is used to justify the establishment of the monarchy in Israel.[64] The study of Matthews demonstrates the value of investigating the motif of hospitality within its social context and its impact on the interpretation of the authorial intention of the texts.

Edenburg's monograph offers the most recent and also most detailed analysis of the differences and similarities between Judges 19 and Genesis 19. As there is resemblance as well as individuality in each of the two texts, she contends that neither story is a blind reflection of the other and each contains independent and purposeful composition.[65] In her analysis of the parallel motifs and structural elements, she observes that the elements of incongruity in Judges 19, such as the mob's willingness to accept the concubine, and the apparent breach of hospitality by the host in offering the concubine, may be explained by borrowings from Genesis 19. The motifs of male rape and the counteroffer of two women by the host were borrowed from Genesis and woven into the Gibeah story, and hence do not fit perfectly well into the logic of the narrative.[66]

Edenburg also analyzes the language of the intertexts and identifies occasions of resemblance, which indicates influence of the Genesis text on that of Judges.[67] This includes the comment about sleeping in the square; shared collocation of "men of the city" in Judges 19:22 and Genesis 19:4;

---

62. Matthews, "Hospitality and Hostility," 3–11.
63. Matthews, "Hospitality and Hostility," 3.
64. Matthews, "Hospitality and Hostility," 10–11.
65. Edenburg, *Dismembering*, 175.
66. Edenburg, *Dismembering*, 177–79. This is a significant contribution, as it offers a convincing explanation to the elements in the narrative that seem unnatural and have puzzled commentators.
67. Edenburg, *Dismembering*, 179–84.

and the syntax in the exhortation to the mob in Judges 19:23 and Genesis 19:7. She contends that "the accumulative weight of these evidences is decisive and leads me to conclude that Judg 19 was patterned upon Gen 19."[68] The author of Judges 19 was familiar with the literary tradition of the story of Lot in which Sodom was known for being an irredeemable sinful city, and the purpose of the patterning is to picture Gibeah as a spiritual "sister" of Sodom.[69] However, she does not go further to investigate the impact of this influence to the rhetoric of the story of Gibeah, except with a general statement: "the analogy between Gibeah and Sodom may be rooted in a polemic directed against Gibeah and Benjamin."[70]

This overview of scholarship on the intertextuality between Judges 19 and Genesis 19 yields two issues that pave the way for further exploration. The first issue concerns the literary dependency of the intertexts. It appears that there is more support for the primacy of Genesis 19 among recent scholars. The textual evidence provided by Block and Edenburg is detailed and convincing, whereas Niditch's argument for the opposite is anchored in her interpretation of a well-integrated narrative of Judges 19, which does not necessarily point to an earlier tradition. The author of Judges may have possessed masterful skills in incorporating a previous tradition, and Niditch's comment of a "more simple" theology and structure in the Genesis text appears subjective. This study hence is based on a working assumption that the readers of Judges 19 knew the Genesis text, while I acknowledge that the matter remains open to discussion.

The second issue concerns the motif of hospitality. As identified by various studies, this motif plays a significant role in the interpretation of the intertextual association. However, the object of comparison between the two texts within this framework remains debatable, and different reference points may lead to vastly different proposals concerning the rhetorical purpose of the narrative, as demonstrated by the interpretations of Lasine and Block. This matter is taken up in the discussion of this motif, and I propose that the Levite, being the protagonist in the narrative, should form the focal point of comparison.

1 Samuel 11

Though less often discussed, the association between Judges 19:29–30 and 1 Samuel 11:7 is recognized, and the precedence of the latter is generally

---

68. Edenburg, *Dismembering*, 184.
69. Edenburg, *Dismembering*, 186.
70. Edenburg, *Dismembering*, 186.

assumed.[71] Analysis of the intertexts often focuses on the comparison between the Levite and Saul, as their actions in the two texts are juxtaposed. However, there is no consensus among scholars in the interpretations of the authorial intention in associating the intertexts. This is demonstrated below in two studies that result in opposite conclusions.

Edenburg lists the verbal parallels between the action of the Levite in dismembering his concubine and Saul's cutting up of the oxen and contends that Judges 19:29–30 is dependent upon 1 Samuel 11:7. The parallel use of the verb *ntḥ* ("to cut up") in Judges 19:29 and 1 Samuel 11:7 is particularly noteworthy. She observes that "[e]lsewhere in the Bible this verb is restricted to cultic contexts dealing with sacrificial offerings, and the object of the verb is invariably an animal (Exod 29:17; Lev 1:6, 12; 1 Kgs 18:23, 33), as it also is in 1 Sam 11:7 (oxen)."[72] The cutting of a human body in the case of the Levite hence deviates from the usual usage, which suggests that the place of Saul's oxen is both substituted by the concubine as a sacrificial victim and also without any divine ordinance.[73]

Edenburg then interprets the Levite's action as a parodic reflection of Saul and, reading together other intertexts developed from the Saul narrative to Judges 20, she concludes that "the authors of Judg 19–21 lifted elements from the history of Saul and reapplied them in a narrative supposedly occurring before there was a king, in order to predispose readers against Saul and subvert any sympathy the narratives in Samuel may raise."[74] In other words, not only is the Gibeah incident written with an awareness of the Saul narratives, its meaning is found in anticipating the intertext rather than possessing an independent meaning within Judges 19–21.

Also presupposing the knowledge of the Saul narratives by the readers of Judges, Lasine focuses on the consequences of the actions described in the intertexts and evaluates Saul in an opposite manner compared to Edenburg. He points out that the Levite's dismemberment of his concubine leads

---

71. For example, Lasine, "Guest and Host," 41; O'Connell, *Rhetoric*, 299.

72. Edenburg, *Dismembering*, 222.

73. Edenburg, *Dismembering*, 221–24. This observation by Edenburg will play a significant role in the discussion of the motif of sacrifice discussed later in this chapter.

74. Edenburg, *Dismembering*, 230. This view of the narrative as an anti-Saul polemic has been rather popular in recent scholarship. For example, the connection between Judges 19–21 and the story of Saul has been elaborately explored in Amit, "Literature," 28–40. More recently, Milstein contends that the Levite is a "stand-in" for Saul, and Judges 19:1–20:13 is as an anti-Saul polemic added to an originally pro-Saul complex in Judges 20–21; "Echoes of Saul," 174–206. Against these scholars, however, I will argue that Saul is seen in a positive light in the sacrificial scene in 1 Samuel 11, and the intertextual association here is an anti-Levite polemic.

to near annihilation of a town, whereas the sacrifice of the oxen by Saul results in the deliverance of Israel. He therefore contends that "the parallels actually function as an 'execration' of the Levite, and all the other Israelites of his 'kingless' age."[75] Saul is thus seen in a positive light in that his action is motivated by the Spirit of God and prevents disaster, whereas the Levite, who is apparently emotionless in his action, causes disaster. This contrast functions to emphasize the perversity of the events in Judges 19–21 and reveals the ludicrous nature of society without a king.

Both the studies of Edenburg and Lasine demonstrate a strong case for the patterning of the Levite's dismemberment of the concubine on the sacrifice of Saul. However, their interpretations of the authorial purpose of this juxtaposition head in opposite directions. Edenburg takes it as an anti-Saul polemic, whereas Lasine considers that it conveys a pro-Saul ideology. Nevertheless, the motif of sacrifice being central to the intertextual relationship is clear in both analyses. This is, however, not the only instance in Judges 19:29 that has intertextual references relating to sacrifice. This same verse in fact is also connected to the sacrifice of Isaac in Genesis 22:10, yet neither the analysis from Edenburg nor from Lasine brings together the two intertexts to read them in the light of each other. This is investigated under the motif of sacrifice.

Deuteronomy 22

Edenburg perceives several textual associations between Judges 19 and the laws about sexual offenses concerning women in Deuteronomy 22:13–29. Although the laws technically do not address concubines, there are three verbal parallels between the texts: the collocation *' b hn' rh* (father of the young woman) appears in the Bible only in Deuteronomy 22:15–16, 19, 29 and Judges 19:3–6, 8–9; the unusual usage *znh* (to commit fornication) in Judges 19:2 corresponds to Deuteronomy 22:21; and *ptḥ hbyt* (the entrance of the house) is mentioned in both Judges 19:17 and Deuteronomy 22:21.[76] Based on these observations, she suggests that the language of the laws in Deuteronomy 22 is intentionally invoked in the narrative in Judges 19. However, she does not seem to find a satisfactory explanation for the purpose of this association, proposing that "the author planted the associative links in order to demonstrate the range of his literary competency."[77] However, if one attends to the motif of rape in the narrative, certain authorial

75. Lasine, "Guest and Host," 42.
76. Edenburg, *Dismembering*, 246–48.
77. Edenburg, *Dismembering*, 248.

purposes may be revealed in the associations. This is examined particularly via a discussion of the motif of rape in 2 Samuel 13.

2 Samuel 13

The Gibeah incident and the story of Amnon and Tamar share a common element in that the rape of a woman causes men to take revenge on the culprits. While there are significant points of difference between the two plots, Edenburg notices similarities in the language that are sufficient to argue for a case of literary dependency. The commonalities include a unique expression "Don't my brother(s)! Do not . . ." in the plea of Tamar and of the host; use of the verb *ḥzq* ("to seize") in describing the actions of Amnon and the Levite; the command to the woman to "get up and go," and the expression "would not hear" occurring twice in each story.[78] Combining these with other inverse applications of language in Judges 19, she contends that "[t]he web of links with the story of Tamar may have been intended to augment the characterization of the three different figures in the Gibeah story—the Ephraimite host, the Levite, and the Benjamites—all of who are likened to Amnon."[79] In particular, the Levite is now portrayed as partaking in the same actions as a rapist in seizing the woman and asking her to get up and go, which in turn highlights his callous behavior. This is examined in the section on the motif of rape and shown to be consistent with the negative characterization of the Levite in the narrative.

Potential for Further Investigation

The review of scholarship above demonstrates that Judges 19 has strong intertextual connections with other texts in the Hebrew Bible. Though Genesis 19 is the most often addressed intertext (and hence warranted a longer discussion in this survey), the associations with other texts such as 1 Samuel 11, Deuteronomy 22, and 2 Samuel 13 are not to be neglected. The issue of intertextuality is therefore crucial to the interpretation of the narrative. Substantial work has been done by Edenburg and others in establishing the associations based on textual grounds, hence discussion in the next section builds upon these findings. As illustrated, there remains room for further investigation as interpretations of the demonstrated textual connections remain diverse and inconclusive. In particular, there is not yet any study that brings the four different intertexts together and

---

78. Edenburg, *Dismembering*, 250–52.
79. Edenburg, *Dismembering*, 253.

considers their collaborative impact on the rhetorical effect on the narrative of Judges 19 as a whole. As the author does not randomly choose intertexts and put them together without any purpose, it is legitimate to assume that there is a rhetorical purpose, not only in individual intertexts, but also in their combination.

Moreover, the above discussion identifies three motifs in the intertexts: the motif of hospitality, which is found in Genesis 19; the motif of rape, which is found in both Deuteronomy 22 and 2 Samuel 13; and the motif of sacrifice, which is found in 1 Samuel 11 (and Genesis 22, which is explored further). These three motifs are integrated as significant components of the narrative and represent the progression of each stage of the plot respectively. It is therefore potentially beneficial to bring together the three motifs for a better understanding of the communicative purpose of the narrative.

In the next section, I demonstrate this combined communicative purpose through studies of each motif. Taking Talmon's definition of motifs, I incorporate findings from historical and anthropological backgrounds and explore the possibilities of the reactions of readers to the use of the motifs in the narrative within their context. I also demonstrate that the Levite, who has been identified as the protagonist of the narrative, is also the central character in all three motifs. In each of the motifs, the Levite is being compared with the characters of the intertexts. These comparisons collaboratively condemn the character of the Levite, conveying a consistent anti-Levite sentiment throughout the narrative.

Motifs in Judges 19

Motif of Hospitality

Motif of Hospitality in the Hebrew Bible

The practice of hospitality is recognized as an important aspect of the cultures in the ancient Near East, and it differs significantly from the understanding of the concept in contemporary Western societies.[80] Studies on the motif of hospitality in the Hebrew Bible, therefore, often focus on providing a descriptive account of the custom. Weston Fields, for example, surveys biblical narratives containing scenarios of hospitality and derives from them twelve features of the convention. The features follow the approximate chronological order of the hospitality scenes, from greeting

---

80. Hobbs concludes that the two are "worlds apart" after comparing the ancient practice and the modern, consumer-oriented convention of hospitality in the Western world; "Hospitality," 28.

and the formal offer of hospitality through to the last step of seeing the guest away. He takes these as a framework of reference, though not all features are observed in every scene.[81] Biblical narratives containing the motif of hospitality are then studied against these features, and deviations from the norm are observed.

While Field's study is beneficial in identifying elements in the texts that are at odds with the common practice, his reference points are mostly restricted to biblical narratives that seldom provide an explanation of the actions of characters. Therefore his framework does not necessarily explain the deviations nor provide clues to the social meanings of such actions. As Talmon contends, motifs are to be understood in a social context, and it is therefore necessary to go further and explore hospitality in the social world of the Hebrew Bible.

Matthews's study contributes in this regard as he extends his scope beyond the biblical corpus to the field of anthropology. He uses theories and findings from anthropological research on Mediterranean societies and develops a model of their practice as a framework for understanding hospitality in biblical narratives.[82] This protocol delineates the social expectations of the responsibilities of both the host and the guest—from the way the invitation is extended, and the implications of a refusal of the offer, to the expected behaviors of both parties once the offer is accepted. He shows that providing for material needs and providing protection are very much social expectations of the hosts in the culture, and that the guests are to reciprocate with honor and respect toward the hosts. Deviations from these expectations are then deemed to be violations of the social conventions and damaging to the honor of the individual.

Hobbs also contributes to the discussion, highlighting the social functions of hospitality in the world of the Hebrew Bible. He contends that "[i]n the First Testament world hospitality is a means to an end. As such, it enhances the cohesion of the immediate group, the host's moral community, in that it provides a recognized method of entry of others into the host's private world of the house. Further, it enhances the host's publicly recognized honour."[83] Hospitality in this culture is not a mere act of kindness but serves multiple social functions. It is offered to people outside of one's immediate household, and to offer hospitality is to recognize the guest's inclusion in the community. It neutralizes any threats that might be posed by the guests, though the threats

---

81. Fields, *Sodom*, 43–46.
82. Matthews, "Hospitality and Hostility," 11.
83. Hobbs, "Hospitality," 28.

could be as transient as the stay.[84] In other words, the interaction between the hosts and the guests is not a private issue between the two parties but carries social implications for the community.

With this understanding, we now turn to the exploration of the rhetorical meaning of the motif of hospitality in Judges 19.

The Rhetorical Use of the Motif of Hospitality in Judges 19

HOSPITALITY IN JUDGES 19:1–9

As shown earlier in the discussion of intertextuality between Judges 19 and Genesis 19, many have explored the motif of hospitality in the two narratives. However, more attention is focused on the second hospitality scene in verses 16–21; the role of the hospitality scene at the house of the father of the concubine is not always recognized. For those who do comment on the latter, the rhetorical function of the scene is often regarded as a simple contrast to the inhospitality of the people of Gibeah.[85]

While it is true that the almost excessive hospitality of the father-in-law is in stark contrast to the behavior of the mob in Gibeah, it may not be the sole purpose of the description. After all, the hostility of the people of Gibeah is very much self-evident in their threat at the old man's house, and the narrator does not need a positive example earlier in the story to let the readers see the wickedness of these characters. In other words, the description of the overwhelming hospitality of the father-in-law does not add many rhetorical nuances in conveying a negative image of the mob.

Moreover, according to the study by Hobbs, hospitality in ancient Israel is offered to those who are not immediate family members. This does not mean, of course, that family members are not offered food and shelter when they travel to each other's households, but that the hospitality offered to family members may be regarded as a different category of social interaction. The expectation of behavior toward a family member and toward a stranger may not have been the same, and the communicative purpose of the description of the hospitality in the father-in-law's household is therefore not designed to be compared with that of the people of Gibeah.

The rhetorical emphasis of the first hospitality scene, then, may be on the protagonist, the Levite. In the account of the interaction in the household, the hospitality of the father-in-law in the first three days is as

---

84. Hobbs, "Hospitality," 28–29.
85. For example, Niditch, "'Sodomite' Theme," 367.

is customary in the culture and is summarized in just one verse in 19:4.[86] The simplicity of the record of these three days indicates that it is nothing unusual meriting extra description. However, what happens in the next two days has implications for the development of the plot and the characters and demands a more detailed portrayal.

The focus of the description in verses 5–9 is the repeated invitation from the father-in-law to the Levite to further enjoy food in verses 5, 6, 7 and 8. It is clear from this repetition that the father-in-law is not intending to rescind his offer until such time as the Levite declines it. The one-sided conversation by the father-in-law and the lack of response from the Levite create an air of suspense where the reader is almost eagerly waiting for the Levite to finally decline the offer so that the plot can move on.[87] This draws the attention of readers to the character of the Levite and indicates clearly that he is responsible for what happens next: it is his decision to leave the house late in the day that puts him and his concubine into danger in Gibeah.

As the Levite has presumably come along the same route, he would be expected to know how long the journey takes, and a late start would inevitably mean not arriving home on the same day. Though he might not have been able to foresee the danger, this extraordinary scene of hospitality illustrates his responsibility in the attack when it could have been totally avoidable had he not delayed. The rhetorical purpose of this first scene of hospitality is therefore an implicit condemnation of the Levite, which paves the way for understanding the next hospitality scene in the narrative.

Hospitality in Judges 19:10–25

The group comprises the Levite, his concubine, and the servant; they realize their need for hospitality as they come near Jebus in verse 11. The Levite rejects the servant's suggestion to lodge in Jebus as it is a city of foreigners, and he insists on travelling to Gibeah instead. The social expectation of the Levite is consistent with the findings in the study by Hobbs, who observes that hospitality is offered only to those who are considered part of the extended community. The preference of the Levite may seem reasonable in the culture, as he would expect the Benjamites in Gibeah to include him as a member of the Israelite community and offer him hospitality.

---

86. The convention of three days of hospitality is generally recognized; Matthews, "Hospitality and Hostility," 7.

87. And if Gale A. Yee is correct in interpreting the action of the Levite as abusing the hospitality of the father-in-law, this may create a negative impression toward the Levite, "Ideological Criticism: Judges 17–21," 163.

From this point onward, scholars have noticed, there are multiple violations of hospitality in the narrative. The Levite does not receive the expected hospitality from the people of Gibeah, and it is instead an old man from Ephraim who offers him food and shelter. The initial attitude of the Ephraimite to the potential guest is less than welcoming, and the inclusion of the concubine in his offer to the mob also falls short of his responsibility of protection. The mob who surrounds the house threatening homosexual rape is, most blatantly, violating the code of hospitality.[88] On the surface, this combination of violations against hospitality seems to paint a picture of adversity working against the Levite. This leads Fields to contend that "after seeing the ways in which the men of Gibeah transgress the laws of hospitality, the author's audience is totally swayed to the side of the Levite and those who later fight to revenge him."[89]

This might be so if the motif of hospitality in Judges 19 is read independently. However, given the significant textual association between Judges 19 and Genesis 19 (as established by Edenburg), it is essential to include the intertextual connection in the interpretation. Assuming a knowledge of the Sodomite narrative by the readers of Judges, the textual resemblance that begins to appear from Judges 19:15 prepares the reader for the sinister progression of the plot. The adversities faced by the Levite are almost expected and not a surprise, for they are foregrounded by the reader's knowledge of what happened in Sodom. The similarities between the two texts, therefore, are not an end in themselves, as they are only meant to urge readers to compare the current story with the tradition. The impact and the power of the story, however, are to be found in those places where the two accounts differ. It is these differences—where the two narratives depart—that are truly unexpected to readers and catch their attention; and this is where the rhetorical purpose for the use of the intertext may be found.

While some studies of the intertextual associations have aptly focused on the disparity between the two accounts, the point of analysis is often diverted to the minor characters in the narrative.[90] However, as the Levite is the protagonist of the story and the first scene of hospitality already focuses on his behavior, the point of contrast should be found in this character also.

The characters in Genesis 19 that are parallel to the Levite are the divine messengers, and the most blatant disparity between the two accounts

---

88. It is generally recognized that the threat of the mob is homosexual rape, and its implications of inhospitality have been discussed in Niditch, "'Sodomite' Theme," 367–69.

89. Fields, *Sodom*, 63.

90. For example, Lasine considers Lot as a model of hospitality that the old man of Ephraim fails to follow, "Guest and Host," 39.

is found at the end of the intertextual resemblance in Judges 19:25, which is also the climax of the narrative. At this point in the story of Lot in Genesis 19:10–11, the divine messengers stretch their hands and pull Lot into the house and resolve the threat by striking the men with blindness. The almost mechanical way of following the Genesis intertext up to this point leads readers to expect a similar act of rescue, yet in the Levite story, the complete opposite takes place: the concubine is seized and pulled out to be ravished by the mob.[91] It is this divergence from the Genesis tradition (where the offer of the women is interrupted by divine intervention) that is most shocking to readers of the Levite story, and where the rhetorical effect of intertextuality lies. What has been divinely dismissed in Genesis is now realized in the narrative in Judges!

The contrast between the action in Judges 19:25 is further elaborated when one recalls the action of the angels in Genesis 19:16. Both scenarios use the combination of the verbs $ḥzq$ (to seize) and $yṣ'$ (to put), and yet in the Genesis account it is describing the benevolent action of the angels in taking Lot and his family away from the destruction of Sodom, whereas, in the narration of Judges, the combination of the verbs is used to describe the victimization of the concubine in being thrust toward destruction.

But whom should the readers blame for such an action? Judges 19:25 is noticeably ambiguous in the identity of the man who seizes the concubine and pushes her to the mob. However, as discussed in the previous chapter, it is likely to be an intentional gap in the narrative, subtly pointing to the Levite. Given the background of the hospitality scene in the house of the father-in-law, it is reasonable to infer that this is, again, a description highlighting his responsibility for the tragedy. The Levite is the one who acts in a manner opposite to the divine rescue in Genesis and is the person to be blamed.

In this sense, while the motif of hospitality forms the background of the narrative propelling the progression of the plot, the ultimate message conveyed is not about the issue of hospitality itself. The point of the intertextual association in the motif is not about evaluating who is a better host or who violated the codes of hospitality. The function of the hospitality scenes is, instead, to draw readers' attention to the character of the Levite and his responsibility in the entire story. It is the pivotal role of the protagonist, and of his action that is decisive to the tragedy, that readers are urged to evaluate.

---

91. Gur-Klein suggests that this is related to the atavist custom of sexual hospitality, in which a woman in the household of the host is offered to the guest for sexual gratification. Gur-Klein, *Sexual Hospitality*, 6–23. Her theory, however, does not match the two narratives, because in both cases the women are offered to the people of the town, not the travelling guests.

Motif of Rape

Establishing the Motif of Rape in Judges 19

The motif of rape in the narrative begins much earlier than the actual gang rape of the concubine in Gibeah in verse 25. As Edenburg has shown, the verbal parallels between Judges 19 and Deuteronomy 22 illustrate that the language of the Deuteronomic laws concerning female sexual propriety is intentionally invoked in the story of the Levite. In particular, the designation of the father of the concubine as *'b hn' rh* (father of the young woman) in verses 3–6, 8–9 corresponds with Deuteronomy 22:15–16, 19, 29, which is the only other passage in the Hebrew Bible that the collocation occurs. As the use of *n' rh* (young woman) is rather unnatural here, for it is usually used to refer to girls before marriage, Edenburg considers this an intentional usage by the author to elicit correspondence to the Deuteronomic sexual laws.[92] Indeed, the phrase *'b hn' rh* appears six times in six verses here and twice immediately following *ḥtnw* (his father-in-law) in verses 4 and 9, which should be sufficient in identifying the character. The repeated use of the phrase seems almost redundant and begging for readers' attention in making the connection.

While Edenburg is unable to suggest a rhetorical purpose for the association, as none of the laws concerns concubines, the study of Leeb on the use of *n' rh* suggests a possible explanation. Upon surveying the various uses of the term in the Hebrew Bible, she proposes that it refers to "women who are, by reason of circumstance or conduct, functioning outside the control/protection of father or husband."[93] As the phrase *'b hn' rh* in Deuteronomy 22 applies to the father of a woman who has had sexual relations prior to marriage, either as a result of rape or seduction, she suggests the possibility that the Levite's concubine may have once been in such a situation. This may have imposed upon her a lower status as "used goods," which explains her secondary rank (as concubine) in the absence of a primary wife in the narrative. It is even plausible that the Levite might have been a rapist—for Deuteronomy 22:29 prescribes an un-renounceable marriage of the raped *n' rh* to the rapist.[94] The repeated use of the phrase *'b hn' rh* may then represent a hint in the narrative that encourages the readers to connect the Levite to this possibility. Although readers are never able to verify their suspicion, this nonetheless creates a rhetorical impact that brings the character of the Levite into doubt.

---

92. Edenburg, *Dismembering*, 246–47.
93. Leeb, *Away from the Father's House*, 129.
94. Leeb, *Away from the Father's House*, 141.

The association of the Levite with rape is then further reinforced as the narrative continues. Edenburg has observed the commonalities between the rape of Tamar in 2 Samuel 13 and the incident in Gibeah. In particular, the use of the verb *ḥzq* ("to seize") in describing the actions of Amnon and the Levite, as well as the command to the women to "get up and go," bring the two characters onto the same page. Though the Levite is not the one physically committing the rape in Gibeah, the intertextual association indicates that he is engaged in actions identical to the rapist Amnon: he is the one who seizes the concubine and subjects her to a situation where she is raped and, when the ordeal is over, he orders her to go as if nothing has happened. This in turn shifts the attention of readers to the Levite in terms of responsibility for the tragedy. Together with the intertextual connection with Deuteronomy 22, the motif of rape in the narrative seems to point to the Levite as the person to blame. In order to further understand the social implications of such a literary association, we now turn to the broader context of the understanding of the concept of rape in the Hebrew Bible.

The Concept of Rape in the Hebrew Bible

Since the 1970s, following the rise of feminism, the motif of rape in the Hebrew Bible has gained increased attention among biblical scholars.[95] There is, however, controversy over the understanding of the concept of rape itself. The debate is mainly focused on two issues. The first issue concerns the translation of the Hebrew in rape narratives. It is noticed that there is no Hebrew word that corresponds exactly to the English word "rape," and ʿ*nh*, which is sometimes translated as rape, is shown to carry other meanings in different circumstances.[96] This leads to challenges to the interpretation of the rape narratives in the Hebrew Bible, especially with the account of Dinah in Genesis 34.[97]

The second issue concerns the legal understanding of rape in ancient Israel, in contrast to the modern Western legal system. It is well recognized that the patriarchal worldview of ancient Israel considered the sexuality of a woman to be under the authority of the patriarch of the household, which

---

95. Scholz, *Sacred Witness*, 3–4.

96. The semantic analysis of Ellen van Wolde contends that it is used as an evaluative term in a juridical context denoting a spatial movement downwards in a social sense and should be translated as "debase"; "Does ʿ*innâ* Denote Rape?," 528–44. For a discussion on the translation of ʿ*nh* in biblical scholarship; see Lipka, *Sexual Transgression*, 88–89.

97. For example, Bechtel, "What If Dinah Is Not Raped?," 19–36.

meant rape was viewed from a perspective different from the modern view that emphasizes a woman's autonomy. In her study of Deuteronomic family laws concerning women, Pressler observes that there is no evidence of the author's acknowledgement of the concept of violation to the sexual integrity of the women. As the laws referring to nonconsensual intercourse with a woman in Deuteronomy 22:25–29 consider the damaged party as either the husband or the father, it therefore does not qualify the action as rape as understood in the modern Western legal system.[98]

These two issues lead scholars to challenge the existence of the concept of rape in the Hebrew Bible. Brenner contends that not only is the Hebrew word for rape missing, there is also a lack of conceptual reference to rape and "neither males nor females are ever 'raped' in the HB."[99] Lipka has a different opinion on the matter and follows Pressler in her comment on Deuteronomic sexual laws. Using Bechtel's definition of rape as a model, she contends that there are two requirements in determining whether an act is considered as rape in the Hebrew Bible. "First, there must be evidence of some belief on the author's part that the sexual act is forced upon an individual against his or her will. Second, there must be evidence of a conception that this forced act violates the victim on a personal level. That is, there must be evidence of an understanding on the part of the author of the psychological effects of sexual coercion."[100] Lipka applies these two criteria to the biblical texts and argues that the incidents in Deuteronomy 22 do not fulfill the second criteria and hence do not qualify as rape. However, since 2 Samuel 13 clearly demonstrates Tamar's trauma, it then can be considered as rape.[101]

While it is true that the legal implications of violent, nonconsensual sexual intercourse in ancient Israel are different from modern Western worldviews, and that there is no Hebrew word that corresponds exactly to the English "rape," to deny the concept of rape in the Hebrew Bible seems to go too far. As Kawashima argues, the lack of acknowledgement in the laws or even narratives does not diminish the woman's experience of the damage from rape.[102] The violation to the sexuality of the woman may not have been the focus of the text, yet this does not imply that the woman or people around her do not perceive it as a humiliation and injury. If we are to restrict the use of the term "rape" for the reason that the action

98. Pressler, *View of Women*, 32–33.
99. Brenner, *Intercourse of Knowledge*, 136–37.
100. Lipka, *Sexual Transgression*, 180.
101. Lipka, *Sexual Transgression*, 90–92, 178–81, 203–23.
102. Kawashima, "Could a Woman Say 'No' in Biblical Israel?," 4.

might have been understood differently across time and culture, then we will be short of descriptive terms to articulate the deed. The term "rape" is therefore used in the discussion in the next section about the social implications of violent, nonconsensual sexual intercourse, without implying that it carries the same social or legal value as that of modern Western cultures. In fact, it will be demonstrated that the social understanding of rape is quite different in the Hebrew Bible.

The Social Implications of Rape in the Hebrew Bible

The study of the motif of rape in the Hebrew Bible has mainly focused on the three rape narratives, Genesis 34, Judges 19, and 2 Samuel 13, as well as the legal provisions in Deuteronomy 22.[103] Scholars have attempted to explore the way rape is perceived in the social world depicted in the Hebrew Bible through analysis of these texts, though it is acknowledged that they do not necessarily reflect historical reality in ancient Israel.[104] Nevertheless, the social perception of the motif of rape as exemplified in these texts is helpful for the understanding of the rhetorical intent of the incident in Gibeah, as it sheds light on how readers are encouraged to view the matter.

The sexual laws in Deuteronomy 22 may serve as a starting point in the process. In Edenburg's study on Deuteronomy 22:13–29, she observes that the formula "expunge the evil" occurs three times in verses 21, 22, 24, addressing the need to prescribe the death sentence to those guilty of illicit sexual relationships. As the formula is used elsewhere in the context of social and religious violations, it implies that improper sexual intercourse is not a private matter between the man and woman involved but is viewed as a threat to the integrity of the social fabric in the community. She contends that it reflects an ideology: "maintaining the proper relations between the sexes—particularly with regard to the uncompromising fidelity incumbent upon women to maintain toward their patron, be he father, present husband, or future spouse—is as critical to preserving the proper social order as maintaining exclusive fidelity to YHWH."[105] This mindset stems from the analogy between the marital bond and the political alliance as applied to YHWH's

---

103. For example, Bader, *Sexual Violation in the Hebrew Bible*; Yamada, *Configurations of Rape*; Schulte, *The Absence of God in Biblical Rape Narratives*.

104. Scholz, *Sacred Witness*, 5–7; Lipka, *Sexual Transgression*, 6; Keefe, "Rapes of Women," 79–80.

105. Edenburg, "Ideology," 57.

relations with his people, making bonds of exclusive intimacy in marriage a symbolic parallel to fidelity to the deity.[106]

The Deuteronomic sexual laws therefore reflect a social understanding that any form of adultery is an act that disrupts the exclusive sexual relationship in marriage, which is analogous to the exclusive relationship between Israel and YHWH. Rape of a betrothed woman as described in Deuteronomy 22:25–26, in this sense, is an aggressive deed of the rapist that disrupts the bond between the woman and her future husband. The death sentence is prescribed, as the act has social implications beyond the couple extending to the disorder of social and religious coherence in the community.

On the other hand, the rape of a woman who has not yet been betrothed, as described in Deuteronomy 22:28–9, is viewed as a different category since a marital relationship demanding absolute fidelity has not yet been formed. Monetary compensation to the father of the woman is demanded from the rapist, and the rapist is to marry the woman for life without divorce.[107] Lipka contends that this is an offence that transgresses communal rather than religious boundaries, and the compensation for both the father and the woman are prescribed in consideration for their loss in social and financial status.[108] This demonstrates that rape of an unbetrothed woman is still considered a debasement in society, yet it is a wrongdoing that has a remedial scheme, unlike the rape of a betrothed woman.

It is therefore evident that rape in the Deuteronomic laws is not a private offence between the individuals involved but is considered a violation on a social and religious level. Indeed, it has been noticed that in all of the three narratives that depict rape in the Hebrew Bible, the incident is followed by military action between men. This indicates that the social concern in the incidents relates to the way it disrupts social cohesion rather than it being a personal tragedy.[109]

The Rhetorical Use of the Motif of Rape in Judges 19

The incident in Gibeah is clearly a matter of the rape of a married woman, which evokes comparison with the Deuteronomic sexual laws. Though a concubine has a lower status than a wife, it is generally acknowledged that sexual fidelity to her husband is expected, and the rape would then be viewed

---

106. Edenburg, "Ideology," 60.

107. There is evidence that the fifty shekels prescribed is the bride price; Lipka, *Sexual Transgression*, 177.

108. Lipka, *Sexual Transgression*, 179.

109. Keefe, "Rapes of Women," 83.

as a transgression of social and religious boundaries as per Deuteronomy 22:25–26. The reaction of the people of Israel to the rape of the concubine in Judges 20 also confirms that it is perceived as a violation on a level beyond the individual, demanding military action against the Benjamites. The incident of the rape is therefore viewed as a significant disruption in society, and the logical question to ask is who is responsible for this catastrophe?

While it is beyond doubt that the wicked mob are the persons who enacted the rape, the intertextual associations of the motif of rape seem to associate the Levite with a rapist and thereby place the blame on him. This portrayal of the Levite is particularly subversive when one takes into consideration the social context. Being the husband of the concubine, he is supposed to be seen, by social convention, as the offended party in the rape, yet the text points to him at multiple moments in the narrative as contributing to the rape himself. The "victim," who is supposed to be the least likely person to want the rape to happen, is in fact the person responsible for propelling the catastrophe to its climax. This is very much unexpected for readers of the narrative and provokes scrutiny of his character. As rape of a married woman is analogous to the breaking of the bond between Israel and God, the Levite is therefore implicitly condemned for promoting disruption in the social and religious realms. The motif of rape in Judges 19, when read with the intertexts, acts as a powerful pointer of judgment toward the protagonist, who acts contrary to the expectations of the Deuteronomic laws.

Motif of Sacrifice

Establishing the Motif of Sacrifice in Judges 19

It has been recognized in intertextual studies of Judges 19:29–30 and 1 Samuel 11:7 that the focus of comparison is the resemblance of the Levite's dismembering his concubine to Saul's cutting up of the oxen. Both serve a communicative purpose, as the parts of the person/animal are sent to the people of Israel, and the people gather for war in response to this symbolic message. As Edenburg has shown, the use of the term *ntḥ* ("to cut up"), is restricted to cultic contexts dealing with sacrificial offerings in the Hebrew Bible (Exod 29:17; Lev 1:6, 12; 1 Kgs 18:23, 33).[110] To use this verb in the description of the cutting up of the oxen/concubine is therefore not a random act of anger, but an indication of the dismemberment being carried out as a sacrificial ritual. Though the procedure of the ritual may not necessarily correspond to sacrifices offered to God in the Levitical system,

---

110. Edenburg, *Dismembering*, 222.

the action of both the Levite and Saul nonetheless have clear sacrificial overtones. It is, at the very least, a cultic ritual that serves a symbolic purpose by means of the sacrifice of an entity.

The motif of sacrifice in the narrative is also evident in the association between Judges 19:29 and Genesis 22:10. It has been noted that the rare term *m' klt* (knife) is used in both instances: to refer to the knife that the Levite uses to dismember his concubine, as well as to the knife Abraham uses in the attempted sacrifice of Isaac.[111] Although there are different opinions regarding this association,[112] Edenburg nonetheless affirms the connection between the two and considers them to be an isolated parallel though the textual evidence remains inconclusive on the relative priority of the two texts.[113] It is true that the textual connection of a single word, *m' klt*, may be insufficient to draw a definitive conclusion on the intertextual association. However, the weight of the argument may alter significantly when the other intertext, 1 Samuel 11, to the same verse (Judg 19:29) is bought into consideration. The motif of sacrifice is common to both intertexts, and it may not be a coincidence that two texts concerning sacrifice are alluded to in the exact same verse.[114] There could be a reason that the two intertexts are brought together in the Levite's dismemberment of the concubine, and an understanding of the meaning of sacrifice in the social context may shed light on this authorial intention. This is explored in the following discussion. It first investigates the social meaning of the sacrificial ritual in the Hebrew Bible and then applies the findings to the interpretation of the narrative of Judges 19.

The Social Meaning of Sacrifice in the Hebrew Bible

Scholars since the Middle Ages have paid attention to the practice of sacrifice in the Hebrew Bible. It has been noted that while the procedure of the complex system of sacrifice is prescribed in detail in Leviticus, little is

111. The two narratives are the only instances where this word appears in the Hebrew Bible, and once more in the plural in Proverbs 20:14; Edenburg, *Dismembering*, 279.

112. Unterman considers this a very strong association and lists ten similarities between the two narratives on top of this verbal parallel, suggesting that the author of Judges 19 borrows from Genesis 22. Unterman, "Literary Influence," 161–66. Brettler, on the other hand, disputes some of the similarities Unterman lists and dismisses the overall connection of the two texts, though he agrees that the use of *m' klt* is "very suggestive." Brettler, *Judges*, 88.

113. Edenburg, *Dismembering*, 280.

114. Lauren A.S. Monroe also considers the combination of the two intertexts as strong evidence of a sacrificial motif in Judges 19; "Disembodied Women," 32–52.

said in regard to the meanings of these sacrifices.[115] In recent years, theories from sociology, psychology, and anthropology have been applied to explain the biblical sacrifices, and universal theories that attempt to explain all occasions of religious sacrifices have been appealing to biblical scholarship.[116] However, as Janzen points out in *The Social Meanings of Sacrifice in the Hebrew Bible*, the field of anthropology has abandoned such universal theories, as they attempt "to impose a theory on all sacrifices enacted in all societies with no regard to their cultural or historical contexts. Anthropologists who study rituals in various cultures point consistently to the contexts in which the rituals are performed and argue convincingly that if we are to interpret their social meanings we need to understand as much as possible about these contexts."[117] In other words, the meaning of sacrifices needs to be studied in each of the contexts in which they are performed. The action of sacrifice in itself may not carry any intrinsic and universal social meaning; rather, it is the interpretation of the social group that performs the sacrifice that grants meaning to the ritual. It reflects the worldview of the community and may change over time.

Janzen proposes that the understanding of this contextual meaning of a sacrifice needs to be placed in the larger context of the functions of rituals performed by a social group. Taking an anthropological approach, he contends that ritual is a form of social rhetoric: it says something to its participants and persuades them to believe and act in particular ways.[118] It may be used to communicate and advance a wide variety of social goods, including unity, hierarchy, rebellion, pacifism, power, subjugation, and much more.[119] Ritual is differentiated from other forms of social communication by its formality and repetition, and as it follows a pre-established order, any variance from the ritual will strike the participants as "odd and wrong."[120] By participating in a ritual, individuals in the social group demonstrate their adherence to the social truth and morality conveyed through the actions. The practice of rituals

---

115. Janzen, *Social Meanings*, 1.

116. A prominent example is the vastly popular use of the theories of Girard. Marty Alan Michelson applies Girard's theory in his reading of Judges 9, 17–21 and 1 Samuel 9–11, arguing that by sacrificing the oxen, Saul enacts the atoning benefits of the scapegoat mechanism and prevents further violence as per the other two passages; *Reconciling Violence and Kingship*, 82–112.

117. Janzen, *Social Meanings*, 3.

118. Janzen, *Social Meanings*, 19.

119. Janzen, *Social Meanings*, 10.

120. Janzen, *Social Meanings*, 23.

hence brings conventions and social good into being and becomes a "culturally constructed system of symbolic communication."[121]

Sacrifice, in this sense, is also a form of symbolic social communication performed to persuade members of the social group to adopt certain values and worldviews. The sacrifices in the Hebrew Bible, therefore, may be understood as a means of promoting such values and worldviews among the Israelites. The exact purpose of a symbolic communication, the value and worldviews being promoted by each sacrifice, is then dependent upon the context. It may vary at different times and in different circumstances for authors of biblical texts, even when similar actions of sacrificial ritual are performed. Janzen then demonstrates the different foci of social meaning of sacrifices in various sections of the biblical corpus. He contends that the authors of Priestly writings, Deuteronomistic History, Ezra-Nehemiah, and Chronicles have specific concerns from their contexts, and the social meanings of sacrifice have differing foci addressing these different concerns.[122]

Before going further into the details of Janzen's discussion on the social meaning of sacrifice in the Deuteronomistic History, it is necessary to give some attention to another theory on the rhetoric of sacrifices, which also is beneficial to our reading of the intertexts.

In his article, "The Rhetoric of Sacrifice," James Watts also contends that a meaning of sacrifice is not intrinsic to the ritual but dependent upon the interpretation of those who perform the sacrifice. Surveying various religions and traditions, he proposes that it is the narrative tradition of sacrificial stories within a social group that determines the social rhetoric of the sacrifice.[123] Correlations of rituals with stories in the tradition compare the act to some paradigmatic action in a hero's or a villain's story, which then "serve to *evaluate* a ritual on the basis of a story, and do so for purposes of persuasion."[124] The insight of Watts points to the intertextual characteristic of sacrificial narratives within the biblical tradition, which will come into play when the reading of the motif of sacrifice in Judges 19 is considered together with the narrative in 1 Samuel 11.

The Social Meaning of Sacrifice in the Deuteronomistic History

Janzen examines the social meaning of sacrifice in Deuteronomistic History. He sees Deuteronomy 12–26 as ideal laws for the exiles to follow when God

121. Janzen, *Social Meanings*, 20–21.
122. Janzen, *Social Meanings*, 243–45.
123. Watts, "Rhetoric of Sacrifice," 12.
124. Watts, "Rhetoric of Sacrifice," 8.

returns them to the land, and Josiah is presented as the ideal king carrying out these laws.[125] Contrary to those who dismiss any significance of cultic practice for Dtr, Janzen contends that throughout Deuteronomy to Kings, sacrifice acts as the litmus test for obedience to the law, which determines the future security and prosperity of the nation.[126]

The law code in Deuteronomy 12, Janzen observes, begins with the commands to destroy foreign altars (12:2–4), to centralize worship (12:5–28), to worship in the manner YHWH directs (12:29–13:1), and to kill Israelites who engage in foreign worship (13:2–19). This gives a first hint in DtrH that sacrifice is a litmus test for monolatry and observance of the law as a whole.[127] Proper sacrifice is hence a concrete sign of submission to the authority of YHWH and a pledge of fidelity. The link between sacrifice and obedience to the law is also evident in Joshua 22, the only story between the division of the land in Joshua 13–21 and the final exhortations in Joshua 23–24. The response to the questionable altar built by the Transjordan tribes, emphasizing that this altar is not for making sacrifices, indicates that sacrifice at the wrong place is considered disobedience to the law and hence detrimental to the fate of the nation.[128]

In the "cycle of disobedience" in Judges, the judges fail to protect Israel from the worsening apostasy that brings about divine punishment. The priests also fail in their duty to bring the people back to YHWH through proper sacrifice, since it a priest who leads Israel in idolatry in Judges 17–18, and 1 Samuel 2:11–36 also highlights the sins of the sons of Eli in despising the sacrifice.[129] Janzen contends that these lead to the search in the history of Israel for a king who can properly guide the nation in worship and sacrifice.[130] The refrain in the final chapters of Judges—"In

---

125. Janzen, *Social Meanings*, 121–22. Janzen takes DtrH as a work in the exilic period embracing Deuteronomy through to Kings as a complete corpus (except for isolated passages in Deuteronomy and Joshua). It is beyond the scope of this discussion to comment on the research on DtrH, yet it is noted that the relevance of Janzen's observations on the motif of sacrifice is not hindered by different opinions on the redaction history and layers of DtrH, as Janzen's theory may be considered as dealing with the final form of the text.

126. Janzen, *Social Meanings*, 122.

127. Janzen, *Social Meanings*, 133.

128. Janzen, *Social Meanings*, 134–35.

129. Janzen, *Social Meanings*, 140.

130. It has been noted by Levinson that there is a discontinuity in the role of the king in cultic matters between Deuteronomy and DtrH: in Deuteronomy, the king does not seem to bear any cultic roles, yet in DtrH, kings are given presiding roles in cultic matters. Levinson, "Reconceptualization," 520–34. The observation of Levinson is correct, yet it does not discredit the relevance of Janzen's analysis on the motif of

those days there was no king in Israel; everyone did what was right in their own eyes" (17:6; 18:1; 19:1; 21:25)—is interpreted as the call for a king to enforce the law through proper sacrifice.[131]

The responsibility of a king to ensure proper sacrifice is evident in the history of the kings of Israel. Saul's dynasty collapses because he fails to sacrifice properly, which represents disobedience to YHWH.[132] All the kings who come to the throne are judged by their sacrificial practices: Solomon and the kings of the northern kingdom are criticized for their engagement in apostate sacrifices, whereas Josiah, the perfect king, is approved for his performance of proper sacrifices in Jerusalem.[133] The king, therefore, is portrayed in the book of Kings as the custodian of sacrifice, whose responsibility is to ensure that the nation worships properly through correct sacrifice. Wrong sacrifices convey wrong moral messages to the community, which in turn bring about destruction of the nation.

Moreover, upon surveying the association between sacrifice and warfare in DtrH, Janzen proposes that sacrifice is also a symbolic representation of the outcomes of military conflicts. Numerous accounts in DtrH illustrate the defeat of enemies following proper sacrifice, and national defeats of Israel follow improper sacrificial slaughter.[134] Sacrifice therefore conveys a social message as either a symbol of promise of YHWH's protection of Israel or a symbol of warning of the destruction that YHWH will bring upon Israel. When sacrifice is correctly performed, the destruction of the sacrificial victim represents what God will do to Israel's enemies on the nation's behalf. In sacrifice wrongly performed, including sacrifice offered to foreign gods, the fate of the victim mimics the fate of Israel.[135] Participants in the sacrifice are therefore witnesses to the promise/warning, being incorporated into the ritual as members of the social group and bearing the corporate consequences anticipated in the sacrifice.

Judges 19–21 is among the passages that Janzen investigates on the topic of warfare associated with sacrifice. In the battle between the eleven

---

sacrifice in DtrH, for the social meaning of sacrifice in the historical books is not necessarily dependent on its agreement with the book of Deuteronomy. Deborah Rooke also affirms the sacral role of kings in the pre-exilic period, "Kingship and Priesthood," 193–95. It is therefore reasonable to discuss the motif of sacrifice in Judges 19 together with the observation of this pre-exilic cultic role of the king, without claiming unity with the book of Deuteronomy.

131. Janzen, *Social Meanings*, 140.
132. Janzen, *Social Meanings*, 143.
133. Janzen, *Social Meanings*, 144–50.
134. Janzen, *Social Meanings*, 163–70.
135. Janzen, *Social Meanings*, 160–61.

tribes and the Benjamites, there is no victory for Israel until they sacrifice and submit to the authority of YHWH in 20:26–28. Janzen considers this to be a demonstration of the rhetorical notion of sacrifice as promise and warning: the proper sacrifice of the Israelites symbolizes protection by YHWH and defeat of their enemy, the Benjamites.[136] He also recognizes that the unexpected defeat of the first two rounds is the result of divine intervention, in that Israel's army vastly outnumbers Benjamin's. However, as he does not recognize the possibility of a sacrificial motif in Judges 19:29–30, he is unable to establish the argument that the defeat is also the result of improper sacrifice. This possibility will be developed further in the next section.

In summary, Janzen demonstrates the social significance of sacrifice in DtrH: sacrifice is not a mere cultic ritual but carries a social meaning that is closely related to submission to the authority of YHWH and obedience to the law. Proper sacrifice is an indicator of monolatry and a symbol of adherence to the law, and it reflects the promise of the protection of Israel in warfare. Conversely, wrong sacrifice serves as warning to Israel of destruction of the nation. Participation in the sacrifice signals one's inclusion within the social group of Israel, and in the book of Kings, it seems to be the king's responsibility to ensure proper sacrifice in the group.

The Rhetorical Use of the Motif of Sacrifice in Judges 19

As established in the previous section, sacrifice is a form of ritual in a social group that functions rhetorically to persuade participants to adopt certain worldviews and values. The social meaning of biblical sacrifices, that is, the particular worldview or value that is promoted through the sacrifice, is neither universal nor monolithic through the entire Hebrew Bible. It is dependent on the context of the text, which, as Janzen demonstrates, may be explored through the themes and purposes expressed within the collection of biblical writings by the same author or within the same tradition. The rhetorical purpose of the motif of sacrifice in Judges 19 may therefore be explored in light of its use in DtrH.

Moreover, as Watts points out, the social meaning of a sacrifice is dependent upon the narratives within the traditions of the social group. Given the parallels between Judges 19:29–30 and 1 Samuel 11:7 and the general assumption of the precedence of the latter in the biblical tradition, the Levite

---

136. Janzen, *Social Meanings*, 171–73. While this "proper sacrifice" is among the examples of sacrifices that are not done in Jerusalem and appears to be incongruent with the theme of centralization in Deuteronomy 12, by the measure of the outcome of the warfare, it is viewed positively in the narratives.

narrative may then be interpreted through images from the Saul narrative. As both texts are situated within DtrH, it is reasonable to infer that consistent social messages are present in the two narratives. The following first explores the social meaning of sacrifice in 1 Samuel 11 as a part of DtrH and then discusses the implications of this narrative for that of the Levite.

The Social Meaning of Sacrifice in 1 Samuel 11

The context of 1 Samuel 11 is clearly a situation of warfare, where the people of Jabesh Gilead are threatened by the Ammonites and seek rescue from Saul. Under the direction of the Spirit of God, Saul cuts up a pair of oxen and delivers them across the land calling for soldiers. As previously mentioned, this action of slaughter carries a sacrificial overtone, and Saul is therefore making a sacrifice of the oxen according to the divine ordinance. The maneuver being portrayed here may then be considered exemplary of proper sacrifice made before warfare.

Taking into consideration the symbolic value of sacrifice in warfare, as indicated by Janzen, the sacrifice of the oxen is representative of the promise of God in protecting Israel and defeating their enemies, who are like the slaughtered animal. The verbal message that Saul sends with the messengers is not a mere threat emphasized by the visual horror that he invents but is consistent with the social message of sacrifice: those who do not respond to the call and join the army are then regarded as enemies of the people, and of God, and will be slaughtered like this animal. The worldview being promoted through this sacrifice is that God is in charge of warfare, and God alone is their rescuer who will defeat their enemies. The people of Israel are urged to respond to this call as a sign of submission to the authority of God, and by participating in the divine warfare, they are incorporated into the social group. The war results in great victory for the Israelites, in that the Ammonites are slaughtered, and the survivors are scattered, as anticipated by the proper sacrifice.

This sacrifice is also the first one Saul performs in the History. Considering the responsibility Dtr ascribes to kings in monitoring proper sacrifice and leading the nation to follow the law, Saul passes this first test, as he acts according to divine instruction and delivers the social message consistent with the sacrifice. This is confirmed by the success of the battle and by the response of the people in receiving him as their king. It is, however, also in direct contrast to the wrong sacrifice he later offers, which removes him from the throne. In a sense, the success of Saul begins with proper sacrifice, and it is also wrong sacrifice that marks the end of his dynasty. The story of

Saul as the first king in the history of Israel thereby demonstrates the significance of proper sacrifice for the fate of a king. A king is established and deemed acceptable by God through correct sacrifice and will be discarded by God if wrong sacrifice is performed. The story of Saul therefore serves, in a way, as a paradigm of warning to the later generations.

The Social Meaning of Sacrifice in Judges 19

The textual parallel between Judges 19:29–30 and 1 Samuel 11:7 suggests that the Levite's dismemberment is portrayed to evoke comparison of his act with that of Saul. As the Levite also sends the twelve body parts throughout the land of Israel and, given the response of the people in Judges 20 in assembling together ready for battle, it is clear that the social message of the Levite's sacrifice is meant to call for military action, as conveyed in the Saul narrative.[137] This kind of sacrifice is meant to be a symbolic representation of God's protection as well as a promise of victory. However, the sacrifice made by the Levite obviously differs from Saul's: there is no divine inspiration; the slaughtered object is a human body, not an animal; and there is no verbal message accompanying the body parts. If Saul's action is divinely instructed and taken as exemplary of how sacrifice for this purpose should be done, then the Levite is severely deviating from the proper way of sacrifice.

As the study of ritual has shown, a characteristic of ritual is its repetition and formality, and any deviation from the practice is readily recognized by participants as wrong. Readers of Judges 19 are therefore expected to promptly identify the problems with the sacrifice of the Levite, and, in so doing, perceive the signal of alarm. In this sense, the actions of the Levite subvert the social meaning of the sacrifice of Saul, and this subversion becomes a symbol of warning for wrong sacrifices in warfare: the slaughtered object now symbolizes the fate of Israel in defeat, which is then illustrated in the first two rounds of battle in Judges 20.

Moreover, it is noticed that Dtr is explicit in prohibiting human sacrifice: it is condemned as a worship practice of the Canaanites (Deut 12:31; 18:10) and listed among the failings of kings and of Israel (2 Kgs 16:3; 17:17; 21:6).[138] Regardless of whether the concubine is alive or dead at the time of

---

137. This practice may find resemblance in the cultures of the ancient Near East, as Matheny cites a Mari document from the early eighteenth century BCE, which attests to an example of the distribution of body parts as a means of quickly assembling the people for battle. She hence argues, that while it is not common practice in Israel, the social purpose is understood by the people. Mathey, "Mute and Mutilated," 644–45.

138. Janzen, *Social Meanings*, 179.

dismemberment, the notion of a human being slaughtered for sacrifice in place of an animal is meant to arouse condemnation of the action.

This is further reinforced by the association with Genesis 22:10, in which a human sacrifice is prevented by divine intervention. Although the textual connection between the intertexts is subtle, the context of human sacrifice is not. There are not many places in Bible narratives that directly refer to human sacrifice, and the only incident in which it is clearly portrayed is Genesis 22. Whether the connection is an allusion to a pre-existing tradition or a redaction from a later stage following the written text of the *akedah*, the rhetorical impact of the Levite account is one that reminds readers of the divine intervention in Isaac's sacrifice, which implied that human sacrifice is not pleasing to God. The subtle intertextual connection therefore confirms to readers that this sacrifice by the Levite is administered against divine ordinance.

The motif of the sacrifice in Judges 19 therefore works to illustrate how the Levite has done wrong in a sacrificial ritual, which paves the way for the disastrous defeat in Judges 20. It is only rectified in Judges 20:26–27, when the Israelites submit to the authority of God and offer proper sacrifices. Putting it together with the idolatrous Levitical priest in Judges 17–18, and the sons of Eli in 1 Samuel 1 who disrupt the sacrifices, the Levite in Judges 19 may then be another example illustrating the social situation that, without a king, sacrifices are not done properly. The identity of the Levite in Judges 19, in this sense, is not merely to mirror the Levite in the previous two chapters for editorial consistency, as some have suggested,[139] but is incorporated within the flow of Judges 17 through to 1 Samuel 1, demonstrating the failure of Levites and priests in cultic matters and the subsequent need for a king. In other words, like the motifs of hospitality and rape, the motif of sacrifice conveys an anti-Levite message that aims to discredit the character of the protagonist.

Conclusion

This chapter has demonstrated the fruitful interpretive potential of reading Judges 19 with the intertexts in the Hebrew Bible. Utilizing the recognized intertextual connections with Genesis 19 and 22, 1 Samuel 11,

---

139. Amit considers the identity of the Levite here to be "irrelevant," and that it is an attempt to enrich the analogical framework between the two successive narratives in the book. *Book of Judges*, 353. Others, such as Soggin, also struggle to propose a significance for the Levite's background; he states that "it is not clear why the protagonist is a Levite"; *Judges*, 303.

Deuteronomy 22, and 2 Samuel 13, it has been illustrated that the intertexts reflect the motifs of hospitality, rape, and sacrifice. Each of the motifs provokes comparison of Judges 19 with the intertexts, which in turn leads to negative evaluation of the character of the Levite. His actions throughout the plot are pictured as contrary to divine ordinances: (1) he seizes the concubine and pushes her to the mob, as opposed to the angels rescuing Lot; (2) he acts in a way that is parallel to a rapist, which subverts the concept of the husband of a raped woman as victim in the Deuteronomic sexual laws; (3) he performs prohibited human sacrifice that diverts from the divine instruction to Saul in sacrificing for military action. Contrary to the common critique of the narrator's silence toward the Levite's behavior, the text is in fact permeated with interpretive clues.

By focusing on the intertextual associations of the character of the Levite, this study also illustrates a helpful reference point for intertextual studies. As there may be multiple points of comparison between two intertexts (which is clearly demonstrated in the diverse opinions on the association between Genesis 19 and Judges 19), there may be many potential interpretations of the rhetorical purpose of the intertextual association. However, interpreters should bear in mind that when different literary tools are used in the writing of a narrative, the rhetorical purpose identified should remain consistent across these realms. In other words, if the author draws readers' attention to the protagonist through narratological techniques in the creation of the plot and the portrayal of characters, then it is logical that the intertextual associations made be also consistent, intending to focus attention on the same protagonist. As shown in this chapter, when the intertextual connections across the various intertexts are considered, the focus on the Levite provides a fruitful and coherent understanding of the rhetorical purpose of the narrative. This is consistent with the identification of this character as the protagonist in the previous chapter.

Presuming a knowledge of the intertexts for readers of Judges 19, the communicative purpose of incorporating the references to the intertexts is therefore to illustrate the degradation of the morality of the Levite in multiple aspects in comparison with the characters in the other discourses. The reasons for such anti-Levite polemics are explored in the next chapter, when the ideological aspects of interpretation are considered.

5

Reading Judges 19 with Ideological Lenses

Gender and Politics

Introduction

THE PREVIOUS CHAPTERS IN this study have identified the Levite as the protagonist of the narrative in Judges 19, and it is evident that the narrator's characterization of him consistently attracts negative evaluations when read from both narratological and intertextual perspectives. This chapter aims to build upon these findings and investigate the rhetorical purpose of the presentation of such an individual. In other words, I examine the ideology behind the anti-Levite sentiment and what the author (or authors and editors) attempts to achieve through telling this story.

This brings ideological criticism into the scope of the study. This method of interpretation acknowledges that literary works are written by authors in an ideologically charged historical context, which is reproduced in the text and interpreted by readers motivated and constrained by varying ideological assumptions.[1] Scholars in recent decades have endeavored to investigate the biblical corpus on different aspects of ideology, such as gender, race, and politics. By focusing on the ideologies conveyed in the text, one may then reveal its rhetorical agenda and possibly reconstruct its historical context. This may also allow interaction between readers with varying ideologies when their reading interests are brought to the fore.

This chapter attempts to read Judges 19 through two different ideological lenses: masculinity and politics. The first lens is chosen because it has been very much neglected in past scholarship. While the prominent issue of gender is noted by the many feminist readings of the text, seldom is the attention focused on the male protagonist, the Levite, and the ideological portrait of his manhood. It is proposed that reading from the perspective of masculinity may enrich the interpretation of the text through understanding its ideology of gender. The reading of the second lens, on

---

1. Yee, "Ideological Criticism," 535.

the contrary, is motivated by the popular focus on the political ideology of the text. As much of the recent discussion of the purpose and dating of Judges 19 centers on the issue of politics and its historical context, it is significant to engage in the dialogue.

This chapter begins with a discussion of the methodology of ideological criticism and its application to the Hebrew Bible. It then surveys the existing interpretations of Judges 19 that have utilized this reading strategy in the realms of gender and politics. I then propose a reading of the text through the lens of masculinity. By applying to the text the findings of hegemonic masculinity in the Hebrew Bible, I demonstrate that the Levite is presented as a character who does not conform to the ideals of masculinity in the culture. This in turn provokes sentiment against him and further confirms the anti-Levite agenda of the text. The last section attempts to reconstruct a historical context that is consistent with the political ideology identified in the text. It builds upon the proposal of Gale Yee of a historical setting of Josianic reform, and the combination of the pro-monarchic and anti-Levite ideologies is best explained by the context of the idealization of King Josiah and his attempt to centralize cultic worship in Jerusalem.

Ideological Criticism and the Hebrew Bible

In this section, I first examine the notion of ideology as perceived in biblical scholarship and then discuss the application of ideological criticism in the Hebrew Bible in general. I then provide an overview of existing scholarship that has engaged in reading Judges 19 with specific ideological foci. This demonstrates that prior interpretations have identified two significant spheres of ideology operating in the text: gender and politics,[2] and that there is potential for further development in both directions.

---

2. Fowl has accurately pointed out that "texts don't have ideologies" in the sense that it is not an inherent property of the text, and that there are many varied and even potentially conflicting ideologies in the interpretive life of a text according to the different reading interests of the readers. Ideological criticism of a biblical text is hence the discussion of "the various relationships between specific ideologies, the production and interpretation of texts and the practices underwritten by such interpretation in particular contexts." Stephen Fowl, "Texts Don't Have Ideologies," 33. However, as it is difficult to precisely delineate these nuances every time the term is used, "ideology of the text" or the like will be used in this chapter (with awareness of Fowl's contention).

Definition of Ideology

The definition of "ideology" is notoriously complicated, and the usage of the term is very diverse in both popular and literary fields. The difficulty, to a large extent, lies in the discord about whether the notion of the term is to be taken as pejorative.[3] David Clines provides an overview of the varying definitions of ideology by listing four "denotations" and thirteen "connotations" of the term, and he notes that the undertones of the connotations range from negative to neutral to positive. Recognizing that ideology is inevitable in any worldview, Clines himself is more inclined toward a neutral perception of ideology and rejects the outright relegation of the term into presentations of false consciousness.[4]

Some scholars, however, place more emphasis on the term's association with Marxism, as established in the twentieth century, seeing ideology as a medium to articulate the relationship between the cultural world of ideas and the realms of political economy, class structures, and means of production.[5] This is reflected in Gale Yee's definition of the term that stresses its social function: ideology is "a complex system of ideas, values, and perceptions held by a particular group that provides a framework for the group's members to understand their place in the social order."[6] She then explains the operations of this framework: "Ideology constructs a reality for people, making the bewildering and often brutal world intelligible and tolerable. Ideology motivates people to behave in specific ways and to accept their social position as natural, inevitable, and necessary."[7] While Yee maintains that ideology in itself may not be negative, she acknowledges that it may be used to disguise or explain away features of society that are unjust.

Some scholars are more adamant about the pejorative sense of ideology. For example, Walter Brueggemann defines ideology as "vested interest, which is passed off as truth, partial truth which counterfeits as whole truth, theological claim functioning as a mode of social control."[8] Ideology, for Brueggemann, is incompatible with true religion or theology. However, as Taylor aptly acknowledges, every writer inevitably writes from some ideological standpoint, and what is required is a comparative critique of

---

3. Taylor provides a thorough discussion of the use of the term in popular and literary realms. "Ideology," 1–23.
4. Clines, *Interested Parties*, 9–11.
5. Taylor, "Ideology," 3.
6. Yee, "Ideological Criticism," 535.
7. Yee, "Ideological Criticism," 535.
8. Brueggemann, *Israel's Praise*, 111.

the respective ideologies, rather than seeing all ideologies as negative.[9] The approach of this chapter is more aligned with Taylor's view.

Upon surveying the definition of ideology in both literary and biblical scholarship, Taylor identifies five features that aptly summarize a meaningful use of the term:

> First, "ideology" consists of a body of ideas or a world-view held collectively by a specific class or group. Secondly, ideology intersects with issues of power and control. Thirdly, the term denotes idea-systems that are action-oriented, purpose driven to bring about change. Fourthly, it is not possible to understand ideology separately from the vested interests of the relevant class or group. Fifthly, ideology is often unconscious or hidden: hence the specific need for ideological criticism.[10]

This chapter adopts Taylor's definition of ideology, which does not fix a pejorative undertone to the term and aptly describes its functions and characteristics.

Ideological Criticism and Its Application in the Hebrew Bible

The root of the applicability of ideological criticism to the Bible has been traced to the early nineteenth century. Sheila Briggs suggests that it was the Enlightenment that rendered the Bible a legitimate object of ideological criticism. However, the publication of Norma K. Gottwald's *The Hebrew Bible: A Socio-Literary Introduction* in 1985 is often recognized as one of the beginnings of the explicit use of ideological criticism in the study of the Hebrew Bible.[11] This was followed by several contributions in the 1980s and 1990s that explored the ideology and history of ancient Israel,[12] as well as the 59th issue of Semeia, *Ideological Criticism of Biblical Texts*, in 1992. The topic has received significant attention in biblical scholarship in the past few decades.

At the early stage of the development of ideological criticism, the attention of biblical scholars was on the socio-historical dimension of its application, focusing on examining the network of economic class relations involved in the production of the biblical text. This approach has

---

9. Taylor, "Ideology," 31.
10. Taylor, "Ideology," 22–23.
11. Briggs, "Deceit of the Sublime," 1–23.
12. Such as Garbini, *History and Ideology in Ancient Israel* and Amit, *History and Ideology*.

since grown in diversity, both in terms of methodologies used and the ideological commitments of the interpreters. There is no one set of unanimously employed reading strategies, and various methodologies have been proposed by scholars with different interpretive foci.[13] Since Yee proposes a clear, succinct summary of her methodology and assumes a neutral connotation of ideology (which is compatible with the stand adopted in this chapter), I discuss her methodology here as an illustration of the operation of ideological criticism in the Hebrew Bible.

In terms of the scope of the methodology, Yee identifies three levels of applying ideological criticism to biblical texts: (1) the production of the text by a particular author in a specific, ideologically-charged historical context; (2) the reproduction of ideology in the text itself; (3) the consumption of the text by readers in different social locations who are themselves motivated and constrained by distinct ideologies.[14] In other words, ideological criticism is applicable to the examination of ideologies operating at the levels of the author, the text, and the reader.

Yee's reading strategy for ideological criticism is a comprehensive approach that uses the findings of various critical methods to investigate both the text and the context, and she divides the approach into "extrinsic" and "intrinsic" analysis. Extrinsic analysis "uses the historical and social sciences to help reconstruct or 'unmask' the material and ideological conditions under which the text was produced." It is particularly concerned with the category of power, and attempts to determine the types of social, political and economic structures wielding power in the realms of gender, class, race and religion when the text was written. It examines the ways that ideologies may have been used to serve the interests of social groups and identifies disempowered voices or interests in the society.[15] In other words, it is a reconstruction of the historical context of the author, with a specific, though not exclusive, focus on the issue of power.

Intrinsic analysis, on the other hand, uses literary critical methods such as structuralism, deconstruction, and narrative criticism to "examine how the text assimilates or 'encodes' socioeconomic conditions to reproduce a particular ideology in its rhetoric." It assumes that "the text symbolically resolves real social contradictions by inventing and adopting 'solutions' for them," and by attending to the literary features of the text, such as irony, plot, characterization, and point of view, it uncovers the manipulation of the power

---

13. Taylor provides a detailed analysis of ten different methodologies from scholars with different interpretive commitments; "Ideology," 80–201.

14. Yee, "Ideological Criticism," 535.

15. Yee, "Ideological Criticism," 535.

of persuasion in promoting and consolidating certain ideologies. It also pays particular attention to the gaps and absences in the text in order to unmask the dominant ideologies and recover the voices of the silenced.[16]

Yee contends that the process of ideological criticism involves an alternating use of extrinsic and intrinsic analysis: beginning with a preliminary intrinsic analysis taking note of ideological gaps, inconsistencies and dissonant voices, it then works "backward" to determine the social location of production hinted in the text. An extrinsic analysis then determines the nature of the material-ideological disputes the text's ideology tries to resolve. And finally a more complete intrinsic analysis determines how the text encodes and reworks the ideological conditions of its production.[17]

Yee's methodology thereby amalgamates various strategies in the investigation of the ideologies promoted or suppressed in a text. By attending to both the text and the context, it attempts to shed light on the economic, political, and historical circumstances of the text's production that may have been neglected by literary-critical methods. It correlates results from literary criticism and strives to go one step further in reconstructing the historical context in order to understand *why* the text conveys such ideologies. This comprehensive approach is pertinent, as ideologies may be conveyed through different literary techniques, and hence demand the use of different reading strategies. Her attention to gaps and absences is also significant, as ideologies are by definition hidden and may be uncovered by attending to these silences.

Yee's methodology is not without its critics, as it has been critiqued for not distinguishing between the author and the implied author.[18] However, as little can be known about the "real authors" of the Bible, and it is the implied author that is reconstructed from the readings, this is more a technicality in terms of terminology and does not jeopardize the applicability of her methodology.[19]

Yee provides an example of the application of this methodology in her essay "Ideological Criticism: Judges 17–21 and the Dismembered

---

16. Yee, "Ideological Criticism," 536.

17. Yee's methodology that involves the alternating use of intrinsic and extrinsic analysis has been criticized for its circular argument (see Taylor, "Ideology," 103), yet her methodology may also be seen as a cross-examination of the findings from intrinsic and extrinsic analysis that emphasizes coherency.

18. Taylor, "Ideology," 103; and similarly Mayes, "Deuteronomistic Royal Ideology," 251.

19. In the discussion in this chapter, the "author" will be understood as referring to the implied author reconstructed from the text, unless otherwise specified.

Body."[20] The second part of this chapter, focusing on political ideology, builds upon her methodology and findings, particularly in her explication of extrinsic analysis in reconstructing the historical-social context of the text. It demonstrates that a coherent rhetoric and ideology may be found by incorporating the results of the "intrinsic analysis" performed in previous chapters in this volume and is consistent with the context of Josianic reform as identified by Yee. For now, let us review the use of ideological criticism in the reading of Judges 19.

Ideological Criticism and Judges 19

Biblical scholars in recent decades have been rather interested in the ideologies reflected in Judges 19. A substantial portion of the studies comes from the perspectives of feminists, while some others address the political ideologies of the text. The following samples studies from each of these spheres and demonstrates the potential for further investigation.

Judges 19 through the Feminist Lens

Being one of the few passages in the Hebrew Bible that narrates the rape of a female, Judges 19 has naturally caught the attention of feminist biblical scholars.[21] Since it was named the "text of terror" by Phyllis Trible, different reading strategies have been used in feminist interpretations of the text. The following surveys a selection of feminist readings and highlights their contributions to the reconstruction of the ideologies of the text.

In *Texts of Terror,* Trible sets the scene by describing Judges 19 as depicting "the horrors of male power, brutality, and triumphalism; of female helplessness, abuse, and annihilation."[22] She highlights the power relationship between the concubine and the Levite that is implicit in the text: "[h]e is subject; she, object. He controls her. How he acquired her we do not know; that he owns her is certain."[23] Trible demonstrates this power dynamic by noting the silence of the concubine in every scene and contends that the focus of the narrative is on the male characters who are dominant

---

20. Yee, "Ideological Criticism: Judges 17–21," 138–60.

21. This is reflected in the collection of essays in *A Feminist Companion to Judges*, in which there are three essays on Judges 19 in a total of nine included in the book that specifically comment on a particular passage.

22. Trible, *Texts of Terror*, 65.

23. Trible, *Texts of Terror*, 66.

in the society, and the negligence of the female seems to justify an ideology that concedes violence against women.[24]

Trible then attempts to redeem the biblical corpus from assenting to this ideology by pointing to the stories of female characters following the book of Judges, namely Hannah in the Hebrew Bible and Ruth in the Greek Bible. She contends that "[t]he absence of misogyny, violence, and vengeance in the two stories juxtaposed to the Benjaminite traditions speaks a healing word in the days of the judges . . . it does show both the Almighty and the male establishment a more excellent way."[25]

Trible is among the first scholars to bring the issue of gender relationship in the text into the spotlight, and subsequent feminist readings often build upon her observations.[26] By attending to the silence and passivity of the concubine, she convincingly reconstructs the ideologies of the gendered power structure reflected in the story. In reading the story of Hannah and Ruth in juxtaposition with the concubine, she offers a way to interpret the text that does not necessarily demand an utter rejection of biblical authority in the narrative based on feminist grounds.

J. Cheryl Exum uses a different strategy to recover the voice of the concubine, by giving her a name, "Bat-shever" ("daughter of breaking"), as a means of recognizing her humanity as an individual.[27] Similarly to Trible, she identifies an ideology reflected in the text that views women as the property of men. She develops this observation further and argues that the action of the concubine in leaving the Levite is an act of the autonomy of her sexuality, and she is labeled as a "harlot" for doing so. Her rape and dismemberment is then a reaction to this expression of autonomy and an attempt to suppress it and regulate female behavior in order to reinforce male control of female sexuality. Combined with her reading of the other females in the book of Judges, Exum contends that this ideology that apparently promotes male dominance and violence against women in fact betrays a fear of women and their sexuality.[28]

The interpretation of Exum is evidently more critical of the ideology presented in the text, as it pinpoints a motivation of self-interest that results in oppression toward women. However, the effectiveness of her strategy in naming the concubine is questionable, compared to its use in some other

---

24. Trible, *Texts of Terror*, 66–73.
25. Trible, *Texts of Terror*, 85.
26. For example, Kuja, "Remembering the Body," 89–95.
27. Exum, "Feminist Criticism," 82–83.
28. Exum, "Feminist Criticism," 82–87.

texts such as Judges 11, where she named Jephthah's daughter "Bat-jiftah."[29] By giving Jephthah's daughter a name, she is viewed as an individual, as are other characters in the story, instead of being an object defined by her father, Jephthah. However, as all the characters in Judges 19 remain unnamed regardless of their gender, the naming of the concubine does not seem to function to resist a gender-related manipulation in the text. Nevertheless, her reading further develops Trible's idea, in terms of the manifestation and critique of the ideology of male dominance in the text.

The attention to the ideology of gender as discussed by Trible and Exum is more focused on the levels of the text and the author/editor. Some other feminist readings of the text, however, place a greater emphasis on the role of readers and the interplay of ideologies between the text and readers. For example, writing from the perspective of an African American woman, Koala Jones-Warsaw resists an exclusive focus on gender in the power dynamics of the text as proposed by Trible and instead argues for a multi-faceted manifestation of victimization that includes social class, both in the text and in the world Jones-Warsaw experiences.[30] Similarly, Ryan Kuja juxtaposes the rape of women in the contemporary world with the fate of the concubine in his reflection on the ideology of misogyny expressed in both situations.[31] There are also feminist readings that do not focus on the current reader but explore the ideology of interpreters of the text as reflected in literary works and art.[32]

This brief survey demonstrates that Judges 19 has been explored from a variety of angles by feminist interpreters. Collectively, these readings have contributed to heightening the awareness of the gaps and silences in the narrative that reflect ideologies concerning women. The readings expose ideologies that are presumably owned by the group of the dominant male gender in the society—which are oppressive toward the female gender—and challenge readings that may pertain to such ideologies. While there are different interpretive strategies, it is clear that all have recognized the dominant position of the male as portrayed in the narrative. It is therefore interesting that in all these discussions focused on gender, seldom is the attention on the male protagonist, the Levite. Gender relationship is not a concept isolated to only female/male, but a dynamic that involves both genders. If the

---

29. Exum, "Feminist Criticism," 74.

30. Jones-Warsaw, "Toward a Womanist Hermeneutic," 172–86.

31. Kuja, "Remembering the Body," 89–95.

32. Such as Bal, "Body of Writing," 208–30, which discusses the work of Rembrandt; and Kamuf, "Author of a Crime," 187–207, which focuses on the interpretation of the text by Rousseau.

reconstruction of ideologies concerning the female has proved fruitful, it may also have much potential for exploring ideologies concerning the male in the text. With the recent rise of masculinity study in biblical scholarship, findings and methodologies from this area may be used to explore the ideology of the masculinity of the Levite. This will form one of the two ideological lenses through which the text is interpreted later in this chapter.

Judges 19 through the Political Lens

Yairah Amit brings the association of Judges 19–21 with political ideology into the spotlight through her article, "Literature in the Service of Politics: Studies in Judges 19–21," published in 1994.[33] Her approach focuses on identifying textual associations between Judges 19–21 and Saul's narrative in the book of Samuel, which is used to uncover a hidden polemic against Saul. This approach may be categorized as an "intrinsic analysis" according to Yee's methodology, as it attends to the characteristics within the text(s) instead of historical reconstructions. On the other hand, Yee's own study, "Ideological Criticism: Judges 17–21 and the Dismembered Body," provides a more thorough "extrinsic analysis" in establishing a socio-historical context fitting for the political ideology found in the text. These two studies are discussed here for illustration, and as Yee's extrinsic analysis will provide the background for my own reconstruction, it is covered in more detail.

Yairah Amit's Ideological Reading

Amit opens with the recognition that "[l]iterature has always been susceptible to involvement in political struggle," and biblical texts are no exception.[34] She contends that there may be hidden polemics driven by political agendas in biblical texts, and they are recognizable through close readings of literary signs. In order to guard against random suggestions of hidden polemic in any texts, she lists four criteria for establishing the legitimacy of its identification.[35] She then identifies multiple literary references in Judges

---

33. Amit, "Literature," 28–40.
34. Amit, "Literature," 28.
35. These criteria are: (1) avoidance of explicit reference to the phenomenon which the author wants to censure or advocate; (2) the existence of signs, no matter how odd or difficult, used by the author to develop the polemic, so that, in spite of the absence of specific references, the reader finds sufficient landmarks to reveal the polemic; (3) additional evidence from biblical material regarding the existence of open polemic in connection with the same phenomenon; (4) reference to the implicit subject of the

19–21 that may be associated with the narrative of Saul and contends that these references consistently put Saul in a negative light.[36]

Amit then interprets this polemic as a political agenda that attempts to consolidate the rule of the house of David by disqualifying Saul, who was the first king in Israel. She places this agenda in the process of the redaction of the historiography of Israel:

> ... it would seem that someone was bothered by the literary construction of the book of Samuel which fosters understanding, compassion and even sympathy for Saul. This editor decided to try to influence readers by planting earlier material which would change the interpretation put upon what is related in the book of Samuel. It appears that the role of Judges 19–21, immediately preceding the book of Samuel, is to reinforce the negative aspect of all that is connected with Saul, to blur the tragic effect, and thus to make it easier for readers to understand the reasons for the change in regime and the preference for David.[37]

In other words, Amit takes the chronological priority of the narrative in the book of Samuel and interprets the ideology of Judges 19–21 as a political struggle against an existing ideology. Although she does not pinpoint the dating of the texts, she proposes the possibility of the relevance of such an agenda in the Second Temple period. She refers to a hypothesis by Abramsky and suggests that "during the Second Temple period an attempt was made to rehabilitate the first monarchy in Israel, for example via the friendly attitude toward the house of Saul in the book of Esther."[38] Judges 19–21 may then be viewed as a response to such an attitude. She does not, however, engage in more detailed exploration of the dynamics of such struggle in the historical context, nor its implication to the ideology in the text.

Gale Yee's Ideological Reading

Contrary to scholarship that has detached the final chapters of Judges from the rest of the book and attributes this "appendix" to an exilic/postexilic date, Yee works from the possibility that the book is a continuous entirety. Based on this presumption, she then applies to Judges 17–21 the methodology of an interplay between intrinsic and extrinsic analysis

---

polemic in the exegetical tradition. Amit, "Literature," 31.

36. Amit, "Literature," 31–34.
37. Amit, "Literature," 39.
38. Amit, "Literature," 39, referring to Abramsky, "Return to the Kingdom of Saul," 39–63.

and demonstrates its potential ideological relevance to a pre-exilic social context. In the first step, the preliminary intrinsic analysis, she utilizes recognized literary findings and states that "the most obvious ideological comment of Judges 17–21 is that the violence and anarchy of Israel's tribal period is explained by the absence of a king."[39]

She then engages in her main extrinsic analysis to determine when such an ideology could have been produced. Taking a sociological approach, she proposes that the text reflects an ideological struggle between different modes of economy at the time of Josiah's reform. The ancient Israelite society in the tribal period prior to the monarchy operated in what Yee calls a "familial mode of production," with the family as the basic socioeconomic unit. Family households were collected into clans, which formed into tribes that were self-sufficient, self-protecting entities. Tribal lineages owned and administered the land, and because "in those days there was no king in Israel," the tribes were "tributary-free" and agricultural and pastoral produce were retained in the groups.[40]

As Israel moved to a "native tributary mode of production" in the monarchic period, tribal government became centralized under a king. The king and his ruling elite constituted the top of the social pyramid, placing the peasant producers at the bottom. In order to finance a centralized bureaucracy, the king and the ruling class extracted wealth from the peasants, and the peasants eventually became deprived. The king also had to subvert the social solidarity and authority of the tribal body in order to consolidate his political power. However, the familial mode of production with tribal kinship loyalties persisted in the rural areas since the state did not have the technical and administrative apparatus to oversee the entire kingdom.[41]

At the time of King Josiah, following the decline in power of the Assyrians, there came an opportunity for the king to intensify his hold on Judah and extend his control into the former northern kingdom of Israel. In order to fund this expansion, Yee suggests that Josiah's religious reform according to 2 Kings 22–23 was promoted for efficient appropriation of the peasants' surpluses. By destroying local shrines and centralizing worship at Jerusalem, the local leaders, which were largely country Levites of the Mushite house, were bypassed, and revenues were then collected for the royal household in Jerusalem. This led to socioeconomic and ideological conflicts between the tribal body and the tributary mode of production, and Yee contends that it is this background of "the competition between

---

39. Yee, "Ideological Criticism: Judges 17–21," 144.
40. Yee, "Ideological Criticism: Judges 17–21," 144.
41. Yee, "Ideological Criticism: Judges 17–21," 145.

the Jerusalem priesthood and the rural Levitical priesthood, the fiscal ambitions of King Josiah, the destruction of regional sanctuaries, and the centralization of worship in Jerusalem" that provided the material and ideological circumstances that produced Judges 17–21.[42]

Yee then moves to an intrinsic analysis, seeking to determine how the text encodes these struggles. The refrain, "in those days there was no king in Israel, every man did what was right in his own eyes," is taken as an editorial remark that implies that the absence of a king accounts for the chaos and cruelty of Israel's tribal period as depicted in Judges 17–21. Judges 17–18 is interpreted as a ridicule of the cultic chaos at that time, where a Levite of the lineage of Moses is portrayed as an unscrupulous opportunist who defies the expectations of a priest. Yee considers this a hint of the rivalry between the rural Mushite and the Jerusalem Zadokite priesthoods, which may be contextualized in the Deuteronomist's propaganda against northern sanctuaries during the reform.[43]

Judges 19–21, narrating a tragic inter-tribal war initiated by a Levite, is then a representation of the dissolution of the kinship bonds in the tribal period. Noting the absences and gaps in the narrative, the Levite in Judges 19 is seen as one who acquires a concubine for sexual gratification and discards her for his own self-preservation when needed. He is disgraced by the Deuteronomist, observes Yee, with his interaction between other male

---

42. Yee, "Ideological Criticism: Judges 17–21," 146–47. It is noted that the role of Levites is not mentioned in Josiah's reform in 2 Kings 22, and controversies surround the association of Levites with priesthood as well as the origin of the tribe itself. (For a survey of these controversies, see Leuchter, *Levites*, 5–13). However, against scholars such as Dahmen, who challenges the cultic role of Levites, Na'aman has presented a case for the presence of Levitical priests in the pre-exilic history of Israel. Na'aman, "Sojourners and Levites," 261–66.

43. Yee, "Ideological Criticism: Judges 17–21," 148–51. The Mushite origin of the Levites is a matter of debate. For a detailed discussion of the matter, see Leuchter, *Levites*, 59–92. However, as the argument of Yee is based on observations from Judges 17–18, the particular Levite in Judges 19 is not necessarily identified as being of Mushite origin. In fact, identifying him as a "country Levite" may be more appropriate, as Judges 19:1 clearly locates his residence outside Jerusalem. Since the proposed rivalry during Josiah's reform is more focused on the matter of geographical location (as centralization of worship implies competition between priests within and outside of Jerusalem), it is possible to adopt the reconstruction of Yee and locate the text at Josiah's reform without assuming a Mushite origin of the Levite in Judges 19. As Leuchter points out, despite the debate surrounding the identity of Levites, it is generally acknowledged that they are priests in the countryside in the pre-exilic period. Leuchter, *Levites*, 3. In my own discussion, I will hence use the term "country Levites" to refer to the group that, according to Yee's reconstruction, is being defamed in the propaganda of Josiah's reform.

characters in the narrative. The generosity of the father-in-law subordinates him, and the threat of male rape by the Gibeanites humiliates and feminizes him. These contribute to a further negative portrayal of rural Levites in the Deuteronomist's political agenda.[44] Yee then concludes that "Judges 17–21 is a systematic attempt by the Deuteronomist to break up the tribal body in service to the monarchy.... It subverts prestate kin-group connections in order to centralize and stabilize monarchic sovereignty."[45]

The extrinsic analysis of Yee provides a reasonable basis for contextualizing the pro-monarchic and anti-Levite ideology reflected in the text. Though it may not be definitive in dating the text to Josiah's reform, and her proposal of the socio-historical circumstances remains open to criticism, as some have argued,[46] it nonetheless allows the possibility of a pre-exilic dating. There is, however, room to expand on her intrinsic analysis of the literary aspects of the text. As the previous chapters of this thesis have provided us with insights on the literary nuances of the text, these findings may serve as a platform for examining an anti-Levite ideology embedded in the text. This is explored in the later section of this chapter.

This survey of current scholarship on ideological readings of Judges 19 demonstrates that interpretations from a gendered perspective tend to be isolated from issues of historical context and redaction of the text. They seem to work on the presumption that gender ideologies have been relatively stable throughout the period of time involved in the formation of the text, and that there have not been identifiable changes that may point the text toward a particular historical context.[47] On the other hand, readings that concern the political ideology in the text are intricately linked to issues of dating and historical context, as ideologies concerning politics are ever fluid due to the changes in political situations through history. The rest of this chapter illustrates that ideologies from both spheres may co-exist in the text, and one may be used to reinforce the other in the rhetoric of the narrative.

---

44. Yee, "Ideological Criticism: Judges 17–21," 152–57.

45. Yee, "Ideological Criticism: Judges 17–21," 157.

46. See Taylor, "Ideology," 108–13.

47. Whether this presumption is true, however, awaits more research and development. As Carol Meyers contends, the status of women may not have been static throughout the history of ancient Israel, *Rediscovering Eve*, 205–11.

Reading Judges 19 through a Lens of Masculinity

The majority of the gendered readings of Judges 19, as demonstrated earlier, have been focusing on the attitude and actions against the concubine.[48] However, as the concept of gender inevitably has relevance to both male and female, the representation of the male characters and the ideology of masculinity in the text should not be neglected. As chapters 3 and 4 in this study have established the Levite as the protagonist of the narrative, a closer look at the masculinity of this particular character is warranted.

Reading through an anthropological lens of honor and shame, Ken Stone has argued that the narrative portrays challenges posed to the masculinity of the Levite—including the opening verses of the concubine's action, and, more explicitly, the threatened homosexual rape by the men of Gibeah.[49] However, Stone's analysis pauses at the illustration of the threat on his masculinity and does not further evaluate the responses of the Levite: how did the Levite thrive in "being a man" against the threats of his masculinity? This forms the focus of investigation in this section.

The following first reviews the concept of hegemonic masculinities in the Hebrew Bible, and then applies this concept in the assessment of the Levite as depicted in Judges 19. It demonstrates that the narrative presents him as a character who does not conform to the ideology of hegemonic masculinity in the society. Throughout the plot, either his masculinity is challenged, or, when he attempts to adhere to the traits, disaster ensues. In this sense, he is not a role model for the propaganda of the ideology. The rhetoric of the narrative hence calls for an anti-Levite sentiment, which views his action as a betrayal of the ideology.

Hegemonic Masculinity in the Hebrew Bible

It has been recognized in anthropological studies across cultures that masculinity is a complex concept concerning gender relations. Being

---

48. With the exception of a recent article published in September 2017: Briggs, "'A Man's Gotta Do What a Man's Gotta Do?,'" 51–71. I presented an earlier version of this section in the "Bible and Gender" seminar on February 27, 2017, at the Malaysia Theological Seminary independent of Briggs's study. There is some common ground, as we both adopt the approach of hegemonic masculinity by Wilson and Clines, with similar observations on some of the traits of the Levite. However, Briggs argues for a subversion of the hegemonic masculinity by the characterization of the Levite, and I contend that it works in the other direction, in that the ideology, as perceived as dominant in the culture, challenges the character of the Levite when he fails the ideals.

49. Stone, "Gender and Homosexuality," 87–107.

biologically male does not entail a man being recognized as "masculine." Rather, it is the performance of certain social behaviors that are intricately tied to power, economics, and social status in the culture that determines whether a man is "being a man."[50]

While in reality there are multiple articulations of masculinity across the population in any culture at any given time, there is often one form of ideal masculinity that stands out in each culture and period as dominant. It is also the standard against which all other forms of masculinities are evaluated, and subsequently, suppressed. The term "hegemonic masculinity" proposed by Tim Carrigan describes this form of culturally exalted masculinity, which is widely accepted by members of a society in determining what it means to be a man.[51] Although the actual number of men who exhibit all of the traits is few, hegemonic masculinity is propagated in the power structure of society, as most men are complicit in sustaining it.[52] It is not a rigid totality, but may evolve over time in adapting to new circumstances in societal norms, shifting politics, and changes in socio-economic conditions.[53]

The theory of hegemonic masculinity has been prominent in contemporary masculinity studies and also proves influential in the study of masculinity in the Hebrew Bible. The attention of biblical scholars began with David Clines's article in 1995, "David the Man: The Construction of Masculinity in the Hebrew Bible." Clines identified four characteristics of masculinity in the description of David, namely strength, wisdom, beauty, and avoidance of women.[54] Since then scholars have built upon Clines's framework and have examined the representation of hegemonic masculinity in other biblical texts. While the trait of beauty is deemed controversial by some,[55] most agree that strength, wisdom (in the form of persuasive speech), and avoidance of women (or avoidance of being seen as feminine) are common characteristics of hegemonic masculinity in biblical narratives. Other traits such as self-control, fertility and marriage, honor, and kinship solidarity also have been identified.[56] The following describes these traits of hegemonic masculinity in the Hebrew Bible.[57]

50. Carrigan et al., "Toward a New Sociology," 89–91.
51. Carrigan et al., "Toward a New Sociology," 92.
52. Carrigan et al., "Toward a New Sociology," 92.
53. Lipka, "Masculinities," 87.
54. Clines, "David the Man," 212–41.
55. For example, Lipka, "Masculinities," 91; Wilson, *Making Men*, 35–36.
56. See Wilson, *Making Men*, 39–45.
57. As the trait of beauty is deemed controversial, it is not included in the discussion here.

Defining Characteristics of Hegemonic Masculinity

STRENGTH

Physical strength is a well-recognized characteristic of hegemonic masculinity in the Hebrew Bible. Clines not only finds ample evidence of the emphasis on this trait in the narratives of David, he also demonstrates that it defines the meaning of manhood for every other male character in 1 and 2 Samuel.[58] The connection between physical strength and masculinity is consistent with archeological evidence from Assyrian and Sumerian inscriptions, and thus reflects the ancient Near Eastern context of biblical texts.[59] This concept has been widely used in the discussion of hegemonic masculinity in the Hebrew Bible.[60] While Wilson cautions against equating strength with violence, it is in fact difficult to delineate the two, for physical strength inevitably entails the capacity to exert violence. Though hegemonic masculinity may not endorse all wanton acts of violence, its emphasis on physical strength does allow the possibility for violence to be regarded as a demonstration of masculinity.

WISDOM AND PERSUASIVE SPEECH

Clines demonstrates that David's intelligence and effective communication skills are evident throughout the narratives in 1 Samuel,[61] and few have since challenged wisdom and persuasive speech as characteristics of manhood in the Bible. It has been applied in the reading of other characters such as Moses and Joshua,[62] and Saul's ineffective use of rhetoric also has been interpreted as undermining his masculinity.[63] Wisdom and its demonstration in persuasive speech is thus an essential element of hegemonic masculinity in the Hebrew Bible.

---

58. Clines, "David the Man," 216–17. It is most evident in 1 Samuel 4:9, where the Philistines encourage each other in battle by calling to one another: "Strengthen yourselves and be(come) men!" and "be(come) men and fight!"

59. Wilson, *Making Men*, 31–32.

60. For example, Haddox, "Favoured Sons," 4–5; DiPalma, "De/Constructing Masculinity," 42–44.

61. Clines, "David the Man," 219–21.

62. DiPalma studies the character of Moses in terms of wisdom and speech, "De/Constructing Masculinity," 49; and Joshua is evaluated in Creangă, "Variations on the Theme of Masculinity," 88.

63. Măcerlau, "Saul in the Company of Men," 62–63.

Avoidance of Association with Women

Clines observes in the narratives of David that he is portrayed as minimizing contact with women despite the fact that he had numerous wives and concubines. He asserts that it is to convey a message that "a real man can get along fine without women; he can have several women in a casual kind of way, but he has nothing to gain from them except children, and he owes them nothing."[64]

The physical and emotional detachment from women as a trait of masculinity also is evident in the broader ancient Near Eastern context. It is suggested that women in this culture were generally viewed as a taming force on men, distracting them from exerting their masculinity.[65] The avoidance of being feminized, especially in situations of warfare, was a sign of mature manhood.[66]

Self-Control

Unlike the previously-discussed traits observed from narratives, self-control as a characteristic of manhood was first identified in the legal texts. Focusing on the legal codes in Deuteronomy, Mark George proposes that it sets up a regimented classification system that requires the audience to exert self-control in a multifaceted manner as a demonstration of masculinity. As "having a name in Israel" is paramount for a Hebrew male, it is achieved—according to Deuteronomy—by faithfully abiding by the restrictions on behaviors and desires concerning such things as sexual contact, plunder, food, and drink.[67] Wilson observes that similar principles can be found behind legal texts outside Deuteronomy, Proverbs and the prophetic books, which qualifies self-control as a fundamental element of ideal masculinity in the Hebrew Bible.[68]

Fertility and Marriage

Virility and the production of offspring are also essential to "having a name in Israel," and a concern with having legitimate heirs is evident throughout the Hebrew Bible. It is accepted among biblical and ancient Near Eastern scholars

---

64. Clines, "David the Man," 226–27.
65. Wilson, *Making Men*, 36.
66. Wilson, *Making Men*, 37–38.
67. George, "Masculinity," 64–82.
68. Wilson, *Making Men*, 39.

that fertility was central to the construction of masculinity in the culture.[69] However, Wilson argues that fertility and marriage are "sufficient conditions for biblical manhood, but not necessary ones," and gives examples of biblical characters being called "a man" before, or without, marriage.[70] Fertility is therefore considered a less significant attribute of masculinity.

Honor

Honor and its counterpart, shame, have been recognized in cultural anthropology as important concepts in the Mediterranean region. Honor is the way a man's reputation and self-worth is determined in a society, and its role in hegemonic masculinity in the Hebrew Bible has been investigated by a number of scholars.[71] It is often observed to be sexual in nature; in particular, the chastity and fidelity of the women in the family determines the honor of the male members—the ability of the male to protect the chastity of the females is considered an enhancement of his honor, and the reverse is also true. Drawing on recent studies, Wilson asserts that the evaluation of honor also includes hospitality and other virtues, and the concept of honor is not merely defined within an individual, but also corporately in terms of familial, tribal, and national relations.[72]

Kinship Solidarity

The role of male bonding in masculinity has been recognized by Clines in the narrative of David,[73] and there has since been increasing consensus in scholarship on the significance of kinship solidarity in the world of the Hebrew Bible. It is argued that solidarity that extends beyond the family unit—to clans, tribes, and the nation of Israel—is a fundamental value in the society and is evident in the kinship language in the Bible, as well as in biblical law involving kinship redemptions. While this solidarity extends to women and children, it is often displayed among men and is a key feature of ideal manhood in Israel.[74]

---

69. Wilson, *Making Men*, 40.
70. Wilson, *Making Men*, 42.
71. See Wilson, *Making Men*, 42, for examples.
72. Wilson, *Making Men*, 43–44.
73. Clines, "David the Man," 223–25.
74. Wilson, *Making Men*, 44–45.

The Masculinity of the Levite in Judges 19

In this section, the character of the Levite is assessed using the above framework. I evaluate his actions against hegemonic masculinity ideals and demonstrate that the issue of masculinity is implicit in each scene: in each instance either he fails to adhere to the ideals, or, when he attempts to do so, he brings further destruction into the plot.[75]

Judges 19:1–3

The opening verses of the narrative have been convincingly demonstrated by Stone as a challenge to the Levite's masculinity. Though it is undetermined whether the verb *znh* ("to commit fornication") describing the action of the concubine in verse 2 connotes sexual infidelity or refers to the woman being angry with her husband,[76] Stone argues from the anthropological concept of honor and shame that both interpretations render humiliation to his masculinity. As male honor in ancient Near Eastern culture demanded that the man be able to "control" the women associated with him, whether the concubine was sexually unfaithful to him or took the unconventional initiative in leaving his household, both cases lead to a questioning of the Levite's manhood in the eyes of the male audience of his time.[77] The narrative therefore draws the attention of the audience from the very beginning to the issue of masculinity.

Verse 19:3 describes the reaction of the Levite after the four months: "Then her husband set out after her, to speak tenderly to her and bring her back." It may not be surprising that the Levite wants to reclaim his authority over the concubine, but the intention "to speak tenderly to her" would be quite unexpected according to hegemonic masculinity ideals. As noted earlier, avoiding association with women was considered a masculine trait, and the Levite is not only described as pursuing the concubine but also preparing to appease a woman. These actions obviously foster association with the female and hence defy the masculinity ideal. The detailed description of the Levite's inner thoughts therefore further challenges his masculinity. It sets the stage for the narrative to unfold, with the audience's attention firmly anchored on the issue of gender performance.

---

75. The description of the character of the Levite extends to 20:7. While here the focus is on Judges 19, the subsequent events that happened as a result of his actions in this unit also will be commented upon.

76. For a summary of the scholarly debate, see Butler, *Judges*, 418–49.

77. Stone, "Gender and Homosexuality," 95–96.

Judges 19:4–10

This unit of the narrative takes place in the house of the father of the concubine. The father-in-law is portrayed as tirelessly offering hospitality to the Levite, and the Levite is both silent and passive in the matter until the fifth day. As hospitality is recognized as an expression of honor in manhood, the insistence of the father-in-law may be read as an eager manifestation of his masculinity. His success in convincing the Levite to stay by repeated use of verbal persuasion also alludes to his masculinity through exhibiting the trait of wisdom in persuasion. The intensity of his persuasion is demonstrated by the repeated use of the emphatic form of imperative throughout his conversation: verse 6 *hw' l-n'* ("please be prepared"), verse 8 *s' d-n'* ("please refresh"), verse 9 *hnh n'* ("please behold") and verse 9 *lynw-n'* ("please spend the night").[78] The portrait of the father-in-law is therefore one that emphasizes his masculinity in two aspects: honor and wisdom. While these do not necessarily impair the masculinity of the Levite, being consistently characterized by passivity and silence, he is in a subordinate position and comparatively disadvantaged in the expression of his manhood. Moreover, the repetition of "ate and drank" in verses 4, 6, and 8 indicates an emphasis on the motif of gastronomic enjoyment. The depiction of the Levite indulging in the food and drink may also hint at his lack of self-control, which defies another trait of hegemonic masculinity.

Therefore, when the Levite finally insists on leaving the house in verse 10, despite the lengthiest attempt of persuasion by the father-in-law in verse 9, it is, for the first time in the narrative, the Levite attempting to assert himself: he is beginning to "act like a man." Yet his expression of manhood might be too late. As the progression of the plot shows, it is this "masculine" action of the Levite in beginning the journey at a late hour that triggers the horrific outcomes.

Judges 19:11–15

This unit of the narrative focuses on one particular incident during the journey, where the Levite rejects the suggestion of the servant to lodge at Jebus and insists on travelling further to Gibeah or Ramah. The Levite labels Jebus as "a city of foreigners," and he emphasizes the alienation of this place from himself by adding "which do not belong to the people of Israel." By accentuating the distinction between foreigners and Israelites, the Levite implies that his identification with the people of Israel is such a significant matter to

---

78. Block, *Judges*, 512.

him that he will not spend even one night among foreigners. The vital issue here is therefore a trait of masculinity: kinship solidarity. By refusing the more convenient option of lodging at Jebus and instead pursuing the choice of Gibeah, the Levite illustrates that kinship solidarity to him is not mere lip service but is demonstrated in his practical actions.

The action by the Levite is an attempt to adhere to the hegemonic masculinity ideal. It is not by chance, or simply unfortunate, that they lodge the night in Gibeah. It is a conscious decision made by the Levite that is prompted by his masculine view of kinship solidarity. Yet, ironically, this decision to reside in Gibeah will lead to a tragedy beyond his imagination.

Judges 19:16–25

In this unit, an old man from Ephraim comes to the Levite's rescue and invites the group to stay overnight in his house. A ruthless mob comes to the old man's house and demands the Levite for homosexual rape. The host tries to negotiate with the mob by offering both his own virgin daughter and the concubine, and he is rejected. The Levite then grabs his concubine and hands her over to the attackers, and they gang rape her throughout the night.[79]

Stone adopts theories from anthropological studies and suggests that the aim of the mob is in fact to mutilate the masculinity of the Levite. By threatening homosexual rape, his masculinity is challenged, as it would subject him to the conventional sexual role of women. As the substitution of the concubine is still an attack upon his manhood (as it damages his honor by sexually abusing a woman under his protection), this explains why handing the concubine out seems to settle the request.[80] Stone also observes that the mob overpowers the Levite through their speech: they do not speak to him directly but to the old man only. This puts the Levite in the position of the object of speech and further degrades his masculinity.[81] This unit is therefore a challenge in terms of gender politics.

The response of the Levite to the challenge should then be considered from the perspective of masculine performance. There is no doubt that he hands over the concubine as a means of self-protection, but the way his action is described seems to emphasize his initiation of the action. There is no discussion between the Levite and the host, and the position of the

---

79. Though the text is not explicit on the identity of the person who grasps the concubine, as discussed in the previous chapters, most agree that it is more likely to be the Levite himself. See Webb, *Book of Judges*, 468.

80. Stone, "Gender and Homosexuality," 98–101.

81. Stone, "Gender and Homosexuality," 99.

Levite changes abruptly from the passive to the active by the verb *yḥzq* ("he seized"). This *hiphil* verb carries a sense of strong hold and violence, which indicates the strength of the Levite in initiating this action. This is further accentuated by the use of a second verb, *yṣ'* ("he put"), in describing the action of the Levite of pulling the concubine to the mob. The combination of the use of the two verbs emphasizes the physical power of the Levite. It alludes to the trait of physical strength that is fundamental in the hegemonic masculinity of ancient Israel. The action of the Levite therefore represents his effort to salvage his own masculinity. Ironically, his action not only leads to the suffering of his concubine, but also his own manhood is still tamed, for he fails to protect her sexuality and hence loses honor.

Judges 19:26–30

The concubine survives the gang rape and falls at the doorstep of the old man's house, and the relational designation of the Levite becomes "her master" from verse 26. The succession of verbs at the beginning of verse 27—"he arose," "he opened," and "he went"—paints a picture of rapid actions without hesitation. Together with the simple command, "arise and go," there is an obvious sense of detachment of the Levite from his concubine. While many interpret this as a description of his cruelty and lack of sympathy toward the woman,[82] it may also be a literary technique to emphasize his avoidance of association with her, which serves to enhance his masculinity. Being the "master" of the concubine, the connection of the Levite with this woman is downplayed, and the rapid actions in the morning reflect that he seems to have been unaffected by the events of the previous night. And by commanding the concubine to get up and go, there is no emotional attachment shown to the female. All of these details together sketch a picture of an attempt at manhood that is independent of the woman and consistent with the hegemonic masculinity ideal of the culture.

The Levite further attempts to demonstrate his masculinity upon arriving home. He takes a knife, grasps his concubine and cuts her into twelve pieces, and sends the body parts to the twelve tribes of Israel. The text is ambiguous as to whether she is alive during the dismemberment, but nevertheless, it still takes a great deal of strength to cut up a human body. The passage emphasizes the strength of the Levite by using a double verb again, "he seized" and "he divided her," and it is further accentuated by the additional description "to her bones." It is not simply cutting up

---

82. Such as Yee, "Ideological Criticism: Judges 17–21," 155; Lapsley, *Whispering the Word*, 48.

twelve pieces of flesh, but a full-scale dismemberment. The Levite must have great physical strength to accomplish this by himself, as the text does not imply he has assistance in the process. Consistent with the focus on gender performance, the display of strength on the part of the Levite is a sign of his masculinity. However, contrary to the strength displayed by Levites in Numbers in cutting animals for sacrifices and promoting the religious well-being of the Israelites, here the actions of the Levite are done to a woman and lead to a civil war among the Israelites.

Judges 20:1–7

The tactic of the Levite proves effective, since four hundred thousand soldiers assemble upon receiving parts of the body of the concubine, and they assume an "evil thing" (verse 3) has offended their kinsman even before knowing what actually happened. This unit focuses on the speech of the Levite in persuading the tribes to go to war with the Benjamites. His version of the incident in Gibeah is heavily tainted: he leaves out the intention of homosexual rape of the men of Gibeah, as well as the fact that he himself handed over his concubine to them. Instead, he repackages the incident as, "they intended to kill me, and they raped my concubine until she died." It gives the impression that his life was in danger and therefore he was unable to help his concubine. This illustrates that he is intentionally misleading the Israelites concerning the facts of the events.

Consistent with the focus on masculinity, the eloquence of the Levite and his skillful repackaging of the incident demonstrate his wisdom in the form of persuasive speech. He successfully mobilizes the tribes of Israel to fight against the Benjamites, and yet the outcome of the war is the loss of almost the entire tribe of Benjamin. The ironic tone is noticeable in the description, "they were as one man": no such unity has been achieved in the book of Judges prior to this, and now they are united in destroying their own people.[83] The action of the Levite leads to the worst destruction in the entire book of Judges.

This analysis illustrates that the narration on the Levite in Judges 19 is consistently concerned with his manhood. As the narrative opens with substantial challenges to his masculinity, readers are tuned from the beginning to be skeptical about his actions. As the plot unfolds, each scene depicts the Levite attempting to salvage his masculinity, and yet it is obvious that each of these attempts leads himself and his concubine into a worse scenario. The destructive effect flows beyond his household to the

---

83. Butler, *Judges*, 441.

level of the tribal union. To those who share the ideology of hegemonic masculinity, this portrayal of the Levite is then a counter-example that betrays the ideals of the ideology.

Similar to the previous chapters that studied Judges 19 from narratological and intertextual perspectives, this investigation through the ideological lens of masculinity once again puts the Levite in a negative light. One may hence conclude that the rhetoric of the narrative consistently promotes an anti-Levite sentiment, and the following section turns to a socio-historical context that may illuminate the political reason for such a literary agenda.

Reading Judges 19 through a Lens of Politics

In Yee's proposal of a Josianic historical context for Judges 19, there are issues that have not been thoroughly discussed. First, Yee assumes a pro-monarchic agenda for the refrain, "in those days there was no king in Israel," and takes it as an interpretive framework for the unit. As opinions concerning the significance of this refrain are diverse, and it is sometimes regarded as a mere editorial connection with the previous chapters, a more in-depth exploration may clarify the issue. Second, while Yee considers various literary perspectives in her intrinsic analysis of the portrayal of the Levite, her discussion is brief, and a stronger case may be built based on a more thorough investigation of the proposal of an anti-Levite rhetoric in the text.

The following investigates these issues, based on Yee's analysis and the findings from previous chapters. It demonstrates that the two facets of political ideology in the text, namely the pro-monarchic and the anti-Levite agendas, both point to the possibility of a historical context of Josianic reform.

Pro-monarchic Ideology in Judges 19

This section reviews the pro-monarchic elements in Judges 19 that may provide clues to the historical context for the text. The repetition of the refrain, "in those days there was no king in Israel," in Judges 18:1 and 19:1, and its extended form, "in those days there was no king in Israel, everyone did what was right in his own eyes," in Judges 17:6 and 21:25, has long been recognized as a series of narratorial comments that binds the last five chapters of the book together in its current form. With few exceptions, most scholars agree that the phrase implies a negative evaluation of the happenings "in those days," and the chaos in the narratives is attributed to the absence of a king. The understanding of the ideological role of the refrain in Judges 19, however, is disputed. Some take it as evident of a pro-monarchic agenda that steers the interpretation of the narrative;[84] others dismiss its rhetorical function and consider it as a mere editorial frame that attaches Judges 19–21 to the previous chapters.[85] As the role of this refrain is pivotal to an understanding of the political ideology in the text, this issue is examined here in more detail.

A survey of the arguments against a pro-monarchic ideology conveyed by the refrain reveals that the core argument lies in the apparent inconsistency of the pro-monarchic content of the plot in Judges 19–21. Soggin argues that "while the phrase fits well with the situation existing in chs. 17–18, where in fact we find examples of political and religious licence, it seems to be particularly ill-chosen for chs. 19–21." The existence of an inter-tribal assembly that gathers in war against the Benjaminites is already seen as a solution to the violations of social order, and hence does not necessitate a king.[86] Similarly, Edenburg contends that "it is doubtful that a king could either prevent the crime or act with greater efficacy to punish the wrongdoers," and nothing in the story implies that it overtly or covertly deals with kingship apart from the refrain. The phrase is hence taken as an editorial frame that has been "tacked on to the narrative in order to insert it into its context, and therefore it cannot indicate anything about the composition's intent."[87] In other words, this phrase plays no ideological role, according to Edenburg, and therefore should not be taken literally as promoting the monarchy.

Amit assesses the dealings of the Israelite tribes even more positively and considers them "acting in a balanced and responsible way," and they were "concerned with the destiny of an Israelite tribe and made every effort to protect its continuity." She therefore perceives a tension between the account and the narrator's claim that the presence of a king would have prevented the portrayed problems. Instead, this story is to be read as a "'song of praise' to the functioning of the pre-monarchic frameworks."[88]

Such a positive view of the events in Judges 20–21 seems to downplay the irony in the account. The "balanced and responsible" handling by the

---

84. Such as Yee, "Ideological Criticism: Judges 17–21," 148; O'Connell, *Rhetoric*, 268–70.

85. Such as Edenburg, *Dismembering*, 325; Soggin, *Judges*, 280; Dumbrell, "'In Those Days,'" 23–33.

86. Soggin, *Judges*, 280.

87. Edenburg, *Dismembering*, 325.

88. Amit, *The Book of Judges*, 398–99.

community leads to the near extinction of one of their own tribes, and the "concern" for the Benjaminites comes as a consequence of their own actions. It is doubtful that the portrayal of the inter-tribal assembly is presented as a success over against kingship when the consequences lead to so much damage to the community. The apparent unity of the tribes, without a royal leader to guide them in their behavior, in fact proves to be a disaster in the story, which may have been avoided by an ideal king.

Contrary to those who contend that such a king has not been realized in Israel's history, any propaganda that promotes the monarchy does not require such a king to be a historical reality. It is the idealization of what the king is capable of doing that is important to the narrator. A new king may be presented in the propaganda as being able to achieve what kings before him have failed to do. Josiah, being acclaimed for the discovery of the book of the Law in the Jerusalem Temple, according to 2 Kings 22, may well be portrayed by his supporters as having this potential to surpass his predecessors. He is idealized as the one who is able to lead the country in avoiding chaos similar to that in the last chapters of Judges. The lack of such a previous success in the history of Israel therefore does not eliminate the potential of the idealization by the narrator in his political agenda.

Moreover, the argument concerning the lack of pro-monarchic elements in the plot seems to have neglected the intertextual reference between Judges 19:29 and 1 Samuel 11:7. As demonstrated in the previous chapter, the dismemberment of the concubine by the Levite carries a cultic overtone and is a failed attempt at sacrifice in comparison to the positive modeling of Saul. Though Saul may have failed as a king in the end, his initial success remains a case for the argument that this is what a king can, and should, do; the ideal king is capable of doing even better than Saul.

Furthermore, as the evaluative connotation of the refrain is clear and undeniable, it is hard to imagine that the author/redactor would neglect this overtone and insert it into the text for the sole purpose of artificially binding the chapters together. In particular, if the meaning of the refrain is in fact contradictory to the content of the plot, it implies that the author is doing an exceptionally bad job by confusing the readers with an evaluative framework that is opposite to his rhetorical purpose. It is difficult to justify that the need of connecting the narrative to the previous chapter is so strong that the author has no other option but to sacrifice his communicative objectives. Rather, it is more likely that the author uses the refrain and its plain meaning because it is consistent with his ideological agenda in promoting the monarchy.

Read from this perspective, the refrain is not a mere editorial phrase that connects the last chapters of the book of Judges, but an evaluative framework designed to prompt readers to interpret the narratives as warnings from the anarchic era. The pro-monarchic ideology in the text promotes the idea that an ideal king is capable of preventing all the chaos portrayed in the stories, and he will steer the nation in proper behavior in the cultic, social and military spheres. Though this royal propaganda may not be exclusive to Josiah's time, the vibrant hope for such an ideal monarch seems fitting for the spirit of the reform of a king who has discovered the book of the Law.[89] While Saul, and even David, may not have achieved such perfection,[90] there is hope that Josiah may surpass them and turn the ideal to reality.

Anti-Levite Ideology in Judges 19

Compared to the often-discussed pro-monarchic ideology, the existence of an anti-Levite ideology has been largely neglected in interpretations of the text. Commentators have either neglected the negative traits of the Levite, or understood it as an anti-Saul polemic, in which the criticism is not directed toward the Levite himself, but toward Saul. However, as the findings of the previous chapters in this study demonstrate, the anti-Levite agenda is actually a prominent theme in the narrative and should be considered in the search for a historical context for such a political ideology. Here, I summarize the arguments for this anti-Levite rhetoric from previous chapters and illustrate its coherence with the social setting of the reform of Josiah as proposed by Yee.

In my narratological analysis of Judges 19, I demonstrated that there are multiple narrative gaps in the text that center on the character of the Levite, including verses 2–3, 5–8, 25, and 27–29. By prompting readers to fill in the gaps in their reading experience, it draws their attention to the Levite and his behavior. This establishes him as the protagonist of the story and generates curiosity, suspense, and surprise in the discourse. The gaps are so crafted that they persuade readers to sway between the possibility of a positive and a negative interpretation of the Levite and his deeds as the plot develops. The final scene of dismemberment not only comes as a surprise, but also it diminishes the possibility of empathy toward the Levite and resolutely pins on him a negative image.

---

89. While the nature, extent and success of Josiah's reform has been debated (see the conversation between Albertz, "Why a Reform Like Josiah's Must Have Happened," and Davies, "Josiah and the Law Book," in *Good Kings and Bad Kings*, 27–46 and 65–77 respectively), this does not affect the argument here as propaganda for the pro-monarchic ideology is not dependent on these issues.

90. The intertextual association between Judges 19 and the rape of Dinah implies David's failure in preventing this from happening in his own house.

Point-of-view study of the narrative also reveals anti-Levite literary devices embedded in the text. By examining the story through the spatial, psychological, temporal, phraseological, ideological, and informational planes, I have demonstrated that the collaborative effect of the various planes of point-of-view in the text are manipulated to keep readers at a distance from the Levite. This forms the basis of an evaluative guidance from the narrator to view the Levite and his actions in a negative light: readers are not encouraged to identify or sympathize with him; instead, the manipulation of the point-of-view in the entire narrative functions to persuade readers to form an adverse judgment on this character.

This is further confirmed in the use of intertextuality in the text. Intertextual connections of Judges 19 with Genesis 19 and 22, 1 Samuel 11, Deuteronomy 22, and 2 Samuel 13 illustrate motifs of hospitality, rape, and sacrifice; the motifs again provoke negative evaluation focusing on the Levite. His actions throughout the discourse are portrayed as contrary to divine ordinances: he seizes the concubine and pushes her to the mob, as opposed to the angels rescuing Lot; he acts in a way that is parallel to a rapist; and he performs prohibited human sacrifice that diverts from the divine instruction to Saul, who sacrificed for military action. By implicitly comparing the Levite to the characters in the intertexts, the narrative vehemently illustrates the degradation of his morality in multiple aspects.

Finally, reading the text from a perspective of masculinity, the Levite is once again portrayed adversely from the view of hegemonic masculinity. The narrative presents substantial challenges to his masculinity, and while he attempts to salvage his manhood, each of these attempts leads himself and his concubine into worse scenarios. He is pictured as a counter-example, who betrays the ideals of the hegemonic masculinity of his time, and he is to be evaluated negatively by readers adhering to this ideology.

The findings from the previous sections of this study illustrate that, while there is no explicit condemnation against the Levite in the narrative, there are numerous evaluative clues that collaboratively prompt readers to adopt a sentiment against this character. This anti-Levite rhetoric not only defames him as an individual; the anonymity of the character also functions to condemn those of his kind.[91] Since he is clearly identified as coming from Ephraim, it may be suggested that he represents country Levites who are not aligned with the Levites in Jerusalem (i.e., in the later historical development during Josiah's rule). The integrity of the group is cast into doubt through this representative figure, provoking skepticism concerning their competence and qualifications to function in the priesthood.

---

91. Hudson proposes that anonymity here expresses universality and parallels loss of individual identity and personhood. Hudson, "Living in a Land," 59.

This polemic against country Levites may correspond to the political agenda of Josiah's reform, especially his destruction of the local shrines. As Yee has demonstrated, the centralization of worship promoted by Josiah was not only a religious matter but also a political means of gathering revenue,[92] which was crucial to his government and most probably was met with resistance. Strong rationales were required to justify such a move; apart from establishing Jerusalem as the chosen location for the temple, it was also important to support the claim that local shrines were unsuitable places for worship. Revealing the loathsome character of the Levite in Judges 19 (and in Judges 17–18) implicitly disqualified country Levites from serving at local shrines. This in turn questioned the value of the existence of local shrines.

The anti-Levite ideology in the text hence again is coherent with the historical context of Josiah's reform. Considering the text also has a prominent pro-monarchic ideology (more specifically, the critique of Benjamin implicitly supports a southern monarchy), this renders the possibility of this historical setting even more probable: this was a political situation that required propaganda that both supported the southern monarchy and dismissed the country Levites.

Conclusion

This chapter has demonstrated the potential of reading Judges 19 with ideological lenses. By reading the Levite from the perspective of hegemonic masculinity in ancient Israel, it is evident that his manhood is frequently challenged in the narrative. His attempts to salvage his masculinity consistently lead to adverse consequences, which presents him as a negative example of the ideology. This forms another aspect of the anti-Levite rhetoric in the text.

The political reading of the text confirms Yee's proposal of a sociohistorical context of Josianic reform. The refrain, "in those days there was no king in Israel," in Judges 19:1 is a strong indication of a pro-monarchic interpretive framework that is consistent with the contents of the plot, suggesting that social and cultic chaos may be avoided by an idealized king from the south. The anti-Levite rhetoric that is consistently evident in narratological, intertextual, and gender readings of the story reveals a political agenda that aims to defame country Levites. The entire discourse may then be read as royal propaganda for the reforms of Josiah, which promotes the regime of the king and his policy of centralizing worship in Jerusalem.

---

92. Yee, "Ideological Criticism: Judges 17–21," 146–47.

6

Chinese Christian Reading of Judges 19

Reflections on Translation and Implications

Introduction

THE READING OF JUDGES 19 in this study has come full circle. We began, in chapter 1, by exploring the Chinese Union Version (CUV) in the context of the Republican era. After an exploration of the puzzling term *pîlegeš* in chapter 2, the rhetorical purpose of the text was investigated through narratological, intertextual, and ideological perspectives in chapters 3–5. It is now time to review the interpretation in chapter 1 in light of the findings of the subsequent chapters and reflect upon its implications, especially for Chinese communities of faith.

It has been evident that there are significant discrepancies between the Hebrew text and the CUV. The analysis of the discourse in the Hebrew establishes the Levite as the protagonist, who is consistently portrayed in an adverse manner throughout the plot. The negative characterization is revealed in narratological, intertextual, and ideological perspectives, and it points to an anti-Levite sentiment. The interpretation from the CUV, however, draws the attention of readers to the character of the concubine, depicting her as a promiscuous woman who brought the misfortune of gang rape and dismemberment upon herself. The translation of the CUV seems to suppress the anti-Levite rhetoric in the reading, and the focus on concubinage within the cultural context also contributes to such interpretation.

My reflection on these discrepancies is presented in two parts. The first part analyzes the translation choices of the CUV in its historical context and proposes reasons that might underlie the decisions. It suggests that the anti-concubinage agenda of Western Christian missionaries, combined with the pressure to gain acceptance among Chinese authorities, rendered them less attentive to the anti-Levite rhetoric in the text, which in turn influenced their translation. The second part discusses the implications of the translation for Chinese Christian communities today. I investigate how Chinese commentaries in recent decades have been influenced by the CUV, and thereby demonstrate its impact on the perception of the narrative in the faith community. I contend that the condemnation of the Levite that is missing in the CUV contributes to the neglect of the issue of violence against women in Chinese interpretations. This illustrates the tremendous power of the role of the translator and the need for more critical evaluation of biblical translations.

Translation of Judges 19 in the CUV

As has been identified in chapter 1, the translation of Judges 19 in the CUV, particularly of 19:2, 25 and 29, conveys a negative view of the concubine and downplays the role of the Levite in the gang rape and dismemberment. This section analyzes the translation choices made in these verses and investigates the historical context of the production of the CUV that may have influenced these decisions by the translators. In order to provide background information, it begins with a brief discussion of the history and translation principles of the CUV.

History and Translation Principles of the CUV

The project of the CUV began with an interdenominational meeting of Western missionaries in Shanghai in 1890. As the various mission societies had previously been using different Chinese translations of the Bible, it was widely acknowledged that a united effort was required for better use of resources in China missions.[1] It was decided that this new united translation would consist of three versions using different levels of the Chinese language: high *Wenli* (higher classical Chinese), easy *Wenli*, and Mandarin.[2] The first two versions were later combined into one, as the use of *Wenli* was becoming outdated,[3] and the Mandarin version (now known as the CUV) that was published in 1919 became the authoritative Chinese version of the Bible. For many decades, it was the only known translation in Chinese churches, and it has been in popular usage for almost a century until today.[4]

---

1. Zetzsche, *Bible in China*, 187–89. This was not the first joint effort by mission societies. As will be mentioned, the Delegates Version was the first such attempt but the cooperation failed with the departure of American missionaries after the completion of the New Testament.
2. Zetzsche, *Bible in China*, 198–200.
3. Zetzsche, *Bible in China*, 287.
4. The dominance of the CUV in Chinese churches is studied in Chong, *Jidujiao shengjing zhongwen yiben*, and will be examined in further detail later in this chapter.

The earliest Mandarin committee was formed by seven missionaries.[5] While there were considerable changes in the appointment and involvement of translators during the process, one thing that did not change was that all the translators were male Westerners.[6] Male Chinese assistants also were acquired, but their contribution was largely restricted to the fluency and accuracy of the use of the Chinese language, and it is widely recognized that the CUV was a product of Western missionaries.[7] Though main translators were recorded for the translation of certain books of the Old Testament, the drafts were examined and adopted by the committee as a team.[8]

The translation of the CUV was based on the Hebrew and Greek texts underlying the Revised English Version. The translation principles stated by Chauncey Goodrich, the chairman of the Mandarin committee, included: "(1) the rendering must be truly colloquial . . . ; (2) the language must be universal as opposed to local Mandarin; (3) the style, while easily understood, must be high enough to be chaste;[9] (4) the translation must be a close rendering of the original; (5) the illustrations must be, as far as possible, translated, not paraphrased."[10] This demonstrates that while the translation emphasizes the fluency of the Chinese language, faithfulness of the translation to the original text is not to be neglected. The specific concern about paraphrasing indicates that formal equivalence is recognized as significant in the consideration of translation choices, which provides insights into how the translation of Judges 19 should be evaluated.

Analysis of the Translation in Judges 19:2, 25, 29

The translation nuances of Judges 19:2, 25 and 29 in the CUV are studied from two perspectives. I first compare its word choices to other passages within the CUV, so as to demonstrate how the Hebrew words were understood by the same translators. I then compare the CUV to other Chinese translations in order to investigate how the text has been understood by translators in different contexts. This may shed light on the translation choices made in the CUV that were particular to its historical setting.

---

5. Zetzsche, *Bible in China*, 221.
6. Zetzsche, *Bible in China*, 318–19.
7. Zetzsche, *Bible in China*, 319–20.
8. Zetzsche, *Bible in China*, 318–19.
9. This attention to stylistic elegance is discussed in Ren, *Shengjing hanyi wenhua yanjiu*, 175–80.
10. Zetzsche, *Bible in China*, 325.

As identified in chapter 1, the translation nuances in the CUV include: (1) use of *xing yin* (行淫, "committed adultery") to translate *znh* in verse 2; (2) omission of the verb *ḥzq* ("to seize") in both verse 25 and verse 29; (3) insertion of *"shi shen"* (屍身, "corpse") in verse 29; (4) omission of *lʿ ṣmyh* ("limb by limb," or literally, "to her bones") in verse 29. The following analysis focuses on these particularities.

Comparisons Within the CUV

The root *znh* ("to commit fornication") in verse 2 appears about 134 times (Logos 8) in the MT, and at least 60 times as a verb,[11] with at least 57 times in the CUV variously translated as *xing yin* (行淫, "commit adultery"),[12] *xing yin luan* (行淫亂, "commit adultery"),[13] *zuo ji nu* (作妓女, "to be a prostitute")[14] and *xing xie yin* (行邪淫, "commit evil adultery").[15] *Xing yin* and *xing yin luan* often refer to extra-marital sexual relationships, though it is also used in a metaphorical sense referring to spiritual adultery.[16] *Xing xie yin* is usually used in connoting spiritual adultery in worshipping other gods, and *zuo ji nu*, on the other hand, specifies prostitution for monetary gain. The use of *xing yin* in Judges 19:2 is therefore consistent with the other passages that refer to husband-and-wife relationships. However, this translation does not reflect the possibility of the verb being a unique occurrence of a homonym meaning "be angry," which is attested in the LXX. As will be demonstrated in the next section, the latter meaning has been conveyed in an earlier version of Chinese Bible, indicating that the use of *xing yin* in the CUV is a choice made between two traditions.

The verb *ḥzq* ("to seize") that has been omitted in Judg 19:25 and 29, on the other hand, is not consistent with the way the verb is translated elsewhere in the CUV. The hiphil *waw* consecutive of *ḥzq* is translated *che zhu* (扯住, "grasp") in 1 Sam 15:27, *si lie* (撕裂, "tear apart") in 2 Sam 1:11, *si* (撕, "tear") in 2 Kings 2:12; and *zhua zhu* (抓住, "grasp") in 1 Kgs 1:50 and 2:28. All of these verbs in Chinese connote a sense of strong force in action that is missing in the translations of Judges 19:25 and 29. Judges 19:25 collapses the two verbs *ḥzq* and *yṣʾ* ("to put") as *la chu qu* (拉出去, "pull out"), which does

11. Logos 8 and *DCH*, *TWOT* counted 89 times in the Qal stem.
12. E.g., Ezekiel 16:28; Jeremiah 3:6, 8.
13. E.g., Numbers 25:1; Deuteronomy 22:21.
14. E.g., Genesis 38:24; Amos 7:17.
15. E.g., Exodus 34:15, 16; Leviticus 17:7; Numbers 15:39; Deuteronomy 36:16; Ezekiel 6:9; Psalms 106:39; Hosea 9:1.
16. Such as in Jeremiah 2:20.

not emphasize the grasping motion implied in *ḥzq*, and the entire action is neglected in the translation in verse 29. Comparing with the word choices in the other passages, it is clear that the translation in Judges 19:25 reflects a conscious choice of wording from at least the listed options.[17] In other words, there are other Chinese words known to the translators of the CUV that correspond to *ḥzq* and convey a greater sense of force in action, yet the word *la* (拉, "pull") was chosen deliberately on this occasion.

The other missing phrase in the CUV of Judges 19:29 is *lʿ ṣmyh*. The only other occurrence of the combination of *l* and ʿ*ṣm* is found in the MT in Proverbs 3:8. Here the CUV translates *bai gu* (百骨), which literally means "hundreds of bones" and can be understood to connote "all bones." This implies that the meaning of the phrase was clearly understood by the translators of the CUV and yet was deliberately omitted in Judg 19:29. Together with the insertion of the word *shi shen*, which is absent in the MT, the visualization effect of the dismemberment scene is significantly reduced by the translators of the CUV. As the translation principles of the CUV incline toward formal equivalence, these particularities seem to defy the translation principles and demand further investigation.

This analysis of the word choices in the CUV reveals the possibility of bias among the translators. The identified nuances reflect either a conscious choice to turn away from a previous translation, or word choices that are not consistent with the translations made in other passages by the same translators. The translation choices collectively contribute to masking the terrifying details contained in the Hebrew text and subsequently downplay the role of the Levite in the entire ordeal. Compared with the anti-Levite rhetoric that has been clearly identified in the previous chapters in this study, the CUV turns the rhetorical focus away from the Levite.

Comparison with Other Chinese Translations

In this section, the CUV of Judges 19:2, 25, 29 will be compared with other Chinese versions in order to demonstrate alternative possibilities in translation. Three translations are chosen here: the Delegates' Version (DV 1858), Chinese New Version (CNV 1992), and Revised Chinese Union Version (RCUV 2010).[18] The following first provides a brief introduction of the

---

17. It is interesting to further note that when the same verb is used in the description of the action of Amnon toward Tamar in 2 Samuel 13:11, the CUV chooses *la zhu* (拉住, pull) over the other stronger verbs. It seems that the force of the man is again downplayed in a rape scene through the translation.

18. It is noted that although the editions of the source texts of the various

background and translation principles of each version, as well as the reasons that they are chosen for comparison.

Delegates' Version

Prior to the DV, Chinese translations of the Bible were mostly undertaken by individual Western missionaries, and the translations were not commonly accepted across different mission societies. The DV was the first joint attempt by a committee of delegates from various Western Protestant mission societies.[19] The project began in 1843, and the completed volume was published in 1858.[20] Although American missionaries split from the committee after the completion of the New Testament due to divergent opinions, and the Old Testament was translated by missionaries from the London Missionary Society, this version is still commonly known as the Delegate's Version in recognition of the joint effort.[21] It was highly regarded by British and German missionaries, and was considered the most significant Chinese translation of the Bible in the nineteenth century.[22] However, as the evangelization of China was at an early stage, the influence of this translation among the Chinese was limited.

The language used in the DV was classical Chinese as commonly used among the literati.[23] Since Chinese readers had experienced difficulties with previous translations that rigidly adhered to formal equivalence, the DV put more emphasis on its fluency in expression, though maintaining faithfulness

---

translations are different, they are all based on the MT. The particular version of the source text of the DV is not mentioned in Zetzsche, *Bible in China*, and I have not been able to locate it elsewhere. However, as the analysis later will demonstrate, the DV translates nuances that are omitted by the CUV, and it can be inferred that the source text of the DV does contain these particularities. As the CUV is later than the DV, it can be assumed that the Hebrew text available to the translators of the CUV does contain the particularities. The CNV uses *Biblia Hebraica Stuttgartensia* 1977 ; Chong, "Guannian yu xianxiang," 551; whereas the RCUV uses the fifth reprint of *Biblia Hebraica Stuttgartensia* 1997; "Heheben xiudingban," lines 18-20. As the two versions do not demonstrate discrepancies in the particular verses concerned, the translation issues identified are not due to discrepancies among the source texts.

19. Zetzsche, *Bible in China*, 77–78.
20. Zetzsche, *Bible in China*, 77, 102.
21. Zetzsche, *Bible in China*, 101.
22. Zetzsche, *Bible in China*, 94–95, 363.
23. Mandarin had not yet become a lingua franca at that time and classical Chinese was chosen for the translation. Zetzsche, *Bible in China*, 94.

to the meaning of the Hebrew and Greek texts.[24] This version is chosen for comparison here as it was a translation known to the translators of the CUV,[25] and hence differences between the two translations can be considered as representing a preference in terms of translation decisions.[26]

Chinese New Version

The translation project of the CNV was initiated by Chinese biblical scholars in 1972. While the New Testament translation was published within four years in 1976, the Old Testament translation took twenty years, being published in 1992.[27] It was the first Chinese translation that both represented a group effort by Chinese scholars and adopted the translation principle of formal equivalence.[28] A new version had been deemed necessary, as the CUV was considered old style in language and difficult for younger generations to understand.[29] The translation guidelines emphasized that the translation, while using contemporary expressions, was to be faithful to the original text.[30] While it has not yet been able to achieve the status of the CUV in Chinese Christian communities, this version has received more attention in recent years and hence is included for comparison here.

---

24. It is noted that one of the translation principles of the committee was to be in "exact conformity to the Hebrew and Greek originals in sense; and so far as the idiom of the Chinese language will allow, in style and manner also"; Zetzsche, *Bible in China*, 79. However, this translation is sometimes considered not faithful enough to the original; Zetzsche, *Bible in China*, 103.

25. It is noted that the DV was listed as a reference for the translation of the higher *Wenli* version. As it was required for interpretations to be consistent between the three Union versions, it is legitimate to assume that the translators of the CUV possessed the knowledge of the DV during their translation process; Zetzsche, *Bible in China*, 199–200.

26. It is noted that there are significant differences in the use of the language between classical and Mandarin Chinese, and the comparison between CUV and DV focuses on the meaning conveyed rather than expressions used.

27. "Shengjing xinyiben jieshao."

28. The Lu Zhen Zhong Version published in 1970, though adhering to the principle of formal equivalence (to the extent of literal translation at times), was translated by an individual and did not acquire popularity among Chinese Christians; Chan, "Lu zhenzong yiben"; and The Today's Chinese Version published in 1979 follows the translation principle of dynamic equivalence; Chiu, *Yijing suyuan*, 106. These two translations are therefore not considered here.

29. Chiu, *Yijing suyuan*, 121.

30. Chiu, *Yijing suyuan*, 122.

Revised Chinese Union Version

The RCUV published in 2010 is a recent update of the CUV that aims to present a translation of formal equivalence in contemporary Chinese. The revision was prompted by the changes in the Chinese language in the past century since the CUV was published, as well as advances in biblical interpretation, including the discovery of the Dead Sea Scrolls and recent studies of the LXX. The committee of consultants for the RCUV included Chinese biblical scholars from various regions including Hong Kong, Taiwan, Malaysia, and China. The four translation principles were: (1) be faithful to the original language; (2) make the least possible changes from the CUV; (3) maintain the style of the CUV; (4) adhere to contemporary Chinese language and expressions.[31]

This version is chosen for comparison as it represents a reconsideration of the CUV by Chinese biblical scholars. It is the first time that the CUV, translated by Western missionaries, has been directly revised by local Chinese. Considering the translation principles, any changes made in the RCUV are significant, as they denote alterations that the translators viewed as being more faithful to the original text, changes that were unequivocally necessary.

Comparison of Translations

The following table shows the comparison between the different versions (italics are used in the English translations of the various Chinese versions to highlight the points that differ significantly in the Chinese expressions):

	和合本(CUV)	委辦譯本 (DV)	新譯本 (CNV)	和修本 (RCUV)
Judges 19:2	妾行淫 (the concubine *committed adultery*)	妾不悅其夫 (the concubine was *upset* with her husband)	他的妾背夫行淫 (his concubine *committed adultery behind his back*)	這妾對丈夫生氣[32] (this concubine was *angry* with the husband)

---

31. "Heheben xiudingban," my translation.

32. This version also includes a note 或譯「行淫，對丈夫不忠」 (or translated "committed adultery, unfaithful to the husband").

CHINESE CHRISTIAN READING OF JUDGES 19   167

	和合本(CUV)	委辦譯本 (DV)	新譯本 (CNV)	和修本 (RCUV)
Judges 19:25	那人就把他的妾拉出去交給他們，他們便與他交合，終夜凌辱他 (the man *pulled* his concubine out to give to them, they had *intercourse* with her, humiliated her all night)	客強出其妾，眾與淫合，永夕戲侮 (the guest *forced* his concubine out, they had *illicit intercourse* with her, humiliated her all night)	那人就抓住自己的妾，拉出外邊去交給他們，他們就與她交合，整夜凌辱她 (the man *grasped* his concubine, *pulled* her outside to give to them, they had *intercourse* with her, humiliated her all night)	那人抓住他的妾，把她拉出去給他們。他們強姦了她，整夜凌辱她 (he *grasped* his concubine, *pulled* her out for them. They *raped* her, humiliated her all night)
Judges 19:29	用刀將妾的屍身切成十二塊 (used a knife to cut the *corpse* of the concubine into twelve pieces)	取刀剖妾，肢解其骨，分為十二 (took a knife to cut the concubine, *dismembered her to the bones* into twelve pieces)	就拿起刀來，抓住自己的妾，把她的肢體切成十二塊 (picked up a knife, *grasped* his concubine, cut her *body* into twelve pieces)	他拿刀，抓住他的妾，把她的屍身切成十二塊 (he picked up a knife, *grasped* his concubine, cut her *corpse* into twelve pieces)

JUDGES 19:2

A comparison between the various versions illustrates that the translators have chosen different traditions in the understanding of the verb *znh*. The DV uses "*bu yue*" (不悅, "upset"), which carries no ethical evaluation upon the character of the concubine. The CNV, however, has gone even further than the CUV and specifies that the concubine "*bei fu xing yin*" (背夫行淫, "committed adultery behind her husband's back"). While "*bei fu*" (背夫, "behind her husband's back") may be considered a literal translation of the prepositional phrase ' *lyw* ("against him"), this detail clearly brings a heavier sense of condemnation compared to the CUV. The RCUV, on the other hand, seems to be undecided between the two traditions. It favors "angry with the husband" in the main text, but maintains "or translated, committed adultery, unfaithful to the husband" in its notes.

As the DV was known to the translators of the CUV, the word choice of the CUV clearly represents a preference for the interpretation of adultery over a domestic dispute.³³ As the RCUV demonstrates in the note, the meaning of *znh* may also be expressed as *bu Zhong* (不忠, "unfaithful") in Chinese, which arguably carries a lesser value of condemnation than *xing yin*. One may conclude that there are different options in the translation of the word, and the CUV translators have favored an expression that carries a sense of ethical evaluation.

JUDGES 19:25

The translation of the DV uses the phrase "*qiang chu*" (強出, "force out") to translate both *ḥzq* and *yṣ'*. As classical Chinese is highly concise in its use of vocabulary, it is possible that "*qiang*" (強, "force") is considered to correspond to the former Hebrew verb and "*chu*" (出, "out") to the latter. It is also evident that "*qiang*" is a strong word indicating the use of strength in the action against the will of the concubine. The description of the DV therefore brings the attention of readers to the force exerted by the Levite.

In the contemporary Chinese versions, both the CNV and RCUV, the downplay of the verb *ḥzq* in verse 25 of the CUV is clearly rectified. Both add a phrase "grasped his concubine" to the translation, which describes the force of the action. This confirms my previous observation that that the word choice of *la chu qu* (拉出去, "pulled out") in the CUV does not convey the grasping motion of *ḥzq*. This is particularly noteworthy in the RCUV, which aimed to make the least possible changes from the CUV—the change here therefore indicates that the addition was considered necessary and significant.

JUDGES 19:29

The translation of the DV, like the CUV, omits translating the verb *ḥzq* and simplifies the action of the Levite to *qu dao pou qie* (取刀剖妾, "took a knife to cut the concubine"). However, unlike the CUV it does not specify whether the concubine is dead or alive, which is more consistent with the MT. Moreover, it is the only translation of those compared that attempts to translate *l' ṣmyh* into Chinese using *zhi jie qi gu* (肢解其骨, "dismembered her to the bones"). Though one may critique that this translation adds a verb, "*zhi jie*" (肢解, "dismember"), which is not present in the Hebrew

---

33. While it might have been influenced by the use of "played the harlot" in the ERV, which was taken as the reference in the translation process, it nonetheless dismisses any sense of ambiguity that the English translation may convey.

text, the phrase does effectively convey the sense of vivid terror, by translating the detail of *lʿ ṣmyh*.

The CNV and RCUV also display differences as well as similarities with the CUV. They both convey the grasping action of the Levite with "*zhua zhu*" (抓住, "grasp") that is missing in the CUV, but the two translations differ in the description of the object of the cutting action: CNV uses "*zhi ti*" (肢體, "body") which does not indicate the life status of the concubine, whereas RCUV remains the choice of "*shi shen*" (屍身, "corpse") in the CUV. Both translations, however, do not convey the visual effect of horror as implied in *lʿ ṣmyh*.[34]

It is apparent from this comparison that for Judg 19:29, the CUV is less satisfactory than both older and newer translations in terms of accuracy. Though the language of the DV, in being classical Chinese, is by nature more concise than the Mandarin in the CUV, it still contains more detail by including the translation of *lʿ ṣmyh*. The CNV and the RCUV both corrected the omission of the verb *ḥzq*, which is significant in drawing readers' attention to the action of the Levite. Although the detail "to the bones" remains missing in the contemporary translations, they still represent a closer affinity to the MT compared to the CUV.

The translation nuances of the various versions lead to interpretative possibilities that differ significantly from the CUV. The differences are particularly pronounced with the DV and the RCUV. In these two translations, as the concubine is not condemned for committing adultery from the beginning, she is not portrayed outright as one who deserves contempt. The emphasis on the force of the action of the Levite in verse 25, combined with the extent of detail provided in verse 29, serves to focus the attention of readers on the strength exerted by the Levite. Compared to the CUV, these versions may lead to readings that are more likely to put the blame on the Levite. While the CNV also takes the tradition of translating *znh* as adultery, like the CUV, and indeed puts even greater emphasis on it, the subsequent translations in verses 25 and 29, unlike the CUV, do not reduce the force of the Levite's actions. This may create some tension in the interpretation, causing uncertainty among readers in terms of evaluating the characters, yet it nonetheless exposes the Levite's violence. The CUV, on the other hand, not only targets the concubine as the character at fault from the beginning, but also it omits details that the CNV and RCUV prove translatable in the Mandarin language in verses 25

---

34. One may suspect that one of the possible reasons is that it is difficult to find an equivalent expression in the Chinese. Indeed the DV needed to insert a verb, "*zhi jie*" (肢解, "dismember"), that is not present in the Hebrew text in order to express the idea.

and 29. The ultimate effect in the CUV is one that masks the violence of the Levite and shifts the blame away from him.

This comparison illustrates that alternative translations with a closer affinity to the Hebrew text of Judges 19 are clearly possible, both in classical Chinese and Mandarin. One may conclude that the particularities in the CUV are unlikely to be due to difficulties in translation, or limitations that are inherent in the linguistic characteristics of the Chinese language. Rather, there were other factors that caused these deviations. As the translation principle of the CUV explicitly demanded close rendering of the original, this observation calls for further investigation in search for explanations. The following discusses factors from the historical context of the translation of the CUV that may underlie its translation decisions in this particular narrative.

The Role of the Translators and the Translation Context

Until recent times, the focus of scholarship concerning the theories of Bible translation has often been on the text and its linguistic properties. As K. Jason Coker aptly describes, "Bible translation has always been and continues to be a text centered enterprise."[35] Studies of translations are essentially concerned about the use of language in the translated text, and the attention of biblical scholars on the debate between dynamic and formal equivalence in the past decades clearly represents such an orientation.[36] The image of the translators is often pushed out of view, and their roles and influence on the translations are seldom acknowledged.[37]

With the increase in awareness on the role of readers in biblical interpretations in recent years, the adequacy of the traditional text-oriented approach in biblical translation is being contested. Scholars have pointed out that the neglect of the role and power of the translator is intrinsically linked to the assumption that translators are essentially objective and impartial.[38] This assumption is highly questionable when the translators are considered as readers themselves, who inevitably interpret the text in the process of translation.

---

35. Coker, "Translating from this Place," 25.

36. Nida's theory of dynamic (later termed functional) equivalence is regarded as the most influential view of biblical translation since the 1970s. For a discussion of its rationale and challenges to its methodology, see Boer, "Dynamic Equivalence Caper," 13–24.

37. As Coker comments, neither dynamic nor literal equivalence theories take into consideration the identity of the translator; "Translating from this Place," 31.

38. Coker, "Translating from this Place," 30.

This incursion of hermeneutics into translation theories has led to a turning point, recognizing that no translation is inherently and completely neutral. Instead, all translations are interpretations.[39]

The recognition of the involvement of interpretation in the process of translation implies that the ideologies of the translators may influence their interpretation of the text, which in turn governs their translation decisions. In the words of Angelica Bammer, "Translation . . . is never just a more or less technical (linguistic) systems transfer; it is always a process invested with complex political, economic, and sometimes personal interests."[40] As much as the translators may wish to be faithful to the original text, their ideologies stand behind their interpretations. For instance, the theological affiliation of the translators may influence their understanding of passages that are involved in exegetical debates, and their translation choices may reflect a bias toward their positions.[41] As the interpretation of the translators cannot be free of ideology, factors that contribute to their ideologies, such as sociopolitical and economic contexts, personal identities and affiliations may be reflected in the translated product. In other words, the translation context plays a significant role in the outcome of translation.

It is therefore fruitful to study the translation context in order to understand the ideologies reflected by a translation. This may be approached through examining the historical milieu, as the socio-political situation of the time when a particular translation was made may reveal certain tensions and ideologies in the society. The personal identity of the translators may also be investigated. However, when the translation in view was made in a more distant past, often little is known about the lives of the translators. This is particularly the case when the translation is a team effort instead of individual. In such situations it may be more feasible to study the corporate identity of the translators, such as "Western missionaries" or "local elites." One can then juxtapose observations on the particularities of the translated text with the translation context and search for possible connections between them.

This approach has been found useful by postcolonial scholars, who challenge the ideologies behind translations of the Bible into non-Western languages made by Western missionaries in the past. Studies have revealed cultural insensitivities, linguistic shortcomings, and hegemonic tendencies

---

39. Smith, "Productive Role," 55–57. This does not imply that translations are "free" interpretations. Translations remain bounded by the expectations of its art, and to say that translations are interpretations is to acknowledge the inevitable involvement of interpretation in translations.

40. Bammer, "On Being Faithful and Disloyal," 136.

41. Lee, "Guoyu heheben shengjing," 73.

in translations made by missionaries during and after the colonial era.[42] As the missionaries were seen as part of the economic and political colonization by the West, these translation decisions are hence attributed to the identity of the translators in the particular socio-political contexts.[43]

As the CUV was a product of Western missionaries during a time of political turmoil between Western countries and China, it is reasonable to venture the hypothesis that the ideologies of the translators were influenced by the socio-political context and the interests of mission societies. However, previous studies on the translation of the CUV have often focused on issues relating to theological viewpoints and translation principles,[44] and seldom has the significance of the identity and culture of the translators been addressed.[45] Even at times when it was acknowledged that the translators were Western missionaries, the focus of critique centered on the fluency of their use of Mandarin, as if language were the only barrier between the two cultures.[46] The vast differences between Chinese and Western cultures that had always existed since Western missionaries arrived in China were seldom considered a factor in translation.

This cultural aspect of translation can become prominent in texts that concern issues in which the perception between the two cultures differs significantly. Judges 19, as chapter 1 has demonstrated, involves the matter of concubinage, which was a major point of cultural conflict between Western missionaries and local Chinese. Given the significance of the issue at the time of translation, it is legitimate to bring together the socio-political context and the identity of the translators, with the particularities in the translation decisions observed. The following therefore focuses on the issue of concubinage and discusses the possible influence of the ideologies of Western missionaries toward the CUV translation of the passage.

---

42. Nadella, "Postcolonialism, " 50.

43. Sugirtharajah, *Postcolonial Criticism*, 157–78.

44. Mak, *Daying shengshu gonghui*, 2–3. For examples of this approach, see Lee, "Guoyu heheben shengjing," 71–89; and Yang, "Union Chinese Version," 85–99.

45. Mak's study on the influence of the British and Foreign Bible Society and the translation of the CUV is an exception, as he recognizes the role of mission societies behind the CUV and seeks to investigate their influence as sponsors of the translation. Although his work focuses on the textual selection of the New Testament, his findings confirms the significance of the ideologies of the sponsors to the translation outcomes.

46. Chow, "Heheben yijing yuanze he pinggu," 1–16.

The Translation Context of CUV Judges 19

Concubinage had been deeply rooted in the Chinese culture, and it persisted into the Republican era when the translation of the CUV was in progress. Chapter 1 of this study has established the socio-political context from primary sources and demonstrated the hostile attitudes toward concubines of both Western missionaries and the local Chinese during that time. The issue attracted significant attention from society, and the abolition of the practice was hotly debated in the media. Concubinage was regarded by missionaries as a major hurdle in the conversion of Chinese to Christianity, and their rejection of the practice was abundantly reflected in their writings and commentaries. It was evident that they attempted to promote monogamy and discourage concubinage whenever the opportunity arose, and this was a prominent issue in their evangelistic strategy. In order to further explore how this mindset may have influenced the CUV translation, I draw upon insights from studies that investigate the ideologies of Western missionaries toward women in China in the nineteenth to early twentieth centuries.

It has been widely acknowledged that from the time that Protestant mission work began to develop in China, the contrast in the status of women and related practices between the two cultures had disturbed the Western missionaries. The lack of opportunity in education, and the practices of foot binding, female infanticide, concubinage and child brides, were among the many issues that they considered unacceptable in Chinese society.[47] They established the first schools for women, encouraged freeing girls from foot binding, and engaged in social work that helped women in need. While these efforts contributed positively to the lives of women in China, this did not necessarily entail an ideology that resisted the patriarchal Chinese culture. Quite to the contrary, some have suggested that the missionaries might have contributed to a reinforcement of the traditional culture.

In Marjorie King's study of the impact on Chinese women's social status by American missionary women in the nineteenth century, King concludes that the "women's work for women" mission movement failed to achieve the original goal of emancipating women in China.[48] As a major force in the American foreign mission, this movement set out to promote the ideology of women being equal, free, educated, and having the right to their own persons. It was believed that converting Chinese to Christianity would result in a social change concerning the status of women in the nation.[49] However,

---

47. King, "Exporting Femininity," 119.

48. King, "Exporting Femininity," 119.

49. King, "Exporting Femininity," 117–18. For an overview of the history and scope of work of the movement, see Kwok, *Chinese Women*, 15–18.

King observes that the evangelistic target pressured missionaries to increasingly compromise the social goal concerning women, especially when political tension between the local Chinese and mission societies heightened.⁵⁰ In order to avoid being seen as a threat by the Chinese government and elites, the schools they established for women emphasized adhering to traditional Chinese values, including obedience to husbands in the household. Instead of encouraging women to seek equality and freedom outside their homes, they promoted the nineteenth century American ideal of Christian wives and mothers, who prioritized serving the household, which in effect reinforced the traditional patriarchal Chinese culture.⁵¹

The ideologies of the women missionaries also were described in a study by Kwok Pui-Lan.⁵² She acknowledges their contribution in improving the status of Chinese women in the anti-footbinding movement, yet she also observes that their privileged position in semi-colonized China resulted in ethnocentrism and cultural superiority. Kwok comments that "[a]s products of their own time, many women missionaries were bound by the Victorian ideology of female domesticity and subordination."⁵³ The missionaries also discouraged female students from participating in the wider feminist movement in early twentieth century China, criticizing the girls as having gone too far and acting too much like men.⁵⁴

These studies reveal the cultural tensions concerning women that Western missionaries experienced in the China mission. On the one hand, the existing social situation was deemed degrading and inappropriate by their Christian faith and Western culture, and yet on the other hand, their ideologies of female subordination collaborated in some respects with the

---

50. This is demonstrated in a Chinese government circular in 1872, which demanded changes in the existing treaties, seeking to remove female teachers and female schools that were considered to be interfering with the peace of Chinese social life; King, "Exporting Femininity," 130.

51. This is demonstrated by the speech of several speakers at the China Centenary Missionary Conference of 1907. Miss S. L. Dodson, a single woman missionary, defined the goal of women's work as the education of "good wives, mothers, and daughters-in-law," and some others expressed the fear that training Chinese women as high school and government teachers would improve their social position and make them discontented and proud, thus discrediting Christianity; King, "Exporting Femininity," 124.

52. Kwok, *Chinese Women*, 7–28.

53. Kwok, *Chinese Women*, 22. This is not to dismiss entirely the contribution of the manifestation of these ideologies by the missionaries, as many are remembered for their ministry and lives of piety. (For example in the life of Lottie Moon, see Qu, "Yishi toushe," 322–37.)

54. Kwok, *Chinese Women*, 22.

traditional Chinese cultural values. At times when they were pressured to maintain the opportunity to evangelize in China, they strategically emphasized the latter and tried to align with the Chinese authorities. The overall message they delivered concerning women was therefore masked by their adherence to patriarchal values, despite efforts in improving the livelihood and education level of Chinese women.

Translating Judges 19 in such a context, the ideology of the translators of the CUV, who were missionaries themselves, seems to cohere with the findings in these studies. The concept of an unrestricted woman, so free as to get upset with her husband and leave his household, might have been seen as too much of a challenge to the Chinese culture in the eyes of the translators. An adulterous concubine would have been deemed more consistent with the image of concubines that was being conveyed in the media at that time and might have influenced the choice of the word "*xing yin*" (行淫, "committed adultery"). The subsequent translation nuances in verses 25 and 29 also can be explained by this mindset seeking to avoid violation of the Chinese culture. To suggest that the Levite was at fault ran the risk of being considered subversive of Chinese cultural values, which would have jeopardized the reception of the CUV Bible, particularly in a political climate that put the issue of concubinage at the center of attention. By masking the actions of the Levite, the translation covers up his brutality and instead turns the blame onto the concubine, rendering the consequent rape and dismemberment a mere consequence of her adulterous behavior. As the translators were all male, they were apparently less sensitive to the horror of this reasoning.

While this reconstruction of the translation context remains a hypothesis, it is clear from the comparison with other versions that the CUV contains less shock and cultural challenge to Chinese readers.[55] On the surface, the CUV appears to smooth out the tension in the text and render it more acceptable to its Chinese readers. It is, however, a violation of the translation principles of the CUV, which aimed to produce a text as close to the original as possible.[56] In fact, such maneuvers render violence *to* the text in order to cover up the violence *in* the text.

---

55. The different translation decisions in the subsequent versions may then be considered as reflecting a change in ideology, as the translations were done when the issue of concubinage was no longer a major concern in the sociopolitical context.

56. This is not the first time that the CUV has been criticized for compromising faithfulness to the Hebrew text. Lee gives ample examples in his study on the CUV that is evidence of the phenomenon and criticizes that these violate its claimed translation principles. Lee, "Guoyu heheben shengjing," 75–85.

Implications of CUV Judges 19 for Chinese Christian Communities

As the only version of the sacred text used among Chinese Christian communities worldwide for decades, the CUV equals the word of God to many Chinese Christians. The translation generates tremendous authority for a particular interpretation, and the message it conveys shapes the readings for generations. This section first addresses the phenomenon of the dominance of the CUV, which provides the background for understanding its influence. I then compare the interpretations of Judges 19 in recent Chinese commentaries and investigate the impact of the CUV on the commentators. In particular, I focus on the attitude of the commentators toward the Levite and the concubine and examine the way their readings address the violence of the Levite in the narrative. I then conclude with a reflection on the impact of these interpretations in shaping the perspective of the Chinese Christian community on the issue of violence against women.

The Dominance of the CUV

At about the same time as the launch of the CUV in 1919, the written language in China underwent major changes as a result of the New Cultural Movement. Mandarin was promoted, replacing classical Chinese as the national written language, and classical Chinese soon fell out of daily use. This rendered the older versions of the Bible in classical Chinese obsolete, and within ten years of its publication, the CUV was widely used in all provinces in northern and southern China, with sales volumes surpassing those of any previous versions.[57] Given that there were no further attempts to translate both the Old and New Testaments into Chinese between 1919 and 1970, the CUV was considered by Chinese Christians, for many decades, as the only sacred Scripture.[58] Although several new translations using more updated Mandarin were published after 1970, they have not yet gained popularity among Christian Christians, and the authoritative status of the CUV remains unchallenged.[59]

In Chong Yau-yuk's analysis of the phenomenon of the authoritativeness of the CUV, Chong lists four areas of influence that it possesses in the Chinese Christian communities:

---

57. Chiu, *Yijing suyuan*, 45.
58. Chong, *Jidujiao shengjing zhongwen yiben*, 20.
59. Chong, *Jidujiao shengjing zhongwen yiben*, 2, 20.

1. Religious authority—the CUV equates to "the Chinese Bible" for many Christians, and they reject the newer translations, to the extent that some Christians in rural China have been reported to burn the new translations as heretical texts.[60]
2. Historical authority—the growth in Christian population among both local and overseas Chinese in the past century is intricately linked with the use of the CUV, and Chinese churches worldwide have been emotionally connected to each other through the common authority of the CUV.[61]
3. Linguistic authority—the CUV forms the foundation for the use of Christian language and terminologies in Chinese, and its linguistic influence is also recognized in contributing to the promotion of Mandarin in China during the New Cultural Movement.[62]
4. Authority in market share—sales statistics demonstrate that the dominance of the CUV has continued after the emergence of newer Chinese translations. The vast majority of the 5.5 million Bibles printed in China between 1981 and 1990 were CUV, with only a small fraction (240,000) printed in other languages for ethnic minorities. From 1988 to 1997, the CUV continued to represent over 70 percent of the sales of Chinese Bibles from the Hong Kong Bible Society, the major Bible printing organization supplying both local and overseas Chinese Christians.[63]

Chong's study reveals the irrefutable authoritative status of the CUV to Chinese Christian communities. This provides the background for studying its influence on the interpretations of Judges 19, which is our next focus.

Chinese Commentators' Attitudes to the Violence of the Levite

As the translation issues of the CUV discussed above mainly focus on the presentation of the Levite and his violence, the impact of the translation may be revealed from the attitude shown toward this character in commentaries. Three Chinese commentaries on Judges are chosen for comparison

60. Chong, *Jidujiao shengjing zhongwen yiben*, 26–27. The rejection of the newer translations is more prominent from the 1970s to the 1990s. In recent years, some churches in Hong Kong and overseas have begun to use the newer versions, such as the CNV and RCUV, in Sunday services.
61. Chong, *Jidujiao shengjing zhongwen yiben*, 28–29.
62. Chong, *Jidujiao shengjing zhongwen yiben*, 29–30.
63. Chong, *Jidujiao shengjing zhongwen yiben*, 30–32.

here,⁶⁴ and they are listed from the highest to the lowest level of demonstrable dependence on the CUV. I examine how the character of the Levite is commented upon, paying particular attention to the details that reflect the level of responsibility he is deemed to bear in the incident. I demonstrate that the higher the level of dependence on the CUV, the more ignorant is the commentator of the violence of the Levite.

*James Cheung—Judges*⁶⁵

This commentary published in 2000 demonstrates the most dependence on the CUV among the three: it cites the CUV in full at the beginning of each chapter, and it does not refer to the MT or consider other Chinese translations throughout the discussion of Judges 19. It is therefore reasonable to suggest that this interpretation reflects a reading that stems from the CUV.

Cheung's summary of the narrative at the beginning of his comments provides some clues to his view of the Levite: "the concubine committed adultery and left her husband and returned to her father's home, but the Levite loved her so much that he went to the father-in-law . . . a sinister incident happened and the Levite's concubine was raped, and afterwards her husband cut her corpse into twelve pieces . . . "⁶⁶ There is no mention whatsoever of the Levite's participation in and responsibility for the gang rape, and the violence of the dismemberment is toned down by referring to the body of the concubine as a corpse. This clearly reflects an uncritical reading of the CUV, as Cheung does not address any of the above-mentioned translation issues.

Interestingly, Cheung then draws lessons from the behavior of the Levite, reproving him for not performing the duty of a servant of God. His criticisms of the character, however, include: acquiring a concubine and owning wealth (servant and donkeys) at a time of poverty (verses 1, 2); indulging in physical enjoyment (verse 4); being perverted and acquiring a concubine and knowingly disobeying the laws of God (verse 2).⁶⁷ Three of

---

64. In recent decades, there have been about five commentaries on Judges written in Chinese (excluding translations from other languages), and the three are chosen here as they best illustrate the varying levels of dependence on the CUV.

65. Cheung, *Shishi ji*, 241–53.

66. Cheung, *Shishi ji*, 248–49. All quotations from the commentaries hereafter are my translation.

67. Cheung, *Shishi ji*, 249–50. There is some resemblance of this interpretation to Chen's (陳崇桂) during the Republican era, (see chapter 1, n88). Both authors depend on the CUV alone, criticizing the Levite for concubinage and totally ignoring his violence.

the four listed "offences" actually point to the same issue, namely the single fact that he marries a concubine; peculiarly, none of his violent behavior in the second half of the narrative counts toward any condemnation. There are two possible explanations for this observation: either the sin of acquiring a concubine is so much heavier, in Cheung's eyes, than pushing a woman into gang rape and dismembering her, that it renders the latter not worth mentioning; or his reading entirely misses the rhetorical emphasis on the brutality of the Levite. As this commentary was written at a time when concubinage was no longer a pressing social issue, it is less likely that Cheung's attention was heavily drawn to the matter due to its contingencies in the society. The second explanation is therefore more likely: that Cheung's interpretation misses the violence exerted by the Levite, which is consistent with his reliance on the CUV.

Cheung's ignorance of the violence of the Levite is further demonstrated in the way that he addresses the issue of gang rape and dismemberment. Both matters do not seem to warrant emphasis in his comments, and he swiftly changes the foci of attention on both occasions. Concerning the Gibeah incident, he comments that "the people at that time freely engaged in gang rape, and it is even more horrifying that they originally wanted to commit homosexual behavior with a stranger!" He then continues to condemn all extra-marital and homosexual relationships, collapsing gang rape within the same scope as premarital sex and affairs.[68] Concerning the violence in verse 29, he remarks: "A Levite who is supposed to belong to God and preach the truth cut his concubine into twelve pieces and stirred up violence amongst his own people." Again, his attention drifts away from the Levite's treatment of the concubine, and the rest of his comments address the violence of the inter-tribal war.[69]

Cheung's reading clearly illustrates the significant influence of the CUV on a Chinese reader in the interpretation of the narrative. It does not recognize the anti-Levite rhetoric in the MT, and the reader's attention is therefore diverted away from the involvement and responsibility of this character. The moral of the story is drawn concerning the evils of the time, as if it were "society's fault." No sympathy is given to the concubine, and the issue of violence against women is subsequently neglected.

68. Cheung, *Shishi ji*, 251.
69. Cheung, *Shishi ji*, 251.

Timothy Wu—Rediscovering the Bible: The Book of Judges[70]

This commentary published in 2009 does not provide a translation of the passage at the beginning of each section but incorporates the CUV in the flow of the exegesis. It also includes occasional references to the MT within the exegesis when the author deems it necessary, usually when it is considered helpful in clarifying the meaning of the text. It therefore represents an interpretation that is primarily based on the CUV and supplemented by the MT.

In his exegesis of Judges 19:2, Wu interestingly omits the quotation of the first half of the verse and avoids mentioning the issue of adultery. He refers to the concubine as "having a poor reputation" and limits the discussion of the problematic interpretation of *znh* to the footnote.[71] He spends more time discussing the absence of the Levite's wife in the narrative and questions why he does not establish the concubine as a full wife if his first wife has died.[72] He then continues with the exegesis of the second half of the verse, concerning the concubine returning to her father's home, which he considers an action stemming from "an unknown reason" and "not permitted in the Old Testament."[73] The imagery of the concubine as a promiscuous woman is obscured through this presentation, though Wu does not tackle the issue of the translation directly.

In the exegesis of the Gibeah incident and its aftermath, Wu attempts to present the happenings from the view of the concubine and highlights her passivity and victimization. He comments on the ambiguity of the MT in verse 29 concerning the life status of the concubine, and considers the addition of "for she is dead" in the LXX and Vulgate as attempts to take away the blame from the Levite.[74] Though he condemns the cruelty of the Levite in neglecting the suffering of his concubine, he does not acknowledge the repetition of the use of the verb *ḥzq* in verse 25 and verse 29 and therefore misses the focus of the MT on the violence of the Levite on both occasions.[75]

Wu's reading demonstrates sympathy toward the concubine and attempts to attribute responsibility for the tragedy to the Levite. However, as it

---

70. Wu, *Beiyue chenlun de xunhuan guiji*, 281–94.

71. Wu, *Beiyue chenlun de xunhuan guiji*, 287, 313. In the footnote, Wu only briefly discusses the different readings in the LXX, the Targum and the MT, and does not make explicit his own view.

72. Wu, *Beiyue chenlun de xunhuan guiji*, 287. To establish a concubine as a full wife after the first wife dies is a common traditional Chinese practice. Obviously, Wu is reading the text within the context of Chinese concubinage practice here.

73. Wu, *Beiyue chenlun de xunhuan guiji*, 287.

74. Wu, *Beiyue chenlun de xunhuan guiji*, 292–93.

75. Wu, *Beiyue chenlun de xunhuan guiji*, 292–93.

overlooks the anti-Levite rhetoric in the MT, the condemnation of the Levite is not as forceful as it could be. Without the textual support, his sympathy toward the concubine seems to be coming from his own context, where patriarchy is no longer perceived as the norm and the violence is therefore scrutinized. Wu's condemnation of the Levite is not coming from within the narrative itself and hence lacks spiritual authority.[76] Overall, Wu's reading demonstrates a certain level of resistance to the CUV, but with limited success due to his neglect of key translation issues.

Jacob C. S. Tsang—Judges[77]

This commentary published in 1998 begins with the author's translation of the passage in each chapter. Using the CUV as the framework, Tsang uses brackets to indicate places where his translation differs. Each of the modifications is subsequently explained with reference to the MT, providing reasons for his translation being a closer reflection of the Hebrew text.[78] The exegetical section also frequently refers to the MT, and it can be inferred that this interpretation demonstrates the least dependence on the CUV among the three commentaries.

Tsang's translation of Judges 19 demonstrates sensitivity to the translation nuances of the CUV discussed above. He brackets "*xing yin*" (行淫, "committed adultery") in verse 2 and comments on the controversy among scholars on the difference between the LXX and the MT. He takes the metaphorical sense of *znh* and proposes that the concubine did not commit physical adultery, suggesting that her unfaithfulness refers to her leaving the home of her husband. Although he considers her action as unacceptable in the culture, he also suggests that the Levite might have been responsible for her departure by mistreating her, and hence both parties

---

76. Wu's reading perspective may also explain his omission of the CUV in Judges 19:2, as the accusation of adultery may be regarded as a hurdle to drawing sympathy from Chinese readers and hence is counter-productive to the development of his interpretation. This strategy is of doubtful value, for diligent readers will nonetheless read the biblical text and be aware of the contents of the story; to avoid mentioning it in the exegesis may not be helpful at all.

77. Tsang, *Shishi ji*, 430–58.

78. It is evident that Tsang is more prone to formal equivalence in his translation, as his modification of the CUV is not only limited to places where he sees exegetical significance. For instance, he translates *hnh* (behold) in all its occurrences in the MT, which are sometimes omitted in the CUV and other translations, even though it may not alter the interpretation of the text (19:9, 22, 24).

are at fault.[79] In verse 25 and verse 29, he replaces the CUV with "抓住他的妾，把她拉出去交給他們 (grasped his concubine, pulled her out to give to them)" and "他取了那柄刀，抓住他的妾，按著她的骨頭，把她切成十二塊 (he took the knife, grasped his concubine and cut her into twelve pieces according to her bones)."[80] Tsang seeks to correct the nuances missed by the CUV with his translation, and he comments on the ambiguity of the MT in verse 29, suggesting that the concubine could have been alive when the Levite dismembers her.[81]

Tsang further highlights the role of the Levite in the tragedy, commenting twice that he is the one responsible for the concubine's death: "his concubine was 'grasped' by him twice and pushed to death," and "his twice 'grasping' of his concubine (verses 25, 29) is the direct cause of her death."[82] Drawing on the insights from an intertextual reading with Genesis 19, he condemns the character of the Levite as "selfish, cold-blooded, brutal and irrational."[83] Moreover, he comments on the victimization of the concubine in the narrative, and "although many commentators see the Levite as the victim here, the greatest victim is in fact the concubine."[84] The overall perception of the characters demonstrates sympathy toward the concubine, and the actions of the Levite are under scrutiny.

It is evident that Tsang's consideration of the MT leads to an interpretation that recognizes the violence and responsibility of the Levite. Compared with the other commentators, the focus of Tsang's reading is on the repetition of the Levite's grabbing action and its causative relationship with the death of the concubine. This in turn provides sufficient information from the text to assist readers in evaluating the Levite and his actions. Instead of taking the narrative as being neutral or silent on the issue of violence against women, the text clearly condemns the parties involved.

Reflections on the Impact of CUV Judges 19

The authority of the CUV to the Chinese Christian community is clearly demonstrated in the three commentaries studied. While they were

79. Tsang, *Shishi ji*, 449.
80. Tsang, *Shishi ji*, 435.
81. Tsang, *Shishi ji*, 447.
82. My translation of "他的妾是被他兩次「抓住」，推向死亡的" and "他兩次「抓住」他的妾（25, 29節）是直接導致她慘死的原因"; Tsang, *Shishi ji*, 447, 457.
83. Tsang, *Shishi ji*, 455.
84. Tsang, *Shishi ji*, 457.

published when newer versions such as the CNV were readily available, none of them refers to these versions in their exegesis of Judges 19. The CUV is taken as the default version of the Chinese Bible, and even Tsang, who presents his own translation from the MT, takes the CUV as the framework for his translation.

Comparing the three commentators' views on the character of the Levite, it is clear that Tsang is most explicit in recognizing his violence and also most direct in attributing the death of the concubine to him. Although Cheung also takes the Levite as a negative figure and censures him for wrongdoings, his sins are related to concubinage, and there is no condemnation of his violent acts within the narrative. Wu stands somewhere between these two commentators, blaming the Levite for his negligence of the concubine, and yet he cannot provide as much evidence as Tsang from the text. This suggests that a higher level of dependence on the CUV leads to a lesser recognition of the Levite's violence, and that it requires a reading from the MT to recognize the anti-Levite rhetoric embedded in the narrative.

Taking the chronological order of the publication of the three commentaries into consideration, it is evident that although Tsang's work was published prior to Cheung's and Wu's, Tsang's observations from the MT failed to impact the readings of the later commentaries. This may again point to the overpowering influence of the CUV, which continues to steer the interpretation of Chinese readers despite challenges from scholarship.

As the vast majority of Chinese Christians do not have knowledge of Hebrew and rely on the CUV for their interpretations, it is reasonable to infer that the CUV is likely to impose readings that are more akin to that of Cheung's upon Chinese readers. The condemnation of the Levite's violence and of his responsibility in the incident are neglected, and even if they are sympathetic toward the concubine, like Wu, their lamentations revolve around the patriarchal society that allowed such evils to take place. There is nothing inherent in the text that condemns such violence, which leaves readers with an impression that what happened was deemed acceptable to the culture. Women were to be victimized in such a culture, and they had no choice but to accept their fate, no matter how regrettable it might seem to modern minds. Worse still, if she were an adulterous woman, this might be seen as a warning to those of her kind, as if she deserved this fate. In a way, Judges 19 might then be interpreted as normalizing violence against women in cultures that practice such violation. One may grieve over the tragedy, but there are no means in the interpretation to resist it.

An appreciation of the anti-Levite rhetoric in the text brings another dimension into the interpretation. Even in the patriarchal society of ancient Israel, the violence of the Levite was not accepted without question, as if it was a normal behavior in the society. In fact, his character is scrutinized by the narrator, who skillfully incorporates a multi-dimensional anti-Levite rhetoric into the text. This rhetoric is meant to bring condemnation upon the Levite, which is an unmistakable element within the narrative itself that subverts the culture and its practices. A man is blamed for the violence against a woman, even in this patriarchal society. A man is blamed for the violence against a woman, as lowly as the status of the woman is. There is no excuse to evade responsibility, and violence is not justified by cultural practices.

This recognition carries hermeneutical significance, particularly for Chinese readers, who perhaps carry cultural baggage that views submission as a virtue of womanhood. Violence against women could have been considered miserable, yet unavoidable, in traditional Chinese culture. Readings of CUV Judges 19 may confirm this kind of passivity, that women were subjected to such brutal violation in ancient Israel without any hint of condemnation from the biblical text. This perception is, however, misinformed by the translation that masks the critique of the Levite in the Hebrew. An understanding of the anti-Levite rhetoric would therefore enable Chinese readers to recognize the resistance to the violence that is inherent in the text and subsequently calls for reflection that challenge the traditional passivity in confronting violations.

In order to arrive at this reading perspective, Chinese Christian communities need to be freed from the "authority" of the CUV and fully recognize that it is a translation produced within the limitations of its context. Ideologies of the translators inevitably influenced their translation decisions, which, in circumstances such as Judges 19, do not enable readers to appreciate the meaning of the biblical text to the full extent. While it is not possible to achieve a context-free translation, one needs to acknowledge the role of the translators and their impact on the interpretations. A contextual reading of the text must therefore recognize the risk of relying on a single translation, and critically examine it within the translation context.

Conclusion

This chapter has demonstrated that the reading with an apparently adverse attitude toward the concubine from chapter 1 is very much a product of the translation context of the CUV. Compared to other Chinese translations, it neglects the anti-Levite rhetoric in the Hebrew narrative and replaces it with translation decisions that obscure the violence of the Levite. This is consistent with the ideologies of the Western missionaries toward the issue of concubinage in the translation context of the CUV. They rejected concubinage as a sin according to their Christian faith and were also bounded by the nineteenth-century ideals of Christian womanhood. In a political climate that threatened the acceptance of Christianity in China, they promoted submissiveness and avoided confrontation with Chinese authorities in the translation. This resulted in a translation that attempted to cover the violence *in* the text through violence done *to* the text, which in turn reinforced the traditional Chinese patriarchal values.

Chinese Christian communities in the past century have been influenced by the CUV in their interpretations of the narrative. Misinformed by the translation, the violation of the concubine is neglected, and the inherent resistance of the text is concealed. The negative image of the concubine from the beginning of the story may be considered as legitimizing the victimization of women in a culture that endorses such practices, and there is ostensibly no condemnation from the biblical text on such manifestations of evil. This misunderstanding can only be corrected when one engages with the context of the biblical text and reveals the anti-Levite rhetoric that is in fact most prominent in the discourse. This in turn would challenge attitudes dismissing the issue of violence against women as a "cultural matter." It was not deemed acceptable in the narrative situated even in patriarchal ancient Israel. As a test case, this reading of Judges 19 illustrates the potential of recovering the subversive message from the text through bringing together the reading context, translation context, and biblical context.

7

Concluding Reflections

WHO IS TO BLAME for the tragedy in Judges 19? The answer is clear: the narrative consistently points to the Levite, yet this rhetorical force is lost in the Chinese translation that was done in an anti-concubinage context.

This study has demonstrated the contribution of reading Judges 19 from a Chinese contextual perspective. Beginning with a socio-historical context of early Republican China, in which the issue of concubinage was a matter of controversy both in the society and in Chinese Christian circles, I reconstruct a reading that is sensitive to the element of concubinage in the narrative as well as to the traditional values in the Chinese culture. The translation of the CUV renders an interpretation that frames the discourse with the image of an unchaste concubine and implicitly puts the blame for the disastrous events upon her. The neglect of the responsibility of the Levite in the tragedy seems to legitimize violence against women, which calls for further investigation from different perspectives.

A comparative historical study of the practice of concubinage between the Hebrew Bible and the ancient Near Eastern is found to be helpful for understanding the identity of the *pîlegeš* in the text. It clarifies certain questions from scholarship and confirms that the concubine was considered married to the Levite though with a lower status than a full wife. The implication of this understanding entails that marital fidelity would have been expected of the concubine, which is significant to the interpretation of the narrative.

The literary artistry of the text was then examined through studying its narrative gaps and point-of-view. The use of narrative gaps reveals a crafted poetics of the interplay of omitted details. The combination of the gaps functions to draw the reader's attention toward the behavior of the Levite and establishes him as the protagonist of the narrative. Using Yamasaki's methodology of point-of-view study, I illustrate that the various planes of point-of-view consistently act to draw the empathy of readers away from the character of the Levite.

Intertextual study of the narrative also confirms an anti-Levite rhetoric in the text. The intertextual associations of Judges 19 (with Genesis 19 and 22,

1 Samuel 11, Deuteronomy 22, and 2 Samuel 13) suggest that the intertexts may be implied in the interpretation of the narrative and reflect the motifs of hospitality, rape, and sacrifice. Each of the motifs provokes comparison of the Levite with the characters in the intertexts, which pictures the Levite as acting against divine ordinances throughout the plot: (1) he seizes the concubine and pushes her to the mob, as opposed to the angels rescuing Lot; (2) he acts in a way that is parallel to a rapist, which subverts the concept of the husband of a raped woman as victim in the Deuteronomic sexual laws; (3) he performs prohibited human sacrifice that diverts from the divine instruction to Saul in sacrificing for military action. Contrary to the Chinese reading that neglects the Levite's behavior, the Hebrew text is in fact permeated with interpretive clues that condemn him.

Further clues are revealed through studying the text from an ideological perspective. By examining the Levite with standards of hegemonic masculinity in ancient Israel, it is evident that his manhood is frequently challenged in the narrative. His attempts to salvage his masculinity consistently lead to adverse consequences, which again provokes negative evaluation upon his character. This anti-Levite rhetoric combined with the pro-monarchic ideology in the text points to a political reconstruction of Josiah's reform, which promotes the regime of the king and his policy of centralizing worship in Jerusalem.

It is evident, therefore, that the reading of the Hebrew text has significant discrepancies with the CUV. This brings our attention to the translation context as well as the role of the translators of the CUV, who were Western missionaries. I propose that an anti-concubinage agenda among the missionaries, combined with the pressure to gain acceptance among Chinese authorities, rendered the translators less attentive to the anti-Levite rhetoric in the text and instead created an anti-concubine tendency in their translation. The apparent legitimization of violence against women from the CUV, therefore, is not founded in scriptural authority but represents a misinterpretation in the translation, which was bounded by its own context.

This contextual interpretation of Judges 19 stems from a Christian commitment to the authority of Scripture and acknowledges Chinese cultural influences in our reading of the Bible. The overall argument has considerable relevance for Chinese communities of faith. Using tools of biblical criticism, it also seeks to contribute to an understanding of the text beyond our own context. This study therefore demonstrates the fruitfulness of such research and provides a fresh model of contextual methodology for interpreting other passages in the Bible.

Bibliography

Ackerman, Susan. *Warrior, Dancer, Seductress, Queen: Women in Judges and Biblical Israel*. Anchor Bible Reference Library. New Haven: Yale University Press, 2009.

Albertz, Rainer. "Why a Reform Like Josiah's Must Have Happened." In *Good Kings and Bad Kings*, edited by Lester L. Grabbe, 27-46. LHBOTS 393. London: T. & T. Clark, 2005.

Allen, Graham. *Intertextuality*. 2nd ed. New Critical Idiom. London: Routledge, 2011.

Alter, Robert. *The Art of Biblical Narrative*. New York: Basic, 1981.

Amit, Yairah. *History and Ideology: An Introduction to Historiography in the Hebrew Bible*. Biblical Seminar 60. Sheffield: Sheffield Academic, 1999.

———. "Literature in the Service of Politics: Studies in Judges 19-21." In *Politics and Theopolitics in the Bible and Postbiblical Literature*, edited by Henning Reventlow et al., 28-40. JSOTSup 171. Sheffield: JSOT Press, 1994.

———. *The Book of Judges: the Art of Editing*. Biblical Interpretation Series 38. Leiden: Brill, 1999.

Baab, Otto J. "Concubine." In *The Interpreter's Dictionary of the Bible*, edited by George A. Buttrick, 1:666. New York: Abingdon, 1962.

Bal, Mieke. "A Body of Writing: Judges 19." In *A Feminist Companion to Judges*, edited by Athalya Brenner, 208-30. FCB 4. Sheffield: Sheffield Academic, 1993.

———. *Death & Dissymmetry: The Politics of Coherence in the Book of Judges*. Chicago Studies in the History of Judaism. Chicago: University of Chicago Press, 1988.

Bammer, Angelika. "On Being Faithful and Disloyal." In *Race, Class, and the Politics of Bible Translation*, edited by Randall C. Bailey and Tina Pippin, 135-46. Semeia 76. Atlanta: Scholars, 1996.

Bar-Efrat, Shimon. *Narrative Art in the Bible*. Bible and Literature Series 17. Sheffield: Almond, 1989.

Bechtel, Lyn M. "What If Dinah Is not Raped? (Genesis 34)." *JSOT* 62 (1994) 19-36.

Ben-Amos, Dan. "The Concept of Motif in Folklore." In *Folklore Studies in the Twentieth Century: Proceedings of the Centenary Conference of the Folklore Society*, edited by Venetia Newall, 17-36. Woodbridge, UK: Boydell & Brewer, 1980.

Berlin, Adele. *Poetics and Interpretation of Biblical Narrative*. Bible and Literature Series 9. Sheffield: Almond, 1983.

———. "Point of View in Biblical Narrative." In *A Sense of Text: The Art of Language in the Study of Biblical Literature: Papers from a Symposium at the Dropsie College for Hebrew and Cognate Learning, May 11, 1982*, edited by Stephen A. Geller, Edward L. Greenstein, and Adele Berlin, 71-113. Winona Lake, IN: Eisenbrauns, 1983.

Blenkinsopp, Joseph. "The Family in First Temple Israel." In *Families in Ancient Israel,* edited by Leo G. Perdue et al., 48-103. The Family, Religion, and Culture. Louisville: Westminster John Knox, 1997.
Block, Daniel I. "Echo Narrative Technique in Hebrew Literature: a Study in Judges 19." *WTJ* 52 (1990) 325-41.
———. *Judges, Ruth.* NAC 6. Nashville: Broadman & Holman, 1999.
Boer, Roland. "The Dynamic Equivalence Caper." In *Ideology, Culture, and Translation,* edited by Scott S. Elliott and Roland Boer, 13-24. SemeiaSt 69. Atlanta, GA: SBL, 2012.
Boer, Roland, and Fernando F. Segovia, eds. *The Future of the Biblical Past: Envisioning Biblical Studies on a Global Key.* SemeiaSt 66. Atlanta: SBL, 2012.
Boling, Robert G. *Judges: Introduction, Translation and Commentary.* AB 6A. Garden City, NY: Doubleday, 1975.
Bray, Jason S. *Sacred Dan: Religious Tradition and Cultic Practice in Judges 17-18.* LHBOTS 449. New York: T. & T. Clark, 2006.
Brenner, Athalya. *The Intercourse of Knowledge: On Gendering Desire and 'Sexuality' in the Hebrew Bible.* Leiden: Brill, 1997.
Brenner-Idan, Athalya. "So Where Are We? Some Reflections on Contextual Interpretations as Practiced." Paper presented at the 2016 SBL International Meeting, Seoul, July 3, 2016.
Briggs, Sheila. "The Deceit of the Sublime: An Investigation into the Origins of Ideological Criticism of the Bible in Early Nineteenth-Century German Biblical Studies." *Semeia* 59 (1992) 1-23.
Briggs, Will. "'A Man's Gotta Do What a Man's Gotta Do?': The Criticism of Hegemonic Masculinity in Judges 19:1-20:7." *JSOT* 42/1 (2017) 51-71.
Brueggemann, Walter. *Israel's Praise: Doxology against Idolatry and Ideology.* Philadelphia: Fortress, 1988.
Butler, Trent C. *Judges.* WBC 8. Nashville: Nelson, 2009.
Carrigan, Tim, et al. "Toward a New Sociology of Masculinity." In *The Making of Masculinities: The New Men's Studies,* edited by Harry Brod, 63-100. Boston: Allen & Unwin, 1987.
Chan, Bill 陳小標. "Lu zhenzong yiben" 呂振中譯本. https://www.translatebible.com/lu_zhenzhong.html.
Chang, Xin長辛. "Naqie de zuie" 納妾的罪惡. *Jia* 家 22 (1947) 384.
Chatman, Seymour. *Story and Discourse: Narrative Structure in Fiction and Film.* Ithaca, NY: Cornell University Press, 1978.
Chen, Chongqui 陳崇桂. "Lingxiu rixin: shishiji di shijiu zhang yige liwei ren qu nüzi wei qie" 靈修日新：士師記 第十九章——一个利未人娶女子為妾. *Budao zazhi* 佈道雜誌7/3 (1934) 68.
Chen, Lin 陳林. "Lun ming qing shiqi jidujiao dui zhongguo jiating guanxi de chongji" 論明清時期基督教對中國家庭關係的衝擊. *Fujian shifan daxue xuebao (zhexue shehui kexue ban)* 福建師範大學學報(哲學社會科學版) 5 (2005) 108-11.
Chen, Wenlian陳文聯 and Gui Yunqi 桂運奇. "Xixue dongjian yu zhongguo jindai hunyin biange sixiang de yanjin" 西學東漸與中國近代婚姻變革思想的演進. *Zhongnan daxue xuebao(shehui kexue ban)* 中南大學學報(社會科學版) 20/1 (2014) 216-22.
Cheng, Yu程鬱. *Qing zhi minguo xuqie xisu zhi bianqian*清至民國蓄妾習俗之變遷. Shanghai: Shanghai guji, 2006.
Cheung, James M張慕皚. *Shishi ji: luanshi zhong de zhengjiu* 士師記—亂世中的拯救. Shengming xinxi xilie生命信息系列. Hong Kong: Tien Dao, 2000.

Chia, Philip. "Biblical Studies in a Rising Asia: An Asian Perspective on the Future of the Biblical Past." In *The Future of the Biblical Past: Envisioning Biblical Studies on a Global Key*, edited by Roland Boer and Fernando F. Segovia, 81–95. SemeiaSt 66. Atlanta: SBL, 2012.

Chiu, Waiboon 趙維本. *Yijing suyuan: xiandai wuda zhongwen shengjing fanyi shi*譯經溯源──現代五大中文聖經翻譯史. Hong Kong: China Graduate School of Theology, 1993.

Choi, Kam To Daniel 蔡錦圖. *Yizhu shisui: qingmo minchu jidu xinjiao shengjing xuanji* 遺珠拾穗：清末民初基督新教聖經選輯. Xinbei: Ganlan, 2014.

Chong, Yau Yuk 莊柔玉. "Guannian yu xianxiang: cong wanjin yiben tanshi shengjing hanyi de yuanwen gainian" 觀念與現象──從晚近譯本探視聖經漢譯的原文概念. In *Zixi cudong: jidujiao laihua erbai nian lunji* 自西徂東──基督教來華二百年論集, edited by Lee Kam Keung 李金強 et al., 547–60. Hong Kong: Chinese Christian Literature, 2009.

———. *Jidujiao shengjing zhongwen yiben quanwei xianxiang yanjiu*基督教聖經中文譯本權威現象研究. Hong Kong: Chinese Bible International, 2000.

Chow, Lien-hwa 周聯華. "Heheben yijing yuanze he pinggu" 《和合本》譯經原則和評估. In *Zi shangdi shuo hanyu yilai: heheben shengjing jiushi nian*自上帝說漢語以來：《和合本》聖經九十年, edited by Philip P. Chia 謝品然 and Chin Ken-pa 曾慶豹, 1–16. Hong Kong: CABSA, 2010.

Clines, David J. A. *Interested Parties: The Ideology of Writers and Readers of the Hebrew Bible*. JSOTSup 205. Sheffield: Sheffield Academic, 1995.

Coker, K. Jason. "Translating from This Place: Social Location and Translation." In *Ideology, Culture, and Translation*, edited by Scott S. Elliott and Roland Boer, 25–38. SemeiaSt 69. Atlanta: SBL, 2012.

Creangă, Ovidiu. "Variations on the Theme of Masculinity: Joshua's Gender In/Stability in the Conquest Narrative." In *Men and Masculinity in the Hebrew Bible and Beyond*, edited by Ovidiu Creangă, 83–109. BMW 33. Sheffield: Sheffield Phoenix, 2010.

Cross, Frank Moore. *Canaanite Myth and Hebrew Epic: Essays in the History of the Religion of Israel*. Cambridge: Harvard University Press, 1973.

Daemmrich, Horst S. "Themes and Motifs in Literature: Approaches—Trends—Definition." *German Quarterly* 58 (1985) 566–75.

Davidson, Richard M. *Flame of Yahweh: Sexuality in the Old Testament*. Peabody, MA: Hendrickson, 2015.

Davies, Philip R. "Josiah and the Law Book." In *Good Kings and Bad Kings*, edited by Lester L. Grabbe, 65–77. LHBOTS 393. London: T. & T. Clark, 2005.

DiPalma, Brian Charles. "De/Constructing Masculinity in Exodus 1–4." In *Men and Masculinity in the Hebrew Bible and Beyond*, edited by Ovidiu Creangă, 36–53. BMW 33. Sheffield: Sheffield Phoenix, 2010.

Du, Yaquan 杜亞泉. "Lun xuqie" 論蓄妾. *Dongfang zazhi* 東方雜誌 4 (1911) 15–19.

Dumbrell, William J. "'In Those Days There Was No King in Israel; Every Man Did What Was Right in His Own Eyes': The Purpose of the Book of Judges Reconsidered." *JSOT* 25 (1983) 23–33.

Dwight, Sereno Edward. *The Hebrew Wife, or the Law of Marriage Examined in Relation to the Lawfulness of Polygamy and to the Extent of the Law of Incest*. Nineteenth Century Collections Online. New York: Leavitt, Lord, 1836. https://go.gale.com/ps/i.do?p=NCCO&u=nla&v=2.1&it=r&id=GALE%7CANBXIZ457854454&asid=1641618000000~f29adffe.

Edenburg, Cynthia. *Dismembering the Whole: Composition and Purpose of Judges 19–21*. AIL 24. Atlanta: Society of Biblical Literature, 2016.

———. "Ideology and Social Context of the Deuteronomic Women's Sex Laws (Deuteronomy 22:13–29)." *JBL* 1 (2009) 43–60.

Embry, Brad. "Narrative Loss, the (Important) Role of Women, and Community in Judges 19." In *Joshua and Judges*, edited by Athalya Brenner and Gale A. Yee, 257–73. Texts@Contexts. Minneapolis: Fortress, 2013.

Engelken, Karen. *Frauen im Alten Israel: eine begriffsgeschichtliche und sozialrechtliche Studie zur Stellung der Frau im Alten Testament*. Beiträge zur Wissenschaft vom Alten und Neuen Testament 130. Stuttgart: Kohlhammer, 1990.

———. "Pilegeš." In *Theological Dictionary of the Old Testament*, edited by Gerhard Johannes Botterweck et al., 9:549–51. Grand Rapids: Eerdmans, 2001.

Epstein. Louis M. "The Institution of Concubinage among the Jews." *Proceedings of the American Academy for Jewish Research* 6 (1934–35) 153–88.

Exum, J. Cheryl. "Feminist Criticism: Whose Interests are Being Served?" In *Judges and Method: New Approaches in Biblical Studies*, edited by Gale A. Yee, 65–89. Minneapolis: Fortress, 2007.

———. *Fragmented Women: Feminist (Sub)Versions of Biblical Narratives*. London: Bloomsbury T. & T. Clark, 2016.

Fields, Weston W. "The Motif 'Night as Danger' Associated with Three Biblical Destruction Narratives." In *"Sha'arei Talmon": Studies in the Bible, Qumran and the Ancient Near East: Presented to Shemaryahu Talmon*, edited by Michael A. Fishbane and Emanuel Tov, 17–32. Winona Lake, IN: Eisenbrauns, 1992.

———. *Sodom and Gomorrah: History and Motif in Biblical Narrative*. JSOTSup 231. Sheffield: Sheffield Academic, 1997.

Fokkelman, J. P. *Reading Biblical Narrative: An Introductory Guide*. Louisville: Westminster John Knox, 1999.

———. "Structural Remarks on Judges 9 and 19." In *Sha' arei Talmon: Studies in the Bible, Qumran, and the Ancient Near East Presented to Shemaryahu Talmon*, edited by Michael A. Fishbane and Emanuel Tov, 33–45. Winona Lake, IN: Eisenbrauns, 1992.

Fowl, Stephen. "Texts Don't Have Ideologies." *BibInt* 3 (1995) 15–34.

Freedman, William. "The Literary Motif: A Definition and Evaluation." *Novel: A Forum on Fiction* 4/2 (1971) 123–31.

Funk, Robert Walter. *The Poetics of Biblical Narrative*. Foundations & Facets: Literary Facets. Sonoma, CA: Polebridge, 1988.

Garbini, Giovanni. *History and Ideology in Ancient Israel*. Translated by John Bowden. London: SCM, 1988.

Genette, Gérard. *Narrative Discourse: An Essay in Method*. Translated by Jane E. Lewin. Ithaca, NY: Cornell University Press, 1983.

George, Mark K. "Masculinity and Its Regimentation in Deuteronomy." In *Men and Masculinity in the Hebrew Bible and Beyond*, edited by Ovidiu Creangă, 64–82. BMW 33. Sheffield: Sheffield Phoenix, 2010.

Gerber, Wayne J. "English Translations of Scripture: The New Life Version of the Holy Bible," 16. http://www.centralkentuckybiblestudents.org/The%20New%20Life%20Bible.pdf.

Gilmore, David D. "Introduction: The Shame of Dishonor." In *Honor and Shame and the Unity of the Mediterranean*, edited by David D. Gilmore, 2–21. Washington, DC: American Anthropological Association, 1987.
Guillaume, Philippe. *Waiting for Josiah: The Judges*. London: Clark, 2006.
Guo, Songyi 郭松義. *Qingdai juan* 清代卷. Zhongguo funü tongshi中國婦女通史 9, edited by Chen Gaohua 陳高華 and Tong Shaosu童芍素. Hangzhou: Hangzhou chubanshe, 2010.
Gur-Klein, Thalia. *Sexual Hospitality in the Hebrew Bible: Patronymic, Metronymic, Legitimate, and Illegitimate Relations*. Sheffield: Equinox, 2013.
Haddox, Susan E. "Favoured Sons and Subordinate Masculinities." In *Men and Masculinity in the Hebrew Bible and Beyond*, edited by Ovidiu Creangă, 2–19. BMW 33. Sheffield: Sheffield Phoenix, 2010.
Hallo, William W., and K. Lawson Younger, eds. *The Context of Scripture*. Vol. 1: *Canonical Compositions from the Biblical World*. Leiden: Brill, 2003.
Hao, Jinxian 郝晋賢. "Feichu naqie zhi pianmian guan" 廢除納妾之片面觀. *Bingzhou xueyuan yuekan* 并州學院月刊 1/7 (1934) 5–9.
Hays, Christopher B. *Hidden Riches: A Sourcebook for the Comparative Study of the Hebrew Bible and Ancient Near East*. Louisville: Westminster John Knox, 2014.
"Heheben xiudingban" 和合本修訂版. Hong Kong Bible Society. http://www.hkbs.org.hk/tw/content/14-revised-chinese-union-version3.
Hobbs, T. R. "Hospitality in the First Testament and the 'Teleological Fallacy.'" *JSOT* 26/1 (2001) 3–30.
Hudson, Don Michael. "Living in a Land of Epithets: Anonymity in Judges 19–21." *JSOT* 62 (1994) 49–66.
Janzen, David. *The Social Meanings of Sacrifice in the Hebrew Bible: A Study of Four Writings*. BZAW 344. Berlin: de Gruyter, 2004.
John, Griffith. *Yin Jia Dong Dao* 引家當道. Hankou: Shengjiao shuju, 1882. https://nla.gov.au/nla.obj-459581 59/view?partId=nla.obj-45958168.
Jones-Warsaw, Koala. "Toward a Womanist Hermeneutic: A Reading of Judges 19–21." In *A Feminist Companion to Judges*, edited by Athalya Brenner, 172–86. FCB 4. Sheffield: Sheffield Academic, 1993.
Jüngling, Hans-Winfried. *Richter 19: Ein Pladoyer für das Konigtum: Stilistische Analyse der Tendenzerzahlung Ri 19,1–30a; 21,25*. Analecta Biblica 84. Rome: Biblical Institute Press, 1981.
Kamuf, Peggy. "Author of a Crime." In *A Feminist Companion to Judges*, edited by Athalya Brenner, 187–207. FCB 4. Sheffield: Sheffield Academic, 1993.
Kawashima, Robert S. "Could a Woman Say 'no' in Biblical Israel?: On the Genealogy of Legal Status in Biblical Law and Literature." *AJS Review* 35/1 (2011) 1–22.
Keefe, Alice A. "Rapes of Women/Wars of Men." *Semeia* 61 (1993) 79–97.
King, Marjorie. "Exporting Femininity, Not Feminism: Nineteenth Century U.S. Missionary Women's Effort to Emancipate Chinese Women." In *Women's Work for Women: Missionaries and Social Change in Asia*, edited by Leslie A. Flemming, 117–35. Boulder, CO: Westview, 1989.
Kiruki, Joseph Kahiga. "Polygamy: A Pastoral Challenge to the Church in Africa." *AFER* 49/1–2 (March 2007) 119–47.
Klein, Lillian R. *The Triumph of Irony in the Book of Judges*. JSOTSup 68. Sheffield: Almond, 1989.

Knight, Mark. "Wirkungsgeschichte, Reception History, Reception Theory." *JSOT* 33 (2010) 137–46.

Knoppers Gary N. "The Deuteronomist and the Deuteronomic Law of the King: A Reexamination of a Relationship." *ZAW* 108 (2009) 329–46.

Kristeva, Julia. *Desire in Language: A Semiotic Approach to Literature and Art*. Edited by Leon S. Roudiez. Translated by Thomas Gora. Oxford: Blackwell, 1980.

Kuja, Ryan "Remembering the Body: Misogyny through the Lens of Judges 19." *Feminist Theology* 25 (2016) 89–95.

Kwok, Pui-lan. *Chinese Women and Christianity: 1860–1927*. American Academy of Religion Academy Series 75. Atlanta: Scholars, 1992.

Lapsley, Jacqueline E. *Whispering the Word: Hearing Women's Stories in the Old Testament*. Louisville: Westminster John Knox, 2005.

Lasine, Stuart. "Guest and Host in Judges 19: Lot's Hospitality in an Inverted World." *JSOT* 29 (1984) 37–59.

Lee, Archie C.C. 李熾昌. *Kua wenben yuedu: xibolai shengjing quanshi* 跨文本閱讀—《希伯來聖經》詮釋. Shanghai: Shanghai Sanlian, 2015.

———. "Guoyu heheben shengjing: jingdian fanyi yihuo zongjiao chuanbo?" 國語《和合本》聖經：經典翻譯抑或宗教傳播? In *Zi shangdi shuo hanyu yilai: heheben shengjing jiushi nian* 自上帝說漢語以來：《和合本》聖經九十年, edited by Philip P. Chia 謝品然 and Chin Ken-pa 曾慶豹, 71–89. Hong Kong: CABSA, 2010.

Leeb, Carolyn S. *Away from the Father's House: The Social Location of Na'ar and Na'arah in Ancient Israel*. JSOTSup 301. Sheffield: Sheffield Academic, 2000.

Legge, James. "Yabolahan jilüe" 亞伯拉罕記畧. In *Wanqing jidujiao xushi wenxue xuancui* 晚清基督教敘事文學選粹, edited by John T. P. Lai 黎子鵬, 47–78. Xinbei: Ganlan, 2012.

Leuchter, Mark. *The Levites and the Boundary of Israelite Identity*. New York: Oxford University Press, 2017.

Levinson, Bernard M. "The Reconceptualization of Kingship in Deuteronomy and the Deuteronomistic History's Transformation of Torah." *VT* 51 (2001) 520–34.

Li, Fayu 李發餘. "Siyang jiaowu suowen" 泗陽教務瑣聞. *Tongwenbao yesujiao jiating xinwen* 通問報 耶穌教家庭新聞 1230 (1926) 7–8.

Li, Fangshu 李方樞. "Naqie yu zuoqie de bihai" 納妾與做妾的弊害. *Xinmin bao banyuekan* 新民報半月刊 5/8 (1943) 37–38.

Liang, Gong 梁工. *Shengjing xushi yishu yanjiu* 聖經敘事藝術研究. Beijing: The Commercial, 2007.

Lipka, Hilary "Masculinities in Proverbs: An Alternative to the Hegemonic Ideal." In *Biblical Masculinities Foregrounded*, edited by Ovidiu Creangă and Peter-Ben Smit, 86–103. Hebrew Bible Monographs 62. Sheffield: Sheffield Phoenix, 2014.

———. *Sexual Transgression in the Hebrew Bible*. Sheffield: Sheffield Phoenix, 2006.

Luo, Zhufeng 羅竹風, ed. *Hanyu dacidian* 漢語大詞典. Volume 4. Shanghai: Chinese Dictionary, 1989.

Măcerlau, Marcel. "Saul in the Company of Men: (De)Constructing Masculinity in 1 Samuel 9–31." In *Biblical Masculinities Foregrounded*, edited by Ovidiu Creangă and Peter-Ben Smit, 51–68. Hebrew Bible Monographs 62. Sheffield: Sheffield Phoenix, 2014.

Mak, George K.W 麥金華. *Daying shengshu gonghui yu guanhua heheben shengjing fanyi* 大英聖書公會與官話《和合本》聖經翻譯. Jingfeng congshu 景風叢書 18. Hong Kong: CSCCRC, 2010.

Mathey, Jennifer M. "Mute and Mutilated: Understanding Judges 19-21 as a משל of Dialogue." *BibInt* 25 (2017) 625-46.

Matthews, Victor H. "Hospitality and Hostility in Genesis 19 and Judges 19." *BTB* 22 (1992) 3-11.

———. *Judges and Ruth*. NCBC. Cambridge: Cambridge University Press, 2004.

Mayes, Andrew D.H. "Deuteronomistic Royal Ideology in Judges 17-21." *BibInt* 9 (2001) 241-58.

McComiskey, Thomas. "The Status of the Secondary Wife: Its Development in Ancient Near Eastern Law. A Study and Comprehensive Index." PhD diss., Brandeis University, 1965.

McKenzie, John L. *The World of the Judges*. Prentice-Hall Backgrounds to the Bible Series. Englewood Cliffs, NJ: Prentice-Hall, 1966.

Medhurst, Walter Henry. "Shentian zhi shitiao jie zhuming" 神天之十條誡註明. In *Yizhu shisui: qingmo minchu jidu xinjiao shengjing xuanji* 遺珠拾穗：清末民初基督新教聖經選輯, edited by Choi Kam To Daniel 蔡錦圖, 17-106. Xinbei: Ganlan, 2014.

Meek, Russell L. "Intertextuality, Inner-Biblical Exegesis, and Inner-Biblical Allusion: The Ethics of a Methodology." *Biblica* 95 (2014) 280-91.

Meng, Zhenhua. "Remembering Ancestors: A Levitical Genealogy in Yehud and the Bohai Gaos Genealogy of Gao Huan." In *Remembering and Forgetting in Early Second Temple Judah*, edited by Ehud Ben Zvi and Christoph Levin, 257-68. FAT 85. Tübingen: Mohr Siebeck, 2012.

Meyers, Carol L. *Rediscovering Eve: Ancient Israelite Women in Context*. Oxford: Oxford University Press, 2013.

Michelson, Marty Alan. *Reconciling Violence and Kingship: A Study of Judges and 1 Samuel*. Eugene, OR: Pickwick Publications, 2011.

Miller, Geoffrey David. "Intertextuality in Old Testament Research." *Currents in Biblical Research* 9 (2011) 283-309.

Milstein, Sara J. "Echoes of Saul: Revision through Introduction in Judges 19-21, 1 Samuel 1, and 1 Samuel 11." In *Tracking the Master Scribe: Revision through Introduction in Biblical and Mesopotamian Literature*, 174-206. New York: Oxford University Press, 2016.

Monroe, Lauren A.S. "Disembodied Women: Sacrificial Language and the Deaths of Bat-Jephthah, Cozbi, and the Bethlehemite Concubine." *CBQ* 75 (2013) 32-52.

Moore, Stephen D. "Biblical Narrative Analysis from the New Criticism to the New Narratology." In *The Oxford Handbook of Biblical Narrative*, edited by Donna Nolan Fewell, 27-50. New York: Oxford University Press, 2016.

Morgan, James M. "How Do Motifs Endure and Perform? Motif Theory for the Study of Biblical Narratives." *Revue Biblique* 122 (2015) 194-216.

Morschauser, Scott. "'Hospitality,' Hostiles and Hostages: On the Legal Background to Genesis 19.1-9." *JSOT* 27 (2003) 461-85.

Moster, David Z. "The Levite of Judges 19-21." *JBL* 134 (2015) 721-30.

Na'aman, Nadav. "Sojourners and Levites in the Kingdom of Judah." *Zeitschrift für Altorientalische und Biblische Rechtsgeschichte* 14 (2008) 237-79.

Nadella, Raj. "Postcolonialism, Translation, and Colonial Mimicry." In *Ideology, Culture, and Translation*, edited by Scott S. Elliott and Roland Boer, 49–57. SemeiaSt 69. Atlanta: SBL, 2012.

"Naqie zhi hai" 納妾之害, *Jiangyan huibian* 講演彙編 8 (1916) 75.

Nelson, Richard D. *The Double Redaction of the Deuteronomistic History*. JSOTSup 18. Sheffield: JSOT, 1981.

Neufeld, E. *Ancient Hebrew Marriage Laws: With Special References to General Semitic Laws and Customs*. London: Longmans, Green, 1944.

Niditch, Susan. *Judges: A Commentary*. Old Testament Library. Louisville: Westminster John Knox, 2008.

———. "The 'Sodomite' Theme in Judges 19–20: Family, Community, and Social Disintegration." *CBQ* 44 (1982) 365–78.

Ng, Vivien W. "Ideology and Sexuality: Rape Laws in Qing China." *Journal of Asian Studies* 46 (1987) 57–70.

O'Connell, Robert H. *The Rhetoric of the Book of Judges*. VTSup 63. Leiden: Brill, 1996.

Pitt-Rivers, Julian. "The Stranger, the Guest, and the Hostile Host: Introduction to the Study of the Law of Hospitality." In *Contributions to Mediterranean Sociology*, edited by J. G. Peristiany, 13–30. Paris: Mouton, 1963.

Punt, Jeremy. "Dealing (with) the Past and Future of Biblical Studies: A New South African Perspective." In *The Future of the Biblical Past: Envisioning Biblical Studies on a Global Key*, edited by Roland Boer and Fernando F. Segovia, 29–45. SemeiaSt 66. Atlanta: SBL, 2012.

Pressler, Carolyn. *The View of Women Found in the Deuteronomic Family Laws*. BZAW 216. Berlin: de Gruyter, 1993.

———. "Wives and Daughters, Bond and Free" In *Gender and Law in the Hebrew Bible and the Ancient Near East*, edited by Victor Harold Matthews et al., 147–72. JSOTSup 262. London: T. & T. Clark, 2012.

Qian, Xiemin 錢協民. "Jinzhi naqie wenti zhi shangque" 禁止納妾問題之商榷. *Lisheng* 離聲 6 (1920) 94–101.

Qu, Ningning 曲寧寧. "Yishi toushe: shijiu shiji meiguo jidu xinjiao zaihua nü chuanjiaoshi yanjiu bing yi muladi (Lottie Moon) wei gean" 意識投射：19世紀美國基督新教在華女傳教士研究—並以慕拉蒂(Lottie Moon)爲個案. In *Xingbie yu lishi : jindai zhongguo funü yuji dujiao* 性別與歷史：近代中國婦女與基督教, edited by Tao Feiya 陶飛亞, 322–37. Shanghai: Shanghai renwen, 2006.

Rabin, Chaim. "The Origin of the Hebrew Word *Pîlegeš*." *JJS* 25 (1974) 353–64.

Ren, Dongsheng 任東升. *Shengjing hanyi wenhua yanjiu* 聖經漢譯文化研究. Zhonghua fanyi yanjiu congshu 中華翻譯研究叢書 2:11. 武漢：湖北教育出版社, 2007.

Riches, John. "Cultural Bias in European and North American Biblical Scholarship." In *Ethnicity and the Bible*, edited by Mark G. Brett, 431–48. Biblical Interpretation Series 19. Leiden: Brill, 1996.

Römer, Thomas, and Albert de Pury. "Deuteronomistic Historiography (DH): History of Research and Debated Issues." In *Israel Constructs Its History: Deuteronomistic Historiography in Recent Research*, edited by Albert de Pury et al., 24–141. JSOTSup 306. Sheffield: Sheffield Academic, 2000.

Rooke, Deborah. "Kingship and Priesthood: the Relationship between the High Priesthood and the Monarchy." In *King and Messiah in Israel and the Ancient Near East:*

Proceedings of the Oxford Old Testament Seminar, edited by John Day, 187–208. JSOTSup 270. Sheffield: Sheffield Academic, 2013.

Ruggieri, Michele. "Tianzhu shengjiao shilu" 天主聖教實錄(節錄). In *Hanyu shenxue duben* Volume I 漢語神學讀本(上冊), edited by He Guanghu何光滬and Daniel H. N. Yeung 楊熙楠, 31–52. Hong Kong: Logos and Pneuma, 2009.

Schneider, Tammi J. *Judges*. Berit Olam. Collegeville, MN: Liturgical, 2000.

Scholz, Susanne. *Sacred Witness: Rape in the Hebrew Bible*. Minneapolis: Fortress, 2014.

Shan, Yuyuan 單毓元. "Zhongguo jinzhi naqie zhi fangfa" 中國禁止納妾之方法. *Xin zhongguo* 新中國1/5 (1919) 103–09.

Shang, Xuzhi 尚緒芝. "Zhongguo gudai shehui 'yifu yiqi zhi naqie zhi' bingcun yuanyin tanxi" 中國古代社會"一夫一妻制納妾制"並存原因探析. *Zhongzhou xueqian* 中州學刊 159/3 (2007) 176–78.

"Shengjing xinyiben jieshao: chuancheng yu kaita" 《聖經新譯本》介紹——傳承與開拓. Worldwide Bible Society. http://www.wwbible.org/聖經新譯本.

Shi, Yongnan施永南. *Naqie zongheng tan* 納妾縱橫談. Beijing: Zhongguo shijieyu, 1998.

"Shuo naqie zhi hai" 說納妾之害, *Jiangyan huibian* 講演彙編 7 (1916) 80–84.

Ska, Jean-Louis. *"Our Fathers Have Told Us": Introduction to the Analysis of Hebrew Narratives*. Subsidia Biblica 13. Rome: Pontifical Biblical Institute Press, 2000.

Smith, Abraham. "The Productive Role of English Bible Translators." In *Race, Class, and the Politics of Bible Translation*, edited by Randall C. Bailey and Tina Pippin, 55–68. Semeia 76. Atlanta: Scholars, 1996.

Soggin, J. Alberto. *Judges: A Commentary*. Old Testament Library. Philadelphia: Westminster, 1981.

Sommer, Benjamin D. *A Prophet Reads Scripture: Allusion in Isaiah 40–66*. Stanford, CA: Stanford University Press, 1998.

Starr, Chloë. "Introduction." In *Reading Christian Scriptures in China*, edited by Chloë Starr, 1–9. London: T. & T. Clark, 2008.

Sternberg, Meir. *The Poetics of Biblical Narrative: Ideological Literature and the Drama of Reading*. Indiana Studies in Biblical Literature. Bloomington: Indiana University Press, 1999.

Still, Judith, and Michael Worton. "Introduction." In *Intertextuality: Theories and Practices*, edited by Michael Worton and Judith Still, 1–44. Manchester: Manchester University Press, 1995.

Stone, Ken. "Gender and Homosexuality in Judges 19: Subject-Honor, Object-Shame?" *JSOT* 67 (1995) 87–107.

Sugirtharajah, R. S. *Postcolonial Criticism and Biblical Interpretation*. Oxford: Oxford University Press, 2009.

Talmon, Shemaryahu. "The 'Comparative Method' in Biblical Interpretation—Principles and Problems," In *Congress Volume, Göttingen, 1977*, 320–56. VTSup 29. Leiden: Brill, 1978.

———. "The 'Desert Motif' in the Bible and in Qumran Literature." In *Biblical Motifs: Origins and Transformations*, edited by Alexander Altmann, 31–63. Cambridge: Harvard University Press, 1966.

———. "In Those Days There Was no מלך in Israel." In *King, Cult, and Calendar in Ancient Israel: Collected Studies*, 39–52. Jerusalem: Magnes, 1986.

———. *Literary Motifs and Patterns in the Hebrew Bible: Collected Studies*. Winona Lake, IN: Eisenbrauns, 2014.

Taylor, James Patton. "Ideology and Ideological Criticism of Old Testament Texts." PhD diss., University of Sheffield, 2006. https://etheses.whiterose.ac.uk/3621/1/485074.pdf.

Tian, Haihua. "Confucian Catholics' Appropriation of the Decalogue—a Case Study in Cross-textual Reading." In *Reading Christian Scriptures in China*, edited by Chloë Starr, 163–80. London: T. & T. Clark, 2008.

Tianjin funü gailiang huibao 天津婦女改良會報. "Lun naqie zhi feili jiqi yihai wuqiong" 論納妾之非理及其遺害無窮. *Zhenguang bao* 真光報 10/6 (1911) 36–39.

Trible, Phyllis. *Texts of Terror: Literary-Feminist Readings of Biblical Narratives*. Overtures to Biblical Theology. Philadelphia: Fortress, 1984.

Tsang, Jacob C. S 曾祥新. *Shishi ji* 士師記. Tiandao shengjing zhushi 天道聖經註釋. Hong Kong: Tien Dao, 1998.

Tull, Patricia. "Intertextuality and the Hebrew Scriptures." *Currents in Research: Biblical Studies* 8 (2000) 59–90.

Unterman, Jeremiah. "The Literary Influence of 'the Binding of Isaac' (Genesis 22) on 'the Outrage at Gibeah' (Judges 19)." *Hebrew Annual Review* 4 (1980) 161–66.

Uspensky, Boris. *A Poetics of Composition: The Structure of the Artistic Text and Typology of a Compositional Form*. Translated by Valentina Zavarin and Susan Wittig. Berkeley: University of California Press, 1983.

van Wolde, Ellen. "Does *'innâ* Denote Rape? A Semantic Analysis of a Controversial Word." *VT* 4 (2002) 528–44.

Wang, Mingdao 王明道. "Naqie yu lihun" 納妾與離婚. *Lingshi jikan* 靈食季刊 62 (1942) 49–64.

Wang, Shaoxi 王紹璽. *Xiaoqie shi* 小妾史. Shanghai: Shanghai Literature & Art, 1995.

Watts, James W. "The Rhetoric of Sacrifice." In *Ritual and Metaphor: Sacrifice in the Bible*, edited by Christian Eberhart, 3–16. Resources for Biblical Study 68. Leiden: Brill, 2012.

Webb, Barry G. *The Book of Judges*. NICOT. Grand Rapids: Eerdmans, 2012.

Wei, Zengdi 味增德. "Gei naqiezhe yi dangtou yibang" 給納妾者以當頭一棒. *Gongjiao zhoukan* 公教周刊 94 (1931) 2–6.

Wilson, Stephen M. *Making Men: The Male Coming-of-Age Theme in the Hebrew Bible*. New York: Oxford University Press, 2015.

Wong, Gregory T. K. *Compositional Strategy of the Book of Judges: An Inductive, Rhetorical Study*. VTSup 111. Leiden: Brill, 2006.

Wu, Timothy 吳獻章. *Beiyue chenlun de xunhuan guiji: shishi ji xidu* 背約沉淪的循環軌跡：士師記析讀. Hong Kong: Logos, 2009.

Wuming nüshi 無名女士. "Zhongguo naqie de wojian" 中國納妾的我見. *Qingnianyou* 青年友 4/10 (1924) 39–41.

Yamada, Frank M. *Configurations of Rape in the Hebrew Bible: A Literary Analysis of Three Rape Narratives*. Studies in Biblical Literature 109. New York: Lang, 2008.

Yamasaki, Gary. *Perspective Criticism: Point of View and Evaluative Guidance in Biblical Narrative*. Eugene, OR: Cascade Books, 2012.

———. *Watching a Biblical Narrative: Point of View in Biblical Exegesis*. London: T. & T. Clark, 2007.

Yan, Lin. "'Who Is More to You than Seven Sons': A Cross-textual Reading between the Book of Ruth and a Pair of Peacocks to the Southeast Fly." In *Reading Ruth in Asia*, edited by Jione Havea and Peter H. W. Lau, 47–55. International Voices in Biblical Studies 7. Atlanta: SBL, 2015.

Yang, Huilin. "The Union Chinese Version of the Bible and Its Hermeneutical Analysis." *Contemporary Chinese Thought* 36 (2004) 85–99.
Yao, Esther S. L. *Chinese Women, Past & Present.* Mesquite, TX: Ide House, 1983.
Yee, Gale A. "Ideological Criticism." In *Dictionary of Biblical Interpretation,* edited by J. H. Hayes, 534–37. Vol. 1. Nashville: Abingdon, 1999.
———. "Ideological Criticism: Judges 17–21 and the Dismembered Body." In *Judges and Method: New Approaches in Biblical Studies,* edited by Gale A. Yee, 138–57. Minneapolis: Fortress, 2007.
Yeo, K. K. *Musing with Confucius and Paul: Toward a Chinese Christian Theology.* Eugene, OR: Cascade Books, 2008.
Yu, Shaoming余紹明. "Ruhe feichu naqie zhidu" 如何廢除納妾制度. *Falü yuekan* 法律月刊 4 (1930) 49–55.
Zetzsche, Jost Oliver. *The Bible in China: the History of the Union Version, or, the Culmination of Protestant Missionary Bible Translation in China.* Sankt Augustin: Monumenta Serica Institute, 1999.
Zewi, Tamar. "The Particles הִנֵּה and וְהִנֵּה in Biblical Hebrew." *Hebrew Studies* 37 (1996) 21–38.
Zheng, Yongfu鄭永福 and Lu Meiyi呂美頤. *Minguo juan* 民國卷. Zhongguo funü tongshi中國婦女通史 10, edited by Chen Gaohua 陳高華 and Tong Shaosu童芍素. Hangzhou: Hangzhou chubanshe, 2010.
Zhuo, Xinping 卓新平. *Jidujiao yu zhongguo wenhua chujing* 基督教與中國文化處境. Beijing: China Religious Culture, 2013.

Author Index

Ackerman, Susan, 30n9, 33n29, 43
Albertz, Rainer, 156n89
Allen, Graham, 87n4, 88n5–n7, n9, n12, 89n13, n15–16, n18, 90n21
Alter, Robert, 53, 57n26
Amit, Yairah, 1n3, 104n74, 127n139, 132n12, 138–39, 154

Baab, Otto J., 2n6
Bammer, Angelika, 171
Bar-Efrat, Shimon, 53, 71, 75n83, 82n100
Bechtel, Lyn M., 114n97, 115
Ben-Amos, Dan, 93n36
Blenkinsopp, Joseph, 37–38n39
Block, Daniel I., 24n90, 30n6, 101–3, 149n78
Boer, Roland, 170n36
Boling, Robert G, 1n1, 2n8, 18n80, 30n6, 34, 59n36, 60n40, 65n51, 100n54
Brenner, Athalya, 19n84, 115
Brenner-Idan, Athalya, xiv–xv
Briggs, Sheila, 132
Briggs, Will, 143n48
Brueggemann, Walter, 131
Butler, Trent C., 1n1, 2n8, 18n78, 30, 148n76, 152n83

Carrigan, Tim, 144
Chan, Bill 陳小標, 165n28
Chang, Xin 長辛, 9n41
Chatman, Seymour, 70–71
Chen, Chongqui 陳崇桂, 13n60–62, 21n88, 178n67

Cheng, Yu 程鬱, 5n19, n21, n23, 6n28, n30, 7n32–33, n35, 8n36–37, 10n48, 11n49–50, n53, 12n57, 13n59, n63, 14n65, 15n71, 27n91
Cheung, James M. 張慕皚, 178–79, 183
Chia, Philip 謝品然, xivn2
Chiu, Waiboon 趙維本, 165n28–30, 176n57
Chong, Yau Yuk 莊柔玉, 4n15, 160n4, 164n18, 176–77
Clines, David J. A., 131, 143n48, 144–47
Coker, K. Jason, 170

Daemmrich, Horst S., 94n37
Davidson, Richard M., 38
Davies, Philip R., 156n89
DiPalma, Brian Charles, 145n60, n62
Du, Yaquan 杜亞泉, 9n42, 16n73
Dumbrell, William J., 154n85
Dwight, Sereno Edward, 38

Edenburg, Cynthia, 18, 60n40, 99–100, 102–6, 111, 113–14, 116–19, 154
Embry, Brad, 65n50
Engelken, Karen, 2n6–7, 39n47, 40n48–49, 41–43, 46n70, 50
Exum, J. Cheryl, 18n81, 30–31, 32n19, 136–37

Fields, Weston W., 107, 108, 111
Fokkelman, J. P., 55, 57, 77, 78n94
Fowl, Stephen, 130n2
Freedman, William, 94–96
Funk, Robert W., 57

201

Garbini, Giovanni, 132n12
Genette, Gérard, 70
George, Mark K., 146
Gerber, Wayne J., 30n5
Gui Yunqi 桂運奇, 13n62
Guo, Songyi 郭松義, 4n17, 6n26–27, n29, 7n34, 11n52, 54
Gur-Klein, Thalia, 112n91

Haddox, Susan E., 145n60
Hallo, William W., 36
Hao, Jinxian 郝晋賢, 9n42, 10n47
Hays, Christopher B., 36n37
Hobbs, T. R., 63n48, 107n80, 108–110
Hudson, Don Michael, 157n91

Janzen, David, 120–25, 126n138
John, Griffith, 13, 14n64
Jones-Warsaw, Koala, 30n10, 137

Kamuf, Peggy, 137n32
Kawashima, Robert S., 115
Keefe, Alice A., 116n104, 117n109
King, Marjorie, 173–74
Kiruki, Joseph Kahiga, 3n13
Kristeva, Julia, 87–90, 92, 98
Kuja, Ryan, 136n26, 137
Kwok, Pui-lan, 173n49, 174

Lapsley, Jacqueline E., 16n75, 18, 21n87, 55–57, 151n82
Lasine, Stuart, 24n90, 101–5, 111n90
Lee, Archie C., xiv, xvn6, 171n41, 172n44, 175n56
Leeb, Carolyn S., 113
Legge, James, 15
Leuchter, Mark, 141n42–43
Li, Fangshu 李方樞, 3n12, 9n40, 16n74
Liang, Gong 梁工, 52n1
Lipka, Hilary, 113n96, 114–17, 144n53, n55
Lu, Meiyi 呂美頤, 3n10, 10n46
Luo, Zhufeng 羅竹風, 5n18

Mak, George K. W. 麥金華, 172n44–45
Mathey, Jennifer M., 126n137
Mayes, Andrew D., 134n18

McComiskey, Thomas, 2n6, 38n42, 44–46, 48n78
McKenzie, John L., 30n13
Medhurst, Walter Henry, 14–15
Meek, Russell L., 92n29–33
Meng, Zhenhua, xivn5
Milstein, Sara J., 104n74
Monroe, Lauren A., 119n114
Moore, Stephen D., 52n2, 53
Morgan, James M., 94n41, 95–97

Na'aman, Nadav, 141n41
Nadella, Raj, 172n42
Neufeld, E., 38–40, 44, 46, 47n74–75, 48n77
Ng, Vivien W., 12n55–56
Niditch, Susan, 18n81, 30–31, 43, 100–101, 103, 109n85, 111n88

O'Connell, Robert H., 104n71, 154n84

Punt, Jeremy, xivn2

Qian, Xiemin 錢協民, 9n42
Qu, Ningning 曲寧寧, 174n53

Rabin, Chaim, 40n50
Ren, Dongsheng 任東升, 161n9
Riches, John, xivn1, 36n37
Rooke, Deborah, 123n130
Ruggieri, Michele, 14

Shang, Xuzhi 尚緒芝, 4, 13n58
Shi, Yongnan 施永南, 4n16–17, 5n20, n22, 6n25, 8n38
Ska, Jean-Louis, 52n4
Smith, Abraham, 171n39
Soggin, J. Alberto, 2n8, 18n80, 30, 43, 127n139, 154
Sommer, Benjamin D., 86n1, 91
Starr, Chloë, xvi, 4n14
Sternberg, Meir, 53–54, 56–61, 62n45, 63n47, 67, 69, 71n68–69, 74
Still, Judith, 87n3
Stone, Ken, 35–36n35, 143, 148, 150

Taylor, James Patton, 131–32, 133n13, 134n17–18, 142n46

Tian, Haihua, xivn5
Tsang, Jacob C. S. 曾祥新, 181–83
Tull, Patricia, 88–89, 90n19

Unterman, Jeremiah, 119n112
Uspensky, Boris, 56, 70–72, 74, 76, 83

Wang, Mingdao 王明道, 16n72, 23n89
Wang, Shaoxi 王紹璽, 7n32
Watts, James W., 121, 124
Webb, Barry G., 30n6, 32, 49n80, 59n36, 66n52, 100n54, 150n79
Wei, Zengdi 味增德, 16n72
Wilson, Stephen M., 143n48, 144n55–56, 145–47
Wolde, Ellen van, 114n96
Wong, Gregory T., 62n46
Worton, Michael, 87n3

Wu, Timothy 吳獻章, 180–81, 183

Yamada, Frank M., 116n130
Yamasaki, Gary, 53, 57, 70–80, 82–85, 186
Yan, Lin, xivn5
Yang, Huilin, 172n44
Yao, Esther S., 10n44
Yee, Gale A., xviiin11, 1n2, 110n87, 129n1, 130–31, 133–35, 138–42, 151n82, 153, 154n84, 156, 158
Yeo, K. K., 2n9
Yu, Shaoming 余紹明, 9n43

Zetzsche, Jost Oliver, 17n77, 160n1–3, 161n5–8, n10, 164–165n19–25
Zheng, Yongfu 鄭永福, 3n10, 10n46
Zhuo, Xinping 卓新平, xvn7

Subject Index

Abraham, 3, 5, 15–16, 21, 38, 82, 119
ambiguity, 18, 29–31, 52–53, 59–60,
    62–63, 65–67, 80–82, 168, 180,
    182
    definition, 57–59
    in Judg 19:2–3, 60–63
    in Judg 19:5–8, 63–65
    in Judg 19:25, 65–66
    in Judge 19:27–29, 67–68
Amit, Yairah, 1n3, 104n74, 127n139,
    132n12, 138–39, 154
Assyrian laws, 44, 47–48

chastity, 5, 11–12, 17, 19, 22–23, 26, 147
Cheung, James M. 張慕皚, 178–79, 183
Chinese New Version (CNV), 165,
    166–70
Chinese Union Version (CUV), 17–26,
    159, 161–70, 172–85
    dominance of, 176–77
    history and translation principles,
    160–61
Code of Hammurabi, 45–48
comparative approach, 29, 50–51
concubinage in China, 4–14
    and Christianity, 12–16
    history of, 4–6
    in Qing and Republican era, 6–12
    family status, 7–8
    legal status, 10–11
    social status, 6–8
concubines, 28–51
    comparison with extra-biblical
    resources, 44–49
    definition of, 29–31
    Hebrew terms for, 38–41

    in the Hebrew Bible, 37–42
    marital status of, 31–33
contextual hermeneutics, xiii–xix,
    186–87
cross-textual reading, xiv–xvi

Delegates' Version (DV), 164–65,
    166–70
Deuteronomic laws, 34–35, 37, 60, 113,
    117–18

Edenburg, Cynthia, 18, 60n40, 99–100,
    102–6, 111, 113–14, 116–19, 154
Engelken, Karen, 2n6–7, 39n47, 40n48–
    49, 41–43, 46n70, 50

feminist criticism, 18, 135–38

Gibeah, 35, 49–51, 65, 78, 81, 83–84,
    101–4, 106, 109–111, 113–14,
    116–17, 143, 149–50, 152,
    179–80

Hagar, 5, 15, 38–39, 45–47
hospitality, 24, 35, 43, 49, 59, 63–64,
    81, 84, 86, 100–103, 107–112,
    127–28, 147, 149, 157, 187
    in Hebrew Bible, 107–9
    in Judg 19, 109–112

ideological criticism, 1, 110, 129–35,
    138, 140–42, 151, 154, 158
    and Hebrew Bible, 130–35
    definition, 131–32
    extrinsic analysis, 133–35, 138–40,
    142

ideological criticism (*continued*)
  in Judg 19, 129–58
  intrinsic analysis, 133–35, 138, 140–42, 153
  Yee's methodology, 133–35, 139–42
ideology, 4, 12, 76–77, 83–84, 105, 116–17, 129–40, 142–43, 153–54, 156–58, 171, 173–75, 187
  anti-Levite, 87, 104, 107, 127–30, 142–43, 153, 156–59, 163, 179, 181, 183–87
  pro-monarchic, 130, 142, 153–56, 158, 187
intertextuality, 86–93, 98–100, 103, 106, 109, 112, 157
  and Hebrew Bible, 90–93
  1 Sam 11, 103–5
  2 Sam 13, 106
  Gen 19, 100–103
  Deut 22, 105–6
  overview, 87–90

Janzen, David, 120–25, 126n138

Kristeva, Julia, 87–90, 92, 98

Lee, Archie C., xiv–xv, 171n41, 172n44, 175n56
Levite, 21, 25–26, 31, 34–35, 53, 63–65, 67, 78, 80, 82–85, 103, 105–7, 110, 114, 126, 128–29, 141, 143, 149, 153, 156, 175, 178–79, 183–84, 186
  see also masculinity
literary criticism, 69–70, 86, 94, 134

marriage, 2–7, 9, 12, 30–32, 37–39, 41–45, 47–50, 54, 113, 117, 144, 146–47
  patrilocal, 30, 32, 42, 54
masculinity, 143–46, 152–53, 157
  in Hebrew Bible, 143–47
  of the Levite, 138, 143, 148–53, 171–72
monogamy, 2, 12–16, 21, 26, 38, 173
motif, 64, 87, 91, 93–99, 102–9, 111–14, 116–19, 121–24, 127, 149
  definition, 97

narrative criticism, 52–56, 85, 133
narrative gaps, 52, 57–59, 62, 66, 68–69, 85, 156, 186
Neufeld, E., 38–40, 44, 46, 47n74–75, 48n77
New Culture Movement, 3, 9, 16, 176–77
non sequitur, 61
Nu Chieh (女誡), 5

pîlegeš
  see concubines
point-of-view, 52–53, 55–57, 69–79, 81–85, 157, 186
  concurrence/nonconcurrence of planes, 77, 84
  definition, 69–71
  ideological plane, 76, 83–84
  informational plane, 72, 74–75, 81–82
  of Judges 19, 77–85
  phraseological plane, 75, 83–84
  psychological plane, 73–74, 79–81, 84
  spatial plane, 72–73, 78–79
  temporal plane, 74–75, 82
  Yamasaki's methodology, 71–77
polygyny, 37–38, 41–42

rape, 10–12, 19, 22, 25–26, 35–36, 43, 50, 77–78, 85–86, 100, 102, 105–7, 111, 113–18, 127–28, 135–37, 142–43, 150–52, 156–57, 159–60, 163, 175, 178–79, 187
  in Judg 19, 113–14, 117–18, 162–63
  in the Hebrew Bible, 114–17
Revised Chinese Union Version (RCUV), 166–70

sacrifice, 24, 86, 104–5, 107, 118–28, 155, 157, 187
  in 1 Sam 11, 104, 124–26
  in Judg 19, 118–19, 124–25, 126–27
secondary wife, 2, 30–31, 33, 38, 43–46, 48
Sternberg, Meir, 53–54, 56–61, 62n45, 63n47, 67, 69, 71n68–69, 74
Stone, Ken, 35–36n35, 143, 148, 150

Sumerian laws, 46

translation, 4–5, 9, 11, 14–15, 17, 19–21, 23, 25–27, 60, 114, 159–73, 175–78, 180–87
    context and translators, 170–72
    see also Chinese Union Version (CUV)
Tsang, Jacob C. S. 曾祥新, 181–83

Uspensky, Boris, 56, 70–72, 74, 76, 83

women, 10, 15, 19, 26–27, 30–32, 35, 46, 115–17, 119, 173–74, 182, 186
    violence against, 136, 160, 176, 179, 182–87
Wu, Timothy 吳獻章, 180–81, 183

Yamasaki, Gary, 53, 57, 70–80, 82–85, 186
Yee, Gale A., xviiin11, 1n2, 110n87, 129n1, 130–31, 133–35, 138–42, 151n82, 153, 154n84, 156, 158

Scripture Index

Genesis

19	xviii, 24n90, 86, 99–103, 106–7, 109, 111, 127–28, 157, 182, 186
19:4–9	100n54
19:4	102
19:9	100n4
19:16	112
22	xviii, 82, 127
22:10	99n53, 119, 119n112, 127
22:24	40
34	114, 116
35:22	2
38:24	162n14

Exodus

21:7–11	46
21:32	39
22:15–16	35n34
29:17	104, 118
34:15	162n15

Leviticus

17:7	162n15
18:18	41
25:44	39

Numbers

15:39	162n15
25:1	162n13

Deuteronomy

5:14	39
12–26	121
12	122, 124n136
12:31	126
18:10	126
21:15–17	37
22	xviii, 99, 105–7, 113, 128, 157, 187
22:13–29	105, 116
22:15–16	105, 113
22:19	105, 113
22:21, 105	162n13
22:22	47, 60n38
22:25–29	115
22:25–26	118
22:28–29	35n34, 117
22:29	105, 113–17

Joshua

13–21	122
22	122
23–24	122

Judges

8:31	42n5
9	120
17–21	120, 138–42, 140n39, n40, n41, 141n42, n43, 151n82, 154n84
17–18	122
17	127
17:6	123, 153
18:1–2	39
18:1	123, 153
19:1–20:13	104n74
19:1–21	78
19:1–9	109
19:1–3	148
19:1	21, 29, 141n43, 148, 153, 158
19:2–3	60, 62n46
19:2	105, 160–63, 166–67, 180–81, 181n76
19:3–6	105
19:3	148
19:4–10	149
19:4–9	100n54
19:4	102, 110, 149
19:5	63
19:7	103
19:8–9	105
19:9	29, 100, 181n78
19:10–25	110
19:10–11	112
19:11–15	149
19:15	111
19:16–25	150
19:16	112
19:17	105
19:22–25	100n54
19:22	102, 181n78
19:23	103
19:25	65, 112, 160–63, 167–68
19:26–30	151
19:27–28	55n12
19:27	67
19:29–30	103–4, 118, 124, 126
19:29	82n100, 104–5, 119, 118–19, 155, 163, 167–69, 181n78
20–21	104n74, 154
20	104, 118, 126–27
20:1–7	152
20:26–27	127
21:25	123, 153

1 Samuel

1	127
1:11	39
2:11–36	122
4:9	145n58
9–11	120n116
11	xviii, 99, 101, 103, 104n74, 106–7, 119, 121, 125, 157, 187
11:7	103–4, 118, 124, 126–27, 155
15:27	162

2 Samuel

1:11	162
3:7	2, 48
5:13	40
13	xviii, 99, 106–7, 114–16, 128, 157, 187
13:11	163n17
14:15	39
15:16	39
20:3	39

1 Kings

1:50	162
2:17	48
2:28	162
18:23	104, 118
18:33	118

2 Kings

2:12	162
16:3	126
17:17	126
21:06	126
22–23	140
22	141n42, 155

1 Chronicles

1:32	2

2 Chronicles

11:21	40

Psalms

106:39	162n15

Proverbs

146

3:8	163
20:14	119n111

Jeremiah

2:20	162n16
3:6	162n12
3:8	162n12

Daniel

1	101

Amos

7:17	162n14

www.ingramcontent.com/pod-product-compliance
Lightning Source LLC
Chambersburg PA
CBHW062023220426
43662CB00010B/1444